V. Grinnell

MUSIC TALKS

Also by Helen Epstein

CHILDREN OF THE HOLOCAUST

THE COMPANIES SHE KEEPS

Helen Epstein

MUSIC TALKS

Conversations with
Musicians

MCGRAW-HILL BOOK COMPANY

New York   St. Louis   San Francisco
Toronto   Hamburg   Mexico

"Vladimir Horowitz" first appeared in the *New York Times Magazine* in 1978.

"Learning to Conduct at Tanglewood in the Eighties" first appeared in the *New York Times* Arts and Leisure section in 1981.

"Listening to Lenny" first appeared in the *Soho Weekly News* in 1981.

"Chamber Music Up in the Hills" first appeared in the *New York Times* Arts and Leisure section in 1976.

"The Marketing of James Galway" first appeared in the *New York Times Magazine* in 1980.

"An American Free-lancer" first appeared in the *New York Times Magazine* in 1974.

"The Juilliard Quartet" first appeared in the *New York Times* Arts and Leisure section in 1981.

"Yo-Yo Ma" first appeared in *Esquire* in 1981.

"The Leventritt Competition" first appeared in the *New York Times* Arts and Leisure section in 1976.

1 2 3 4 5 6 7 8 9 DOCDOC 8 7

ISBN 0-07-019544-7

LIBRARY OF CONGRESS CATALOGING-IN-PUBLICATION DATA

Epstein, Helen, 1947–
  Music talks.

  Includes index.
  1. Musicians—Interviews. I. Title.
ML385.E67   1987   780'.92'2   86-33725
ISBN 0-07-019544-7

Book Design by Kathryn Parise

For my music teachers,
especially Ruth Katz and Ralph Dale

Contents

~ *Contents* ~

Introduction

Writing about Musicians

When I was a child, I believed that a musician carrying his instrument in the streets of New York City was free from any danger. It did not matter whether it was a tuba he carried, or a saxophone, a fiddle, a harp, or a flute. His instrument protected him and signaled who he was. All he had to do was keep it visible and sidestreet muggers or heavy trucks would freeze in their tracks, stopped by his magic. I had paid attention to stories about musicians, the one in the Bible where David played harp for a king who could not sleep, the fairy tale about a piper who forced the hand of the city council of Hamlin, the myth of Orpheus, who went to Hades and came back alive. But more convincing than any story was my mother's face at concerts—calm, rapt, and in love, sometimes with two or three men at once.

We left my father behind on those evenings, asleep in his work clothes on the living room couch, an open newspaper rising and falling on his chest. My mother dressed up in silk and jewelry; she put on a fur coat or, at least, a fur collar. She dressed me up too, in a velveteen dress and black patent leather shoes, and I danced because it was a week night, there was school the next day, and here I was going out to Carnegie Hall with my mother. At seven-thirty we walked to the bus stop on Broadway which was crowded with people. The women were all painted and dressed up like my mother, the men looked lacquered and posh, the occasional child was made slow and careful by the weight of party clothes. They all wore an expectant look as though they were going to a party and they stood out from the other people on the bus. Those were the years when there were still gangs on the upper West Side, and when large numbers of families rented sprawling apartments between Riverside Drive and Central Park West, and Yiddish and German were heard in neighborhood stores. Musicians and music lovers had always lived in our building, you often heard the sounds of singers vocalizing if you took the stairs, and in the lobby I crossed paths with a whole generation of violinists on their way to lessons with master teacher Ivan Galamian.

At least half the people on the bus got off when it pulled up in front of Carnegie Hall, and they held the doors for one another with a special courtesy. My mother almost always spotted friends in the crowd of people milling before the steps. It never occurred to me that there might be adults who did not go to Carnegie Hall, let alone not know what it was. Entering its doors, I sensed more reverence in its jammed lobby than in any place of worship I had ever visited. Indeed, for many of the concertgoers there, Carnegie Hall served as a church or synagogue, a place where they celebrated eternal life.

My mother gave me our tickets to give to the ticket taker and I listened to his instructions with a little air of superiority, for I knew then better than I know now the names of the tiers and the location of the seats. My parents had no discretionary income when I was a child, but concerts were necessary to my mother's mental health; she chose our seats shrewdly. Either we hiked up to the last tier, to one of the first rows, or else we sat on folding chairs onstage, in a place where I would have an unobstructed view of the pianist's fingers. As a girl in Prague my mother had wanted to be a concert pianist and, as I later discovered while interviewing musicians, was one of many parents who had transferred their own ambitions to their children. In her case, the Crash, the War, and Emigration had made irrelevant any such career. She had become a dressmaker and made clothes for opera singers, actresses, and other artists instead of becoming one herself. Sometimes our seats in Carnegie Hall had been a gift from one of her customers; sometimes they would invite us to their box at intermission; at the very least I would see a dress or coat that had been hanging in our apartment hall being worn by its owner in a proper setting.

About half the seats were filled by the time we settled down. My mother began looking around for friends, fashions, famous people, sometimes with the aid of her mother-of-pearl opera glasses. "There's Firkusny!" she would exclaim, grabbing my arm, and I would look through the opera glasses at the face of the Czech pianist whose presence so excited her.

"Who is he?" I'd ask. "Why do you like him?" And my mother would tell me all she knew about Rudolf Firkusny or Rudolf Serkin or Artur Rubinstein, stories she had heard in Europe, things she had read in the Sunday *New York Times,* things she had heard from a customer or a friend, over the refugee grapevine. The names of the performers we went to hear were all Polish, Czech, German, Russian, or Hungarian. I don't remember ever hearing an American at Carnegie Hall during my childhood and, dimly, I understood that all these people onstage were part of a world that could survive wars and natural disasters, that it had no international frontiers, and that, somehow, its traditions remained constant while, outside it, circumstances changed.

Finally my mother would stop searching the hall, read the program, and begin telling me about the music we would hear, what a requiem was, why this piece was called *Pathétique,* why Liszt was so difficult to play. Then the lights went down and the musician or musicians would stride onto the stage, acknowledging the applause with a smile or a frown or a bow or a wave, looking haughty or friendly or harried or businesslike, depending, my mother said, on what sort of temperament they had. Years of studying music and musicology had not yet dulled my immediate visceral reaction to them. They were all equally famous to me; I imposed no body of knowledge onto any of them and was indiscriminately open to that inexplicable chemistry between performer and listener/watcher that makes of one gifted musician a charismatic star and of another, equally gifted, musician a dullard. I did not care what the person looked like; what I remember is the excitement he (for it was always a he) generated. Like most grown-ups, as I later discovered, I favored musicians who could translate their excitement into things I could see as well as hear. I loved Leonard Bernstein and Emil Gilels; the Budapest String Quartet put me to sleep. It was not until my teens that I heard Jacqueline Du Pré and recognized someone like myself onstage; until then, I thought only men could make that kind of magic and I had no sense of the importance of extramusical factors—luck, education, correct management, date and place of birth, money—that were required for an artist to wind up playing in Carnegie Hall.

At the time, I was largely unaware of the moments of beauty in the extraordinary performances I heard. For most of the first movement, I would sit still. Then came the second movement and suddenly it seemed as though there was less to listen to. It would not be until much later, when I was married with a child of my own, that I would appreciate just how necessary a night out at Carnegie Hall was to my mother, how the occasion of a concert allowed her to step off the treadmill of routine, relax, and refuel. After the first half, we toured the corridors and I would listen to the conversations carried on over my head, about the music, about the musicians, about private life. The music was a stimulant to the grown-ups around me. My mother, too, seemed unusually animated, passionate, more ready to laugh. Flirtation was in the air during those intermissions and, by the time I returned to my seat, I usually had something I had seen or heard to mull over.

Years later, my mother would claim I had sat transfixed through concerts. She bought me a piano, sent me to the Mannes College of Music at age seven, and would have held onto the idea of my becoming a concert pianist for much longer had she not one day happened to sit down beside a European woman of her age with a little boy my age at Tanglewood. The two mothers began discussing their children, the budding concert pianists, and it was not until the mother of André Watts remarked that her son practiced four hours a day without prodding that my mother let go of my potential career.

By that time I had discovered performing. Not playing the piano but singing alone and in groups, accompanied by a piano, a guitar, or nothing at all. It was while singing in choruses and madrigal groups that I began to have, regularly, the experience of losing all sense of time and self that I would later hear Leonard Bernstein talk about with conducting students, the sense of connection to the universe that many musicians would later tell me kept them to a career in music despite all the difficulties. For a time, I too thought I might study music. I majored in musicology at the Hebrew University in Jerusalem, where there are said to be more musicologists per square mile than anywhere else in the world, but while I loved listening, I found I loved reading more. Those intense moments in music came to me once in a while; they were almost always there when I wrote or devoured a book. There was the question of certainty too: I had never totally trusted my ear; my teachers had been of the sort that intimidated rather than developed me; and, in the end, feeling more secure with the acuteness of my eye rather than my ear, I became a writer.

I began writing about musicians in journalism school. There, cultural reporting—let alone reporting about classical musicians—was considered marginal, unchallenging, and certainly far less lucrative than becoming a foreign correspondent or exposing corruption at home. Investigative reporting was the rage, and its application was narrowly limited to

politics. This did not bother me too much because just as I had always
been uncertain of my musical instincts, I was sure of my journalistic ones.
To me, art and music were the most important and interesting things in
the world to write about.

I felt part of cultural history and still do when I sit in Carnegie Hall.
I have the sense that I am listening to life as well as music and that the
stories of the musicians onstage as well as of the people sitting around me
are as gripping as the music being performed.

The music world is, of course, far more complicated than I ever
imagined. Some performers who inspire from a distance turn out to be
horrible people up close; intelligence in music does not always transfer
to intelligence in life; and contrary to what I heard André Previn tell
young conductors one afternoon, I believe there are extraordinary musicians who do *not* make it to the top of their profession. I have met them
and heard them play. Music is like any other field in America: Success
requires talent but it all too often depends on a flair for public relations
and a willingness to engage in extramusical activities that musicians
would have once disdained as inappropriate. Musicians who refuse to be
marketed like exotic fruit and who are not ready, or perhaps able, to
appear jovial on television talk shows, musicians who cannot afford or
cannot bring themselves to hire a press agent, musicians who are not
extroverted or eye-catching, may never get to perform in Carnegie Hall.

Despite all that, I hold onto the notion that musicians are somehow
immune to things that impede the rest of us. The sight of a young man
or woman carrying an instrument in the street fills me with elation, pride,
and a certain envy. Of course, musicians are as likely to be mugged as
anyone else and as likely to be hit by a truck, but I like to think it's not
so. I like to think that people who for centuries have provided such
pleasure, who, every time they perform, are engaged in a re-creation of
life, are closer than the rest of us to immortality.

MUSIC TALKS

Vladimir Horowitz. (*Henry John Corra*.)

1

Vladimir Horowitz

Vladimir Horowitz performs no more than twenty times each year, only on Sunday afternoons at four, and only in places he likes. He does not play in Denver because he finds the altitude disagreeable or in St. Louis because he thinks the acoustics of its hall compare badly with those of his bathroom. He does not play in Poughkeepsie, New York, where "the public is not musical enough," or anywhere in Montana or Idaho, which he has no desire to see. He does not like to play in Europe because he dislikes flying long distances, and, although he would like to visit Japan, the mere thought of getting there casts a pall over his large, extraordinary face. "You fly Saturday and arrive on Friday," he says, as if announcing a funeral. "You have to stay ten days to be right again and that scares me."

The cities that Horowitz does choose to visit must have an acoustically sound concert hall free both on a Sunday and on a preceding day at four so that the pianist may come by for a dress rehearsal. He uses this time to reacquaint himself with the sound, space, and light in a given hall and to position his piano in a way that suits him best. (In Carnegie Hall his chosen spot has, since 1965, been marked in the floor of the stage by a "Horowitz screw," which other pianists look for when *their* pianos are positioned.) The size of the hall is also important: It must hold at least 1,800 people willing to pay the highest single admission price regularly asked by any recitalist. Horowitz dislikes talking about how much money he makes or admitting to being a shrewd businessman. "My expenses are very high," he murmurs instead. And indeed they are.

Wherever the seventy-three-year-old pianist performed in the late

1970s, he was accompanied by his wife, Wanda, the stout, brisk daughter of the late conductor Arturo Toscanini; his Italian tour manager, Giovanni Scimonelli; his valet/advance man/truck driver, Duane Lewin; and Horowitz's "baby"—a gleaming Steinway concert grand that was a wedding present from the company in 1933. His entourage had to be accommodated in hotels which would allow the pianist to do whatever necessary to replicate exactly the conditions in which he lived in his upper East Side town house in New York City; that is to say, something on the order of a presidential suite was required. His bedroom windows were completely covered (sometimes with aluminum foil) and the telephone silenced so that Horowitz might sleep till noon. The living room had to be large enough to accommodate visitors as well as another grand piano in the event that Horowitz felt inclined to play. There had to be a fully equipped kitchen with an oven so that the pianist's meals might be prepared exactly as they were prepared at home, and when Horowitz got fussy, as he did one time before a concert in Miami Beach, he might refuse to perform unless a certain kind of *food*—in this case, fresh gray sole—was made available.

On January 8, 1978, a Sunday at four, Horowitz was playing a benefit concert for the New York Philharmonic. It was the fiftieth anniversary of his American debut and a full twenty-five years since he last performed with an orchestra. And, as usual, the pianist required special arrangements. In a blithe reversal of concert protocol, which traditionally leaves the choice of soloist and repertoire up to the conductor, Horowitz told the New York Philharmonic not only that he wanted Eugene Ormandy to conduct but also what he wanted the orchestra to play. Because Horowitz disliked the orchestra's home base, Avery Fisher Hall ("I will never play there. Never!"), the Philharmonic betook itself to Carnegie Hall. And because Horowitz was under contract to RCA Records while the New York Philharmonic made records for Columbia, that company had graciously ceded its recording rights, a gesture that cost it one of the potentially best-selling classical records in recent times.

Vladimir Horowitz did not gloat over these victories; he took them for granted. For a full fifty years now, the pianist had been having his way with the public, with his friends, with his family, even with the most temperamental of his musical colleagues. When he first appeared on the American stage in 1928, playing the Tchaikovsky B flat minor Piano Concerto with the New York Philharmonic under Sir Thomas Beecham, the audience went wild. "A mob is a mob; blood is blood," wrote *New*

York Times music critic Olin Downes. "The call of the wild is heard whether it is a savage beating a drum or a young Russian, mad with excitement, physical speed and power, pounding on a keyboard."

For the next seven years—the Depression years—Horowitz played to seventy sold-out houses each season and earned more than a quarter of a million dollars each year. His reputation for dazzling virtuosity, effortless technique, and demonic interpretation spread throughout the United States and Europe. "During the last few months, a number of musicians have given me to understand that the greatest pianist alive is Horowitz," wrote the music critic of the *Manchester Guardian* in May of 1933. "As I came away from the concert I realized that the half had not been told me. I am ready to believe he is the greatest pianist alive or dead. His techniques and style are comprehensive, masterful and sensitive. He brings out the essential qualities of the piano; he achieves a most satisfying synthesis of all those attributes of piano playing which usually we have had to look for in different artists." The international press soon took to describing the pianist in hyperbolic terms. "It is literally true," wrote one interviewer confidently, "that he has not played an exercise, scale or arpeggio since he was fifteen. Nature is the only source."

The glamour surrounding his performances was enhanced even further in the early thirties when Horowitz began to concertize with conductor Arturo Toscanini, and to court his younger daughter, Wanda. They were married in December of 1933, and Horowitz took a short vacation from his strenuous concert schedule. Then, in 1935, he underwent what was variously reported as "an appendectomy," "phlebitis," and "a crack-up." He disappeared into Switzerland, and rumor had it that he did not touch the piano for two years. Then, in 1938, he played a concert in Zurich and within a year was concertizing regularly again. After this return, critics found him even better than before. "Mr. Horowitz returns to us as extraordinary a virtuoso as he ever was but a far greater artist," wrote one New York critic. "He is still a dazzling player with a command of the piano and a mastery of its resources that are uncanny even in these days of technical prowess. But he is now bent solely on expression, at whose service he has placed his prodigious pianistic equipment."

For the next fifteen years, he was regarded as the consummate musical artist, a fit son-in-law for the Maestro, Toscanini, and an international celebrity. Music critics adored him and reviewed his concerts so uncritically that composer and critic Virgil Thomson was provoked to counter: "If one had never heard before the works Mr. Horowitz played, one might easily have been convinced that Bach was a musician of the Leopold Stokowski type, that Brahms was a sort of flippant Gershwin who had worked in a high class nightclub and that Chopin was a gypsy violinist." Thomson was, however, a virtual minority of one in his objection to Horowitz's highly personal interpretations, which, he felt, reduced the composer to a shadow of the performer. Most critics emphasized Horowitz's maturity and personal growth. "He has transformed himself from a fire-eating virtuoso into a self-critical, searching artist," wrote Howard Taubman of the *New York Times* in January 1953.

The following month, in Minneapolis, Horowitz canceled a recital and did not play again in public for twelve years. During this second disappearance from public view, people said that he was in a sanatorium, that he had become a drug addict and was undergoing treatment, that he suffered from the delusion that his hands were made of porcelain and would break if he touched the keyboard, and, not least, that he had died.

The pianist said nothing to dispel any of these rumors. "I wouldn't be surprised if some of them originated in his own living room," said a close associate. Horowitz himself likes to attribute both of his disappearances to "the trains." He will smile helplessly and wave his hands and say, "I cannot go in trains. I didn't have time to give encores—I already had to go to catch the trains. On the trains I could never sleep well, it was too noisy and too shaking. If you live like that for twenty years, something happens to you. You get tired. In one town I was exhausted so I thought I'd stop for one or two years. I did records and I let the records travel. But after two years I liked it so much that it became one year more and one year more until it was ten like that."

In 1965, Horowitz made front-page headlines across the United States simply by returning to the stage. "He has the best sense of promotion I've ever come across in any artist," says his press agent, who is one of several people paid to run interference between Horowitz and the outside world. "He's aware of the dangers of overexposure. The whole image he projects is that you never do know whether or not his hands will fall off."

In 1969, Horowitz caught cold in Boston and retired for another three years. Since 1972, however, he has been concertizing regularly in the large cities of North America as well as college towns like Ann Arbor and Bloomington, adding thousands of "the young people" to the public which has grown old with him. And although music critics no longer display the unilateral idolatry of the past, he does not often receive poor reviews.

"I don't know of any other artist who grips an audience the way he does," the former *Times* head music critic Harold Schonberg has said. "There's a kind of inner tension, an electricity, in the man that's scary. It's like you're fooling around with 10,000 volts. You *know* this artist is unique. There are a lot of good ones but Horowitz is unique."

~

Up close, Vladimir Horowitz is a surprisingly slight man with shrewd, lively brown eyes. His hands are not particularly large, nor are his fingers unusually long. His ears are enormous. He likes to talk and does so with great animation, in a throaty, resonant voice that can range from a dramatic whisper to an uproarious guffaw. He has told some of the same musical anecdotes for fifty years: They form the core of his conversation and he is accustomed to telling them without interruption to a deferential, appreciative audience. When he is asked about something for which he cannot find an appropriate anecdote, his eyebrows rise in reflection and surprise, and he appears to be momentarily disoriented by this detour from the beaten track. "This is not a stupid question," he will allow, his English smothered by the thick Russian accent he has retained more than half a century after leaving his native city, Kiev, in the Ukraine.

"I'm from a rich family," he says with dignity. "My father was very important engineer. He built a sugar factory; he represented big companies like Westinghouse. He was going to Germany and spoke German and French like Russian. He translated books and gave his family the best education he could. He was a little bit snob and he was half Jewish. He made a great friendship with all the anti-Jewish world. I know I was in a school with a quota and they took me without quota.

"My family never thought about leaving Russia. The pogroms didn't affect them. Not my father. No. The pogrom in 1905 nearly killed me. They told me the bullet came through the window. But we were living in very good quarters, in aristocratic quarters where the Jews usually don't live...."

Horowitz falls into open confusion when he is asked about his feelings toward Judaism or Jewish identity. He does not like to talk about those things any more than he likes to divulge his business practices and will fend off questions with improbable pronouncements. "I think the anti-Semitism in Russia is all since the establishment of Israel," he will say in all seriousness. "I believe it is political. It is not of feeling." He likes to describe his life entirely in terms of his musical education, and when he speaks of his mother, for example, he says that she was an accomplished pianist who gave up a career for four children. It was his mother who began to give Vladimir Horowitz piano lessons when he was six years old.

Horowitz recalls hearing salon pieces at concerts and excerpts from the opera as a child. "In my formative years I heard most and I love still today *bel canto* Italian singing. Tetrazzini. Caruso. I was listening to that from morning till night and I loved it. I wanted to sing at the piano like that. That was the major influence on everything. I listened to excerpts, not the whole opera. And the orchestra was crummy; it sounded like a balalaika orchestra. But that is not important.

"When I was a child, I was bringing to my professor the music I liked and not the music which I had to play. My mother went to him and asked, 'What are you doing? Instead of Bach, he's playing Rachmaninoff!' I was supposed to be studying the same things piano students study today: Preludes, fugues, and suites of Bach; sonatas of Mozart; concerto of Mozart; sonata of Beethoven; concerto of Beethoven; Schumann; Schubert. But I was bringing my teacher the modern music. I went to the stores and bought the new music. I took it home and I played it. Today, when you don't know some music you buy a record and listen to it and then you say, 'I know it.' But when I was a child there was nothing like this. For example, nobody knew Brahms in Russia. I learned Wagner when I played the piano transcriptions of *Tannhäuser* and *Lohengrin* and *Parsifal*. I have never till today heard *Parsifal performed* but I knew the score from memory. It was the same with Rachmaninoff. I memorized all of Rachmaninoff."

Horowitz turned thirteen the year of the Russian Revolution, but his life, he says, was not severely disrupted until three years later and for a time was actually enriched by it. "The Revolution started in the north," he says, "and the best forces in music came to Kiev from Petersburg and Moscow to escape the bolshevism and because we had food and there they had famine. So in our conservatory I played four hands with the teacher of Gilels and Richter. Glazounov was there. Glière was there. At this time I wanted to be a composer and I wrote a tremendous amount. I wrote poetry in Russian and I wrote music to my own words and it was performed on the stage. God was very generous to me and gave me facility to perform so I didn't have to work too much. I had right away success. I didn't expect it. I didn't want it even. I wanted to be a composer.

"The Revolution forced me to give concerts. Every two months we had a new government. Every day there was fighting in the streets. And I was going to the conservatory. When I had my final examination before all the faculty, they were seated like judges in the Supreme Court, but instead of nine there were nearly forty. We had to play a piece of Bach, Mozart, Beethoven, modern, then bravura. When I finished my last piece the whole forty people stood up and were applauding. That was never before in the history of the conservatory. *They* made me know I was above the typical pianist. I didn't know it. I was always very modest with myself and I wanted to study composition.

"I am a product of the Revolution. The Revolution forced me to leave my studies and to start to give concerts. In twenty-four hours came the soldiers. They took everything. They threw my piano through the window. *Through the window*, my dear. Into the street. They took everything. All the clothing in the closets. We were the bourgeois and they were the proletariat. I'm an old trooper. I remember lots of things. The bullets were going around me in the street. Hundreds of people I knew were killed. I could have been killed too. Everybody was going away. I didn't know where. I didn't know what was outside Russia. I didn't know another world; I didn't realize there was something better. You don't realize that. I thought this Revolution was a passing thing. You can only shoot a certain amount of time and then it calms down. After 'twenty-two, they were not shooting anymore. But my father had lost all he had. We lived with three families in three rooms, and I had to help my father.

"I am a product of general privation, not personal privation. We were deprived sometimes of food. We had rations. Pushing out of that gives a certain amount of dynamic quality to the personality of people, especially young people. This is something young people today are lacking. They're a little bit phlegmatic, a little bit complacent because everything is too easy. For us, it was difficult. For us it was important to do something and be somebody. When I came to New York the critics wrote, 'unleashed from the steppes,' and all that business. That was the Revolution. I had a feeling of wanting to make a place for myself. I had a zest for living and a sense of survival. I wanted to *go* somewhere. So instead of finishing my studies, I began to concertize."

~

At two-thirty on a Sunday afternoon in the prime minister's suite of Toronto's Sutton Place Hotel, Vladimir Horowitz began to prepare for his second recital of the 1977–1978 concert season. Although the pianist now earned up to $45,000 per concert, whereas in Russia in the early twenties he was often paid in butter or flour, his idea of what an artist should be had remained unchanged. "Without false modesty," he said, "I feel that when I am on the stage, I am the king, the boss of the situation, and I have to look like that. I want my suit to fit, my hair to be combed; I want to have a completely clean body and hands, perfume. It is not that I am a showman; this is absolutely natural. If I play at home in pajamas, I behave differently. I'm looser. You can have genius ideas at the moment that you get out of bed, but when you are explaining them before people you become more concentrated and your ideas are more focused.

"In Mozart's time, there was the most elaborate and refined dress. Every gesture was reverence. Lace, a little tobacco, a little black spot on the face. If you play Mozart you have to be close to what the composer was at that time. Look at Chopin! He was a dandy. Everything about his dress was important. He picked out every silk. Liszt too. It was a superficial thing but you could see that this was a person not of common denomination. The public pays money and they want to see and hear something aesthetic. It's not the Barnum circus—it's aesthetic!"

On the day of a concert, Horowitz rises at about noon. He has his breakfast, ignores his piano, and does not answer the telephone or talk to anyone. At about two-thirty, he begins slowly to wash and shave and dress. "I think about the small details," he says. "To put on the socks that they don't press me. To see the shoes are closed. To see the fly is closed. If they are open, they are terrible...(he giggles throatily at the thought, as he does at nearly any allusion to the genitals).

"I try not to be nervous before a concert. Not to rush. All the movements quiet. I don't think about music at all because, you know, the tragedy of the artist is like Pagliacci. At a certain time you have to be inspired and wanting to play and being in good form. It could be that at four—just at four—that I could have a stomachache. And I would have to go onstage anyway. So I am trying to be very quiet. Nobody should interfere with me, and *if* anyone interferes with me they get such a scandal that they never heard!"

Horowitz dresses in afternoon formal attire: black pants with faint white stripes, a white shirt, a gray vest, one of his hundreds of bow ties, and a black cutaway. "The moment that I feel that cutaway—the moment I am in uniform—it's like a horse before the races. You start to perspire. You feel already in you some electricity to do something. At this moment,

I am already an artist. I feel a pressure to be on time although I am always late a little bit—because I am so meticulous. I would like to be ten or fifteen minutes early to warm up the fingers. I am a general. My soldiers are the keys and I have to command them."

By three-thirty, Toronto's Massey Hall was filling up with concert-goers, some of whom had come from as far away as New York and Montreal to attend the recital, although its only advertisement had been a small newspaper notice. By four o'clock, 2,763 of the hall's 2,765 seats and an extra 150 folding chairs onstage were occupied. Mr. Horowitz and his entourage arrived in a large sleek limousine, and the local impresario, Walter Homburger, was smiling and clasping his hands and trying to move things along without appearing pushy. There was a feeling of festivity as well as tension in the chatter that filled the auditorium. At four-ten, Madame Horowitz and a friend hurried toward the two remaining seats. The lights dimmed. There was utter silence.

"The only minute which is unpleasant is the minute I stand in the wings, just before coming in," says the pianist. "But you know, I happen to be a little nearsighted, which makes me happy because I don't see the public. I see just the piano and about three rows of seats. I don't want to see the public. I want to *feel* them."

As soon as Horowitz's slim, immaculately tailored figure emerges from the wings, there is a surge of movement in the audience. People leap to their feet, cheering, applauding in an almost reverential way. The pianist smiles into the hall of faces, bows, sits down quickly on his piano stool. At once the members of the audience sink down into their seats, and again there is total silence as he begins to play.

"Once I sit down at the piano," Horowitz says. "I transform myself. I see the composer. I *am* the composer. The music gives me that sense. It needs a lot of concentration to achieve and a lot of electricity. Then the current has to reach the public and wrap them. I want the public to feel what I feel. I want when I cry on the piano, or when I laugh, that the public also cries and laughs. That is my goal. It takes time to achieve. So with me, the longer the recital progresses, the more people are with me. I can measure it by the silence. To applaud loud is very easy, but it is when they are silent that you are doing something. Sometimes I feel they are not with me and I am unhappy. So I gradually try to seduce them. If I don't succeed with one piece, I try another, with another sound, from another century, with a more spectacular playing. What's important is contrast. Always contrast. And if the audience is not with me, then for ten or fifteen minutes there is a little hole. But in the end—unless I am not feeling well—they will be with me."

Horowitz compares planning a concert recital program to building a house. "The structure is made at home, but all the rooms are individual and the details can be improvised," he says. "What's important is contrast. I don't like to play the same composer straight through. If I do it, I choose the pieces that are completely different. There are geniuses who in their life span composed pieces so different that you cannot recognize that they are the same composer. Beethoven, for example. And Scriabin. I try to have two or three full programs at my disposal with pieces from different centuries, different styles, because I want my public to be with me.

"Artur Schnabel was a very intellectual pianist. His first half was always two sonatas by Beethoven and the second half also something difficult. Once he said, 'You know the difference between me and my colleagues is that when I build a program, the second half is *as boring* as the first!'"

Horowitz guffaws loudly. "He thought he was very witty! He would play a Schubert sonata in the second half, which is difficult to take for a public. I don't want to do that. I don't want to do that. A recital program is a little bit like a dinner; at the end you have something sweet. The second half of the program should have smaller things, a little bit more virtuoso. Also I am choosing pieces which are idiomatic for the piano, which are written by people who knew the instrument: Schumann, Liszt, Chopin.

"I like to play recitals because, you see, I do my own nuances. Everything is mine. I can push the tempo a little bit or I can play loud as I want. When you play concerto, the orchestra sets the pace for you. *They* make it loud or soft. I like to do it myself because I know I can. And my repertoire is much more interesting. There are many more pieces to play for recitals. You can count on your fingers the number of concertos. They always play the same ones. I can play hundreds of pieces and better pieces than concerti. Chopin wrote two concerti, for example, but these are not his best pieces. Schumann's concerto is not his best piece. Beethoven, yes. Mozart, yes. I have not yet played Mozart concerti but I will. Someone said you should play Mozart before twelve and after eighty!

"There is also very beautiful music that I will play at home but I will not play on the stage. There is very, very much music like this—I don't even want to tell what. The late Beethoven sonatas for example. I met in 1938 the daughter of Hans von Bülow and Cosima Liszt, whose stepfather was Richard Wagner. One time she was in the room when Wagner asked Liszt to play the last sonatas of Beethoven. Liszt was an old man but he played them, and afterward Wagner said, 'You know, these are the confessions of a great genius, but the confession belongs in a closed room. It doesn't belong to the stage. This is not music that should be conveyed to the public; this is the music of a very sick man.'

"Sometimes I feel this way too. I have my diary but I don't want to read it to you. It's my own business what I write there. Maybe when I die, my wife will read it. It may be the most beautiful music, these last Beethoven sonatas, but they are the private confessions of a great man."

Horowitz himself is a rather private performer. His body remains immobile as he plays slow movements, his face impassive—as if he were looking down at a display case in a department store instead of at the keyboard. When he plays fast movements, the pianist of necessity moves more, but there is rarely a flicker of recognizable emotion across his face. The emotion goes into his fingers. Each of his musical phrases is so informed by tension that it becomes as direct and comprehensible as speech. This clarity is a signpost of the Horowitz style and it is coupled with a sensualist's veneration for the sheer beauty of sound. "The sound came before the word," Horowitz is fond of repeating. He will occasionally launch into a series of baby sounds, "oooo... mmmaaahhhh...eehhh," to illustrate his point and explain that the sound is sufficient to convey great depth of feeling. Musicians and critics, for their part, agree that no one coaxes more kinds of sounds from a piano than Vladimir Horowitz.

"He's very much influenced by the human voice," says Gary Graffman, the concert pianist who was one of Horowitz's few students. "He made me listen to opera, to the way great singers did certain phrases, where they breathe, how they breathe, and then wanted me to imitate that kind of approach, to Chopin and Schumann especially. A preoccupation with sound characterizes the Russian school of string players and pianists to which Horowitz belongs, while the German approach (like that of Horowitz's contemporary and friend Rudolf Serkin) is more concerned with form. He hears sounds and he wants to reproduce them. It's a combination of a fantastic technique and an extraordinary power of communication."

"What separates Horowitz from everyone else is his characteristic, deeply individual piano sonority," writes the concert pianist and *Commentary* music critic Samuel Lipman. "Its secret would seem to consist in Horowitz's way of controlling a Steinway concert grand of a loudness and brilliance that in anyone else's hands would reduce an audience to a shattered wreck. The advantages of such a piano—highly different as it is from the usual rich, mellow and quietly brilliant Steinway—lie not only in its carrying power and easy articulation of rapid passages; still more important is the range of dynamic contrast possible and the resulting differentiation of bass, middle and treble registers. This differentiation enables the melodic line to be highlighted and the piano's extreme dynamic contrasts to be used without blocking the audibility of the pitches being played."

Fifteen minutes into the first half of the Toronto recital, nearly 3,000 people were listening so attentively that even a stifled sneeze or cough became an outrage, evoking thoughts of violence toward the offender. Horowitz himself claims that he has never, not in fifty years, sneezed during a concert, and feels that if he can refrain everyone else can too. "But they *don't*," he says emphatically. "They cough. Sometimes there is the flu. Sometimes I have bad public and then I don't go back to this town.

"Sometimes what I see is terrible and it can spoil the concert. Once there was a woman sitting in the first row and anything I did she would shake her head. An old woman. Everything I did, she disapproved. Afterwards she came to see me and I saw it was a nervous tic. But I did not know that during my recital. In Milwaukee, there was one man about three hundred pounds sitting back in his seat with the legs out, picking his nose. I was to begin with Beethoven and I was in a rage. So I sat down facing the public and put my legs apart and stared straight at him. Nobody understood what was going on. He became red. I wasn't embarrassed. I've done many things in my life, you know. All this about being shy is *baloney—complete baloney*! I never was nervous. I'm nervous to do what I want to do. I'm nervous to play the conception I have in my head. I'm nervous to know if it will come out from me or no. Maybe I will have a stomach cramp. I'm a human being. But the public does not make me nervous. Still, I don't want to see their faces."

At intermission, Horowitz took his bows and then hurried back into the artist's room. His valet helped him to undress and the pianist then lay down to nap for fifteen minutes in the dark. He says his blood pressure immediately goes down during these naps and that he is capable of forgetting that he is in a concert hall in the middle of a performance. When he gets up, he puts on a new shirt, combs his hair, and spot-checks all the items of his attire. "He does this without thinking," says Madame Horowitz, who shares with her husband a horror of the casual style of dress and manner many young performers now prefer. "He feels he represents people who have a certain name, people like Chopin and Beethoven. To come out onto the stage in turtleneck and blue jeans shows a lack of respect to the public and a lack of respect to the composer. When you go to a concert, you are looking up, and when you look up, you want to see something a little bit different, a little bit better."

When Horowitz returned to the stage of Massey Hall, his welcome was even more clamorous than when he left it at the end of the first half. Once again, the applause died away and there was a hush before he began. In the first half, he had played two sonatas, one by Mozart, one by Chopin. Now, true to his notion of a recital as a kind of dinner, he played smaller, "dessert" pieces by Fauré, Rachmaninoff (who was the pianist's good friend and admirer), Scriabin, and, again, Chopin. He had played many of these pieces for half a century and yet was conscious of still growing into some of them. "You get less wild," he says. "When you are young you think more of physical prowess than intellectual prowess. But the situation is the same for me always: I am the medium between the composer and the public. I must achieve the right spirit and emotions of the composer. *That* concentration gives the aura to the artist. *That* concentration produces the electricity."

Unlike many other performers, Horowitz is not averse to building a program from a dozen small pieces. "A mazurka of Chopin can be greater than symphony of Mahler," he says. "There can be more music in a five-minute piece than in a piece for one hour." At the same time, of course, programming of this kind is easy on the audience because it demands only short periods of intense listening and allows for sharp contrasts in pace and mood. The shrewdness of the pianist's strategy is apparent: His audience is, in fact, "wrapped by electricity," and each time Horowitz finishes a piece, there are smiles, sighs, those moments of tranquil appreciation just before the burst of applause. Moments like those have a religious quality to them and it is in religious terms that a great many of Horowitz's fans couch their praise.

"To compare me or any other pianist with Horowitz is a sacrilege, a profanity, like spitting on a saint in church," Russian pianist Lazar Berman has said.

"His playing defies analysis," says Horowitz archivist Caine Alder, who has assembled in Salt Lake City, Utah, a museum of Horowitziana.

"He doesn't look like anyone else; he doesn't sound like anyone else. He's the only one who's still cast in that great heroic mode of legendary concert pianists," says Tom Shepard, the director of the company for which Horowitz recorded, and a composer himself. "Before he puts a foot onstage, the excitement is there because you know that for two hours every fiber of this man's body and soul is going to be shared with you. No matter how much you've paid for those tickets, you feel like he's doing you a favor by sharing his time with you."

"It transcends anything he does musically or technically," says critic Samuel Lipman. "His is the last great demonic piano career. He is the last musician whose success his colleagues consider *supernatural*."

After four encores, one of which was his own transcription, Horowitz retired to the artist's room, changed his clothing, and then entered the reception area to greet visitors. After signing autographs and hearing the good wishes of numerous pianists who had come to pay tribute to him, he took a seat behind a small desk and like a general in a war movie held court before a small group of well-dressed, middle-aged men who stood around in a semicircle shifting their weight from foot to foot, as shy as small children. They were managers, representatives of his record company, friends who had come to pay their respects.

"We want you in Italy," said a silver-haired RCA representative from that country. "La Scala is waiting for you. The young people are waiting."

"You must come to England, Maestro," said a man with a British accent.

"I *must*, uunnhh?" repeated Horowitz and raised his eyebrows. "I'm afraid you will be disappointed. I don't like Festival Hall. It's such a huge country, America. There are so many places to play."

After a few more such interchanges, Madame Horowitz indicated with a nod that the audience was over and the group of men filed back into the corridor. Horowitz asked for his black overcoat and his black felt hat. Then he, Madame, tour manager Scimonelli, personal manager Harold Shaw (who had flown up for the concert), and local impresario Walter Homburger moved out the stage door, past a flash of professional and amateur photographers' cameras and scattered applause, to the waiting limousine. When the party arrived at the Sutton Place Hotel, Horowitz went into his bedroom, which was totally dark. "I sleep half an hour. I wake up. I dine," he said. "I feel like there was no concert."

~

At home in his upper East Side town house off Fifth Avenue in New York City, Horowitz follows a rigid routine. Unlike most other artists, he does not teach, and his concert schedule, consisting as it does of twenty concerts per year, leaves him with a lot of free time. He employs a secretary to take care of his correspondence, a cook to worry about his meals, a manager to take care of business, and a press agent to handle the almost daily decisions that must be made regarding publicity. His wife serves as a kind of backstop for all these people so that Horowitz himself is able to lead a life which is as insulated as possible from the kind going on just outside his sealed-off bedroom windows. In this self-created environment, he controls the definition of night and day as well as everything else. He customarily rises at noon, eats his breakfast, and works for about an hour with his secretary. Then he spends some time at the piano, naps for half an hour and, at three-thirty, has lunch. He says he eats no meat, drinks no alcohol, and allows himself a maximum of six cigarettes per day ("I have tremendous willpower. Tremendous!"). Then he takes his daily forty-block walk, returns home, answers telephone calls, and goes to bed for half an hour before dinner.

Horowitz gives interviews, transacts business, and entertains personal friends beginning at nine-thirty at night in his warm, elegantly cluttered living room. The caller enters on the ground floor of the Horowitzes' five-story town house and mounts the stairs to the living room. Vladimir Horowitz likes to make dramatic entrances, so the visitor is seated and given a drink. A few minutes later, the pianist descends the stairs, impeccably dressed, a perky bow tie grazing his chin, all smiles and cordiality. Whoever else is in the living room rises to greet him. Then he sits down. Then everyone else sits down. Horowitz does not think much of the press, and interviewers find themselves in a strictly controlled situation, governed by the peculiar Horowitz protocol. "We are not like Lenny Bernstein. We do not want to be in *People* magazine," says Madame Horowitz by way of setting the tone for the evening. She sits down beside her husband and asks the tour manager, Giovanni Scimonelli, to stay as well. "Tch, tch," she will cluck when her husband says something she considers indiscreet, or she will step in to rephrase either the interviewer's question or her husband's answer. Horowitz himself seems to enjoy her participation. He prescreens his interviewers (I was asked to audition at nine-thirty on a preceding night so that the pianist could decide if he wished to talk to me) and addresses himself to interviews as if they were a kind of card game.

"You know," he says deliberately, crossing his legs and toying with one of his six allotted cigarettes, "this article for me is not important. I have made my career. For you is important. For your career. You will write good article, uunnhh?" Then he settles back on the plump black chintz sofa and talks animatedly till nearly one in the morning.

Horowitz prides himself on his continued musical growth. "Every year," he says, "I work on something new. I have a challenge to myself to learn something I have never played before. To see if my mind is right, the reflexes are still right. The composer closest to me is the composer I play at the moment. Every week, I have a different friend; I am promiscuous; what I feel, I play right away. This year, I play for the first time two pieces of Fauré. First of all, I study the whole composer. I play everything he wrote. Ensemble music—everything. I play *myself*, not listen to recordings. I'm a very good sight reader. There are wonderful artists who are not so good sight readers, but I happen to be a good one.

"I play everything the composer wrote because the *mood* of the composer is the same if it is a big piece or a small piece, for the piano only or for ensemble. You feel the music. The texture talks to me. The style: One composer is epic; the other, poetic; or heroic, or dramatic. I play the music myself because records are not the truth. They are like postcards of a beautiful landscape. You bring the postcards home so when you look at them you will remember how beautiful is the truth.

"I know also everything *about* the composer. I read his letters because, usually in those times, they were writing a lot. The letters give me the character of the composer, the honesty of the composer, the taste of the composer. What he liked in other music, what he disliked. The letters give me a clue to his spiritual concept, to the spirit of the music. I don't read books *about* the composer. I always believe the composer himself and not what others write about him.

"The first time I play a piece of music, I *listen*. I think: There is something hidden here. Artur Nikisch said we have five lines and dots. If you play only the dots, it is not music. You must go behind the dots to the other side, to the emotional sense of the music, to what is hidden. So I read it again the next day. Then for two days I leave it alone. Then I repeat the third day. Five days. Six days. And then I am in that music just like I play 'Tea for Two'!"

The pianist breaks off into a throaty giggle which terminates in a cough and a frown. "When I am playing, I don't listen to other people, not even to my own records. I don't want to be influenced, even unconsciously. I take the music and I want to see it as if I have never seen it before. When I play a piece, every note is clear in my mind. Otherwise I cannot do it.

Never. Even from the great composers there are pieces I don't like and I will never play them. Even the most introspective composer of them all—Robert Schumann—I love him but there are lots of pieces that are hackneyed and I will never play because they don't speak to me. Maybe it's my fault. Is possible. I don't blame Mr. Schumann. But I don't do it. I must confess without boasting that I have a kind of inner integrity which dictates what to do and what not to do.

"A concert is not a lecture. For me, the intellect is always the guide but not the goal of the performance. If a composer is too intellectual, like some modern composers, I don't get it. A concert is not a lecture. I myself introduced in forties and fifties modern music. I played the first performances of three sonatas of Prokofiev, of sonata of Barber, and lots of small pieces of Barber. I did not respond immediately to Barber. First, I knew the composer. He was a friend of mine. I get to know his feeling. It was very much beautifully, idiomatically written. But the music? There were places where I didn't understand even playing it. But the whole was good. You cannot always be a genius. My father-in-law said you cannot be twenty-four hours a genius. There are moments....But the music now? You can write a fugue like Bach and you can write a fugue like, pardon me, Hindemith. A soulless fugue."

Madame Horowitz, who has been listening to her husband carefully, settles back into the couch: He is enjoying himself.

"I think that every performer should have some composing instinct," he continues expansively. "Good composers or bad composers, the best pianists were always composers—all of them! It gives you the fantasy, the freedom, the understanding of music! And there's another part of art: Improvisation. I can sit and improvise for two hours. Sometimes nothing comes out and sometimes beautiful things. For me, the intellect is always the guide but not the goal of the performance. Three things have to be coordinated and not one must stick out. Not too much intellect because it can become scholastic. Not too much heart because it can become schmaltz. Not too much technique because you can become a mechanic. Mechanics is something physical like calisthenics to build up muscle. Because we have a percussive instrument. But what every composer was asking—from Mozart to Beethoven to Chopin—is that we must try to make a percussive instrument which is singing. When you have highly developed mechanics, the technique is how to apply it. But if it is only dexterity, it is like...like Detroit, you know..."

"Assembly line," says Madame Horowitz.

"You will go to a concert and the pianist will play passages, every trill is so perfect. It's fine but in ten minutes you will be bored. Everything will sound the same. Always there should be a little mistake here and there—I am for it. The people who don't do mistakes are cold like ice. It takes risk to make a mistake. If you don't take risk, you are boring. These youngsters who win a competition are like the..."

"Assembly line," says Madame Horowitz.

"Assembly line," says Horowitz. "In ten minutes you will be bored and go home. The *critics* don't like it when you do mistakes. I read all the critics but they don't influence me. In the beginning, yes. From a materialistic point of view. My manager told me it was very important to have good critics because then I will be engaged. But they never influenced me musically. Not from the first day I came. They cannot change my mind.

"When I went to Germany in the beginning, when I first played outside Russia, I had to change. I played the music I liked—a whole evening of Medtner, for example—but *two* pieces were too much for them in Germany and in France they were not interested. So I changed my repertoire and put in Chopin, Liszt, Schubert. In France I learned Ravel, Debussy, Dukas, and Poulenc. I shrank the Russian repertoire. Germany was the citadel of music at that time, from 1925 to Hitler, and everybody was there. And I knew them. And they had no effect on me. I kept my personality like a piece of steel. Schnabel wanted to give me lessons. Cortot wanted to give me lessons. But I didn't want. The only person I wanted to go to was Busoni, but I came one year after he died. There was a chauvinism in Europe. In Paris you had to play French music. In Italy, Italian. In Germany, German. I felt it from the audiences. I played in Vienna some Ravel and the audience was *laughing*! So I did not play it the next time.

"When I went to Germany in 1925 I was sitting there for four months and going—absolutely without exaggeration—going three times a week in the concerts. Just to hear everything. I was *verrrrry* disappointed. Terribly. Because I liked all the music but I heard it played very scholastically. *Boring.* I was writing home and I was saying, 'My God this whole Germany is like the Gotterdämmerung. It all goes to pieces here!'"

Madame Horowitz sits up and says "Tch, tch."

"This is a very extraordinary thing which I'm telling you now," he says, disregarding her and leaning forward as if what he is saying were a state secret. "I imagined much more warmth and sensuality, much more life.

I heard everything in the music and when it was played it was much more narrow. Till today, I am not a pedantic. I am an individualist. *Every* artist should be." He breaks off and gazes into the air.

"You were speaking about the critics," Madame prompts. Scimonelli straightens up in his chair and tilts his well-coiffed head toward the pianist.

"I read all the critics but they don't influence me," Horowitz repeats. "After a concert, I remember everything I did. Sometimes I play very good and the critics don't know it. But I will tell you now something a little bit conceited: *Even when I play not as good, it's good enough.* I know it, you see, but the audience doesn't know it and sometimes the *critics* don't know it. For myself, if I succeed to play all the notes, if I succeed to play all the value of the notes, if I succeed with all the colors, then I know it is a success. It's like a painting. Here you plan a little rose, here a little blue, and some parts you don't know what the colors will be. When I finish, I hear the whole thing in my mind and I see it is beautiful."

Although Horowitz makes a case for including mistakes in live performances, he is not eager to have them immortalized in his recordings. Modern recording techniques have, through splicing, eliminated the problem of "succeeding to play all the notes," and the pianist uses them to their fullest advantage. He exercises a control over his records which is unique in the classical music industry: His contract specifies his final approval over every aspect of the recording process, from the production of the LPs, to the appearance of the record jackets, to the wording of the copy advertising them.

At Columbia Records, where he was under contract until 1974, Horowitz had "a higher yearly guarantee than any other artist, including Leonard Bernstein," says a man who worked there. "He also was the only artist whose contract read that he had to *sign* a test pressing before we could release it. The following kind of situation would occur, and I am not exaggerating. We would record a piece, splice the various takes, and send him a copy. He says, 'That's pretty good but I play the trill better elsewhere.' So you go through the takes, find the trill he likes and put it in. Then, a week later, he says, 'I think I play a more exciting coda on another take.' So you go back, find the coda, and put *it* on. You finally get the master tape so that the performance is good. You send him that. You go over to his house at nine-thirty at night even though you've been working all day and got up at six-thirty that morning. Then he says, 'You know, slow movement could be one decibel lower.'

"Now you know that one decibel is the smallest level of differentiation—it can barely be detected. The technical term for this kind of thing is *bullshit*. But it's Horowitz, so you go back, remix the slow movement, and make it one decibel lower. Finally, he's happy. The next step is a test pressing, something which very rarely occurs apart from dealings with Horowitz. The factory actually presses six to twelve records and, instead of going on with the next thousand, one of them is sent to Horowitz. He listens to it at home. Then he'll say, 'You know, is a little bit noisy on the second side.'

"So you make the plant stand on its head (I don't have to tell you how much all this costs the company), take the record apart, and make a new one. You press six more. You send him one to listen to. You go to his house again at nine-thirty and then he says, 'You know, I don't think I like the way I play the second movement.' Now you have to go all the way back to the beginning of the process and start again. *No* other artist in my experience behaves this way."

Horowitz behaves this way with managers, sometimes refusing to sign contracts until days before a concert and, of course, canceling appearances abruptly when he so wishes. He behaves this way with his audiences, who sometimes camp out on the sidewalk the night before a local box office puts Horowitz tickets on sale, only to find in the morning that a number of seats have already been sold and another group are held by the Horowitzes themselves. He behaves this way with his friends, who are for the most part people affiliated with his career and who also serve more as an audience than a peer group. They treat him like a fragile Chinese vase, catering to his whims and rigid routines, listening to well-worn anecdotes and jokes, supporting his decisions with unquestioning loyalty. They believe that they have been honored by the opportunity to be near a genius and they do not wish to endanger it. They say they do not know when asked about the pianist's rumored nervous breakdowns, his rumored homosexuality, the rumor that his only daughter killed herself. *Isn't that all somewhat beside the point?* they are apt to ask.

At eleven-thirty at night in the Horowitzes' living room, it is easy to see what they mean. The pianist is feeling well and, after two hours of talk, has begun to relax and to take a genuine interest in what he is saying. "The public is a very strange animal," he speculates. "Singly, they sometimes don't understand anything, but when they are together, sometimes they do understand. I love to play in Chicago—there are no extremes there. Boston is good. Washington is very good, cosmopolitan.

In New York they are provincial as not one town in America. New York, you see, is not a town—it's a country. So when you give a recital, you don't know who's in the audience. You never know. There are always too many students who listen only to particular things and criticize already in advance. There are too many aristocrats there: That is, they have money and I have a name so they *have* to be there. They will sleep one hour but they have to be there! New York is the most difficult city in that respect. It has the most intellectual and knowledgeable public but they are not always in Carnegie Hall—they cannot always get tickets. I don't know about the west coast but what a wonderful city is Ann Arbor! The colleges are the aristocracy of the public. I like young people and they like me."

Vladimir Horowitz smiles with satisfaction. "The public has learned a lot in the fifty years I am playing here. Because they heard very much music. From radio and from the records. The first year I came here, I played Chopin's G minor Ballade, one of the most hackneyed pieces today. But then, in 1928, my manager told me that people complained that I shouldn't play such intellectual pieces! Fifty years ago, you could play a program of Strauss waltzes and transcriptions of opera. You had to play more pyrotechnical things, more explosive things which made the public stand up from the seats and clap. When I was young, I liked that too. I wanted to *épater le bourgeois*. I had a tremendous facility and I could make people throw their hats off. That was my goal: I wanted them to acknowledge me; I wanted to be a success right away. But today, the public wants music written by geniuses for the piano. Genuine music. It was more Barnum-like then. Not now.

"The artists have also changed. One thing is very important: No one travels by train anymore. Now when they want a success, they ruin their chance because of the planes. They can sing or play in San Francisco in the afternoon and Los Angeles in the evening. They do four or five concerts a week. The question is not physical fatigue. The problem is that when you play all the time, you repeat the same thing. And when you repeat the same thing, you start to imitate yourself instead of doing something fresh. You need time to think. You need time to absorb. When you perform, you are giving. You need time to get back something. I always took six months to refuel. You have to reflect a little bit, to sit back, to *see* yourself. To talk with your colleagues.

"Now colleagues don't meet together so much. They are all separate. They are all traveling in planes. They are all enemies. There's no communication. In the twenties and thirties, we would meet and discuss the music and why you do this and why you do that. The youngsters are afraid and they are busy all the time. We are closer to the music, to the time it was written, than they are. We're closer to the truth. My teachers were even closer than me. It is a human chain in music that goes from teacher to pupil."

Horowitz breaks off and recites a proverb in Russian. "Everyone goes to the forest," he translates. "But some people go for a walk to be inspired and some go to cut down the trees." He repeats the Russian and stares gloomily across the room. The pianist sees himself as a link in a chain of pianists that goes back 150 years. "Now the chain has been broken," he says, "but that's the way it goes today."

Horowitz says he is like an "old-fashioned spinster" who is convinced that in her time, things were far better than they are now. He dislikes much of the modern life he sees around him, and it is for this reason, as much as for reasons of privacy, that he prefers to stay home in his own world. "I read the paper every day," he says. "But in this town the standard has gone down on account of the monopoly. The *New York Times* is getting worse and worse all the time. Cabbages are mixed up with Cézanne; you don't know where to look for things! I cannot follow it anymore! I don't open the radio too much— it's too much noise. I never look at the television. I love theater—do you know a Russian who doesn't love theater? My God. I'm born under Stanislavski! But I must tell you, in these eight years there is not so much good theater. I don't go to concerts. I don't want to be unconsciously influenced, and also that is the time I dine.

"I read the letters of composers. They were writing a tremendous amount in the nineteenth century and I can read in three languages. I have already read all the classics: Dickens, all the Russians, all the Victor Hugo, Proust, you name it. I knew very well Thomas Mann personally, and that I read in German. But the modern literature that is written today I don't read so much. It's too much for me. It takes too much time. I prefer to listen to opera. I go sometimes to the movie but I prefer to go to discothèques. I like to see how the young people behave. You can see *anything* today. It's not like in my time when everything was under the table. Now it's *on* the table. I like to see how far it goes. My wife dances. I don't dance. I have no rhythm. I move so much with my hands that I find it superfluous to move with my feet!"

Horowitz breaks off into another of his loud, delighted giggles, and his face, so gloomy just moments before, radiates gaiety.

"But I talk more than I do," he concedes. "I go once every two or three months. I put the earplugs in my ears and I look at it. Even when I walk in the street, I have a good time. It's like theater, the streets of New York. When I go to Greenwich Village, it's like another town. I sit there. I am like in the opera. It's funny, you know.

"There are very few things in life that make me suffer. Only physical pain. I had pain when I lost my cat. And my daughter when she died, and when I lost my mother. I suffer frustration that I wanted and never became a composer. But every individual is half happy, half frustrated. I have no time now. You can't combine both the composer and the performer. When Liszt played, he composed unbelievably badly. Schubert, the worst of all.

"I think the most important thing in a man's life is health—mental and physical. If you have both these things then you can do anything. When you get older, something happens to you and of that I am a little bit frightened. I had bronchitis now, you know, and I needed a little more time to get better. But I don't *have* the time. That Rachmaninoff concerto that I play with the Philharmonic is so difficult. I need the time to practice."

It is nearly one o'clock in the morning. Madame Horowitz is making small but perceptible signs to her husband, indicating that there has been enough talk. Her husband's face clouds over again and he says, "You will write good article, uunnhh?"

Giovanni Scimonelli, who has not said one word for three and a half hours, smiles and says it would be difficult to do otherwise.

Then, abruptly, Horowitz quotes the composer Domenico Scarlatti, who, in an introduction to thirty harpsichord pieces published in 1738, wrote: "Show yourself more human than critical and your pleasure will increase."

"I think that is beautiful," the pianist says pointedly and then says nothing more.

As I take my leave and thank Madame Horowitz and Mr. Scimonelli, Vladimir Horowitz sits frowning on the black chintz couch.

"You know the pianist Michelangeli?" he asks out of the blue.

"From records," I say.

Horowitz shakes his head. "*That* one," he says of the Italian recluse, "I think he is a little bit *meshuga*."

Seiji Ozawa teaching conducting at Tanglewood. (*Walter H. Scott.*)

2

Learning to Conduct at Tanglewood

It is a profession largely misunderstood by concertgoers, vilified *and* extolled by musicians, described as "crazy," "unnatural," and "impossible" by its most successful practitioners. Conductors are the only musicians who cannot by themselves create a sound people will pay to hear. Their instrument is no inanimate object but a group of (often difficult) human beings. Unlike instrumentalists or singers, who take for granted the fact that they can hear themselves practice, conductors may study for five or ten years before they obtain fifteen minutes of the sound they want to produce. Until then, they conduct imaginary ensembles in empty rooms, church choirs, madrigal groups, bands, or two pianists who play the music that a composer conceived for a full orchestra.

During this bizarre course of study, the aspiring conductor must develop the strength of a dancer, the expressiveness of an accomplished actor, the organizational acumen of a business executive, the interpersonal skills of a psychologist, and the charisma of a religious leader. All this, of course, on top of a musicianship so sensitive and compelling that one hundred other musicians who have also trained long and hard will tolerate the conductor's reading of a given work and play it for him, if not accept it as their own.

This nearly superhuman profile of a conductor is of recent vintage. Until the nineteenth century, a conductor was just another musician who beat time with a roll of paper or a stick so that two dozen players could play more or less together. But as composers wrote increasingly intricate scores for ever larger ensembles, orchestra size doubled, then tripled. Players soon could neither see nor hear one another and needed the services of a conductor who would give them their cues, coordinate meter changes, work out the balance of sound between various sections, and make decisions for the group. Richard Wagner was the first man to take on the role of autocratic disciplinarian, the conductor who was no longer content with beating time but who drilled his musicians and who interpreted the score. Wagner in many ways anticipated the duties of the contemporary music director of a major orchestra: He thought about such things as the optimal duration of intermissions and even about the quality of refreshments, since "everybody knows quite well that art alone is not what the majority of people want."

Wagner was followed by a line of intensely charismatic men, including Artur Nikisch, Gustav Mahler, Arturo Toscanini, and Bruno Walter— all of whom cultivated a mystique that rivaled those of the most demonic pianists. Conductors now held their batons over the heads of one hundred musicians; they could commission new music as well as select which of the old the public would hear; they presided over huge institutions with budgets running into the millions. Television consolidated the conductor's power and preeminence. With the advent of light, mobile equipment, television could capture what even the concertgoer in the hall could not see: The maestro's face. And the way the cameras lingered over that face confirmed what musicians had long known: The conductor had become the most important figure in orchestral music, often eclipsing not only the soloist and the orchestra but the composer as well.

There used to be only two ways of becoming a conductor. One was to spend years in an orchestra; the other, to spend years in an opera house, rehearsing singers. Today most aspiring conductors attend conservatories and colleges and summer programs such as the conducting seminar at Tanglewood in Lenox, Massachusetts, where, every summer, about a dozen young men and the occasional young woman who have survived an arduous selection process undergo an eight-week immersion in the "impossible."

They meet at Seranak, the hilltop estate of the late Serge Koussevitzky, who founded the Tanglewood Festival, gave up his summer vacations in Europe to conduct the Boston Symphony Orchestra year-round, and taught the first batch of student conductors himself. It is an idyllic place. Named for Serge and Natalie Koussevitzky, Seranak sits high above the grounds of Tanglewood, its low-walled terrace offering one of the best possible views of the Stockbridge Bowl and the surrounding Berkshire hills. Inside the white-shingled house, a six-foot-high oil painting of Koussevitzky playing his bass dominates the living room, echoed by smaller paintings, drawings, and busts of the man. There are two baby grand pianos in the living room for the conducting seminar, a conductor's stand, Koussevitzky's lamps and books, a camera and a videocassette recorder, and several rows of plain metal folding chairs jammed amid the once elegant, now somewhat fading rattan and wood furniture.

Every summer since 1940, when the five conducting fellows were Leonard Bernstein, Gaylord Brown, Richard Bales, Thor Johnson, and Lukas Foss, seminars have been anything but calm. In the 1980s, with former star instrumentalists such as violinst Pinchas Zukerman, pianist Christoph Eschenbach, and trumpet virtuoso Gerard Schwarz moving into an already crowded field—the American Symphony Orchestra League in 1986 identified a grand total of 1,297 conductors in North America (including youth and college orchestra conductors)—expectations are high and competition is fierce. Seranak—this very living room—is where Koussevitzky said to Leonard Bernstein, *"It vill be open to you whole the gates from the vorld!"* Lorin Maazel studied here. So did Seiji Ozawa. So did Zubin Mehta. Over the course of a summer, Bernstein, Ozawa, Kurt Masur, André Previn, Erich Leinsdorf, Andrew Davis, Klaus Tennstedt, and other brilliant, powerful music directors of world-class orchestras would come to teach the seminar, impart their insights, and, perhaps, be struck by the talent of one of the conducting students.

About 200 young conductors apply to be conducting fellows every summer. In 1986, four were chosen; five years earlier, there were only two. Those two—Ken Takaseki from Tokyo and Gary Sheldon from Bay Shore, New York—paid no tuition and, more importantly, were slated to conduct the Tanglewood student orchestra every week in public concerts, which are often attended by local as well as Boston and New York critics and other people important in the music business. Another nine men (three Japanese, two Americans, one Pole, one Italian, one Dutchman, and one Russian-Jewish emigré) were seminar students, restricted to conducting pianos. The twelfth man, Wei-Zhi Weng from Peking, China, was designated an auditor, restricted to watching.

These distinctions are meaningful in a group where stakes are high and ego needs are, if anything, even higher. There have been summers at Seranak where fellows did not talk to students, let alone to an auditor.

During the summer of 1981, everyone was talking but conversation resembled a competition, and a question such as "How old are you?" could suddenly take on threatening overtones.

The conductors ranged in age from twenty-one to twenty-nine. All had had at least five years of conducting experience and all had played at least one instrument, usually the piano, since childhood. All had a certain smoothness of manner and the half-attentive eyes of company men at a company cocktail party: During those eight weeks at Tanglewood, each of them did all he could within the realm of propriety to grab the spotlight, for, as one of them put it, "There are many people here who can do something for you."

A hush fell over the room that first week as two such people pulled up in the circular driveway outside the main door of Seranak: Leonard Bernstein in his open beige Mercedes convertible, Seiji Ozawa in his red-and-white Chevy truck. Both men were deeply tanned, glamourous as movie stars, poised and graceful as cats. Their faces looked etched, their arms and backs sculpted, in stone. Ozawa wore all white: White jeans, white Mao jacket, white running shoes; Bernstein wore faded blue jeans, a canvas jacket, and cowboy boots. Each was trailed by his assistant. Each exuded personality and a presence so commanding that it reduced all the other people in the room to a blur.

Up front, beneath the six-foot-high portrait of Serge Koussevitzky, Ken Takaseki ("Poor Ken," one of the students murmured) waited for things to settle down. He had been scheduled to work on Béla Bartók's Concerto for Orchestra that afternoon and had not been sure until he heard the cars in the driveway that Bernstein and Ozawa would show up. Now, after the two took seats, he raised his baton and the two Japanese pianists—the only women in the room—began playing. Seiji Ozawa soon raised an arm.

"Very good. You know the music," he said, nodding to Takaseki and to Gustav Meier, the Swiss-born island of sanity who runs the seminar. "But *to me*, Bartók is..." He ended his sentence with a movement of his arm and body that was difficult to describe. "In words you can describe eight kinds of sadness," he would say later. "In music, so many more."

Then he looked around the living room. "Somebody speaks Hungarian here?"

A few of the students glanced around.

"Lenny? You speak Hungarian?"

Seiji Ozawa with a student at Saranak. (*Walter H. Scott.*)

"Oh, I guess I know a little Hungarian," Bernstein said in his dramatic, resonant voice. "Just a few words."

He struck a pose, his cigarette at eye level, and began an oration in what appeared to be Hungarian.

"All the language is like..." Ozawa ended his sentence in movement again, pounding his right fist into his left palm along with Bernstein's emphases.

"You know the *reason* for that," said Bernstein, "is that almost every word in Hungarian is accented on the first syllable, just as it is in the Czech language. You look at every piece Bartók ever wrote and everything goes: *va*-va, *va*-va, *va*-va, *va*-va-va."

He stubbed out his cigarette and launched into an imitation of Gregor Piatigorsky doing an imitation of Bartók's wife speaking Hungarian, discussed the influence of language on folk themes and the use of folk themes in the music of Bartók and Schubert, then walked up behind Ozawa. "Now," he said, "Seiji and I and this fellow here are all playing trumpet in your orchestra."

He lit up another cigarette as Ken Takaseki watched, stuck it into his aquafilter, and held it to his mouth with two hands as though it were a trumpet.

"We're always nervous at this point," he said. "We need all the help we can get from you. We need to get that *Hungarian* sound and you have to show us how. Now show us, two miles away, three trumpets making an entrance. Show us the attack!"

Ken Takaseki raised his fiberglass baton.

"Excuse me for interrupting," Bernstein said, his voice silencing the two Japanese pianists. "Can you grab us at the bar before? We are *completely* in your control. *Show* us how to do it: With your teeth, with your left earlobe, with your feet if you have to!"

Takaseki stared hard at Bernstein's cigarette and started again, compressing his lips as he attacked.

Bernstein raised his tanned hand. "That's much better. Can we hear it again?"

Takaseki raised his baton again and, this time, Bernstein fixed his large, glittering eyes on him with such intensity that one could almost see the energy flowing from the older to the younger man.

"Can you sing to me how you hear those trumpets in your mind?" Bernstein asked when he had finished the phrase.

Ken Takaseki gulped, then tried to sing. It came out a squeak.

Ozawa nodded.

"Are you afraid?" asked Bernstein. "Are you embarrassed? Are you nervous?"

Ken Takaseki nodded. The class burst out laughing.

"I just think you're so *gifted* that it's worth spending all this time," said Bernstein. He moved forward, scattering ash like baptismal water over the heads of the students. "I'd like you to sing that trumpet line because I think I feel what you hear but I don't *hear* what you hear or *see* what you hear. Do you understand? Whatever is inside of you has to be communicated to the orchestra, but *first*, you have to express it to yourself."

Ken Takaseki listened, then tried to sing again. Again it came out a squeak.

"Again," intoned Bernstein.

Ken Takaseki sang the trumpet line again and again until he would never in his life forget it. Bernstein told the students that he worked with orchestras in that very same way, exploring one detail of the music until he felt it was perfectly executed. "What is a great novel but details?" he would ask later, rhetorically, after reciting verbatim a passage of Thomas Mann.

"Let's make up a word in Hungarian to go along with those trumpets," he said now. "Anyone have a word?"

The students, the fellows, the auditor, Ozawa, and Meier were silent.

"I have a word," said Bernstein. "*Budapestü*! Let's say it means 'I am a citizen of Budapest.' Can you repeat it?"

The students, the fellows, the auditor, Ozawa, and Meier all repeated, "*Bu-da-pes-tü . . . Bu-da-pes-tü . . . Bu-da-pes-tü.*"

"Now sing it the way Bartók wrote it!" Bernstein ordered Takaseki. Ken Takaseki sang. "*Bu-da-pes-tü . . . Bu-da-pes-tü.*"

"*Sing* it!" exhorted Bernstein.

"*Bu-da-pes-tü . . . Bu-da-pes-tü . . .*"

"Now do it again," said Bernstein. "But *mysteriously*. Just between us. It's something that appears in the night. Bartók's always writing this night music. Translate that to the beat and sing it with your *hands*!"

Ken Takaseki's face had by now grown grim. He glared at the two pianists, then gestured with his baton.

"*Now* we're getting something," said Bernstein.

~

Over the course of a summer, the conductors watch Boston Symphony Orchestra and Tanglewood Student Orchestra rehearsals and attend as many master classes and concerts as they can. But most of their time is spent studying orchestral scores, analyzing musical structure, dynamics, phrasing, and tempi; learning how and when to cue various instruments; and watching their colleagues conduct the two Japanese pianists in a dusty former barn or in the living room at Seranak. They spend hundreds of dollars on orchestral scores and then hundreds of hours studying them, forming a musical concept, and then finding a way to express their musical intentions.

One by one they stand between the two pianos every weekday, four feet away from their audience, with a score of Beethoven's Fifth or the Brahms Third, trying to force themselves to reveal more through their bodies and faces than they might to themselves, alone, before a bathroom mirror.

They must learn to let go while staying in control, to risk looking ugly, ill, or ridiculous, and to do this before competitors, teachers, journalists, and anyone else who happens to drop by.

Some of the students cannot do it. Their motions are prim and stilted, pretty and self-contained. Their bodies freeze. Their faces become drained of expression and take on the smoothness of masks.

"Don't be so Oriental," Seiji Ozawa admonishes them when it is his turn to teach. "The worst thing is when conductor is stiff. Orchestra becomes stiff. If you are stiff, you cannot write a good poem, you cannot play instrument or sing. I got the message from Munch here in 1960. He said one word: *supple*. Maestro Karajan said three things: Listen. Hand must be free. Hand must be available. Means *supple*."

Some of the conductors gasp for air, then erupt into movement so convulsive that they look like madmen. Their eyes flash, the pupils disappear. Their faces contort in pain, then show a panorama of emotion. It is like watching a lover's face, and the intimacy of expression clashes with the tense atmosphere like a persistent, dissonant chord.

"I think you feel music very well," says Ozawa politely when one of them has finished a phrase, "but conductor must be—how you say?—a little *distant*? What you do is *too much*, too. . ." He rolls up his spine like a caterpillar. "You do so much your ear stop. You don't hear what orchestra is doing. Also. If you go like this, end of symphony you need ambulance."

He explains to the class how a gesture is likely to be misinterpreted by an orchestra in the way a good editor explains to a writer how a certain word may be misconstrued by a reader.

"Most important part of conducting is *listening*," he says. "Not like audience listening but listening for what orchestra needs. Almost you have to listen *before* the sound comes."

A conductor's concept of a piece, he says, should be implicit in the conducting: "If you and I are not children and we speak the same language, you will understand my personality without me saying, 'My personality is such and such.' Same thing in music. In orchestra, there is time limit. You come in one note early, that's *wrong*. One note is too loud or too high, that's *wrong*. Rhythm *wrong*. Balance *wrong*. When I study score, I try to find composer's wish but, in rehearsal, I don't talk about it. To *me*, technique is everything you do alone and with orchestra. When I was student here, I was very good at technical things but I didn't know Mahler or Bruckner. If you know Mahler and Wagner and Strauss, it becomes absolutely clear what is Mozart. When I learned Stravinsky, it changed how I understood Bartók. This is also technique."

By the third week of the seminar, only Gustav Meier remains good-humored. A tall, informal man whose manner is a corrective to that of the more theatrical conductors, Meier first came to Tanglewood from Zurich in 1957 and returned the following summer in the company of Claudio Abbado, Zubin Mehta, and David Zinman. Of the four fellows that year, he was the only one who chose to combine the professional and academic worlds, taking positions first at Yale, then at Eastman, then at the University of Michigan while guest conducting in Zurich, New York, and Santa Fe and serving as music director of the Bridgeport and Lansing symphonies. As director of orchestra and opera at Michigan and as director of the conducting seminar at Tanglewood, his subject matter includes everything from unscrambling scores to discussing "road maps on how to proceed and hopefully succeed as a conductor."

He reminds his students to breathe and to keep their bodies quiet.

"Be grounded," he repeats every summer. "One of the great things about Bernstein is that he's so connected to the earth he can move away from it with the agility and power of a boxer."

Meier claims that anyone can learn the basic physical signals of conducting in a relatively short time and that his students' major problem is not technical but musical. He says most of them do not study the scores well enough, and that even when they do, they do not become involved enough with the music. "A conductor has to study the score for structure and harmonies, for instrumentation, for balance of sound," he says, "but he should also know where the piece fits in the composer's life. He has to read *about* the composer. His letters, for example. He has to listen to other works that the composer wrote at the same time and earlier—to do all he can to get into the composer's head."

There is no prototype of the young conductor at Tanglewood. The men and the handful of women who have studied there have come from all over the world; they are between the ages of twenty and thirty-five; they are mostly bright, well educated, multilingual, and very polite. "They have to be nice—the days of the nineteenth-century conductor are over," says Meier. They come from various socioeconomic backgrounds—some so poor that they cannot get to Tanglewood without extensive financial assistance, others so rich that their families can buy them an evening's worth of an orchestra's time. All play at least one instrument, some play two or three, and all can find their way around a piano. Some exhibit a Machiavellian grasp of politics; others soon go under because they can't handle them. If there are any components of a "typical" conducting student, according to Meier, they would be a commitment to music, an unusual drive to succeed at it, and, "on the negative side, a lack of rhythm and the ability to convey the emotional part of the musical content."

Lack of rhythm?

"It sounds very strange, I know," he says. "But it's true. Rhythm only becomes natural when you are free physically and spiritually, when you can let go. That's Bernstein and Ozawa. That's what these young conductors are not yet. As to the emotional commitment, the passion needs to be so overriding that it will inspire an orchestra that does not easily get inspired."

In 1986, there were fifteen seminar participants: one from Hong Kong, seven North Americans, and seven Europeans. For the first time ever, three of them were women.

One of the three and the first fellow ever to come to Tanglewood from East Germany was Romely Pfund, a calm, quietly confident thirty-year-old whose warmth and musicality quickly made her a favorite of the student musicians. Born and raised in Dresden, she had, like most of the young conductors, begun her musical training at the piano. Soon, however, she was accompanying singers and working with choruses, following her inclination to work with other people. At eighteen, after finishing high school, she was accepted as one of four piano and conducting students at the Dresden Hochschule für Musik.

Her course of study there, she says, was similar to what Americans learn about conducting, with some important differences: In her classes, technique was discussed less and questions of style and philosophy of the composer more; students generally listened while professors lectured; and conductors were encouraged to go out and get practical experience as soon as possible, with the result that Pfund at thirty had already been working steadily for eight years by the time she got to Tanglewood.

The most striking similarity her career had so far shown to the careers of Americans was the role that a mentor had played in it. At nineteen, Pfund had auditioned for an international music seminar in Weimar and was chosen to attend by a jury that included Leipzig Gewandhaus conductor Kurt Masur. Although she never formally studied with Masur after that summer, she had kept in close touch with him, consulting with him on musical problems, first as a student and then as she prepared for the

Romely Pfund conducting the Tanglewood student orchestra with
Leonard Bernstein coaching. (*Walter H. Scott.*)

Ernest Ansermet Competition that she won in Geneva in 1984 and the
Vaclav Talich Competition that she won in Prague in 1985.

The most striking difference between Pfund and the three other fellows
was that she knew her professional future was assured. "It's hard to get
a *good* job," she said, "but to start as a young conductor in a small theater
is no problem. Now I have a contract, year-round, as a conductor in
Dessau. I have been there for three years and am ready to change. I have
to audition to go somewhere else. There are three top orchestras in my

country—the Gewandhaus in Leipzig, the Stadtskapelle Dresden, and the Stadtskapelle Berlin. Then there are about fifteen excellent orchestras and about twenty-five smaller ones. Every theater or orchestra has several conductors. My problem will be to work my way to the top ones. That will take time, but it is not as difficult as here."

Having been a fellow at Tanglewood will help Romely Pfund's career as it will help all the careers of the seminar participants, but for Pfund, it may have been the only opportunity she will ever have to hear and see most Western conductors in the flesh. "I think this is the climax of my life till now," she said. "The greatest impression for me was Bernstein. I never will forget it. He did his rehearsals like concerts—every note was intense. It was *life*. He showed me what was possible. And Ozawa—how he prepared for rehearsals! And Rozhdestvensky—it's all music! In a way I am glad I did not come here earlier. The rest of my seminar knows all these conductors already. Maybe it would be better to find your own way first, to form your own musical personality, before you are exposed to them."

Her colleague Richard Hoenich, the thirty-one-year-old assistant conductor and principal bassoonist of the Montreal Symphony Orchestra, had been exposed to Bernstein and Ozawa from the beginning of his musical career. A short, articulate former piano prodigy, Hoenich had performed with the Montreal Symphony as a teenager, then went on to major in bassoon at the Curtis Institute of Music. But even as a child, he had always had an "irrational" desire to conduct, which he could explain only years later. "People think that being a conductor is a power trip," he said, "that we go into it because we want to tell people what to do. I don't think that's true. I had strong feelings about the symphonic repertoire. I have something to say with those pieces. I love them, and I love the orchestra as an instrument capable of innumerable possibilities. To examine how various composers have used these possibilities is a lifelong challenge."

Hoenich was playing bassoon in the Montreal Symphony when its assistant conductor, knowing of Hoenich's interest, gave him the opportunity to conduct the student orchestra at McGill University. Some time later, the assistant conductor told Hoenich he was planning to leave Montreal and suggested that Hoenich talk to music director Charles Dutoit about moving into the assistant position.

"I asked him if it was possible," Hoenich said with a smile at his own *chutzpah*, "with no formal conducting training at all, without the benefit of a single course or a book, to become assistant conductor while I continued as principal bassoon. He said yes."

Hoenich immediately made plans to attend the Los Angeles Philharmonic Institute for Conductors, where he worked with Michael Tilson Thomas, and then settled in for three years as assistant conductor of the Montreal Symphony, with eventual guest conducting engagements with various Canadian groups such as the Manitoba Chamber Orchestra and the Symphony of Nova Scotia. Like Romely Pfund, Hoenich takes a measured and patient view of his future. "A conducting career is a *long* career," he said. "Better to grow into it than to make a big bang and then disappear. Kurt Masur was saying last summer that it's only in the last decade he's become an 'international conductor.' For years he was in an orchestra in Dresden and thought that was his place in the world. That's one of the great things you get in this seminar; to hear what these wonderful conductors were thinking when they were younger or in the same position as I am now. The key is always integrity in your work, understanding your limitations, working on them, expanding your capabilities. Another thing is to see that you can be a normal, wonderful, healthy person—and want to be a conductor. Look at Romely!"

Although both Pfund and Hoenich emphasized that their summer seminar seemed to be friendlier than some of the ones that had preceded it, they, as fellows, had been conducting the student orchestra on a regular basis while the eleven other members of the seminar had not. For those eleven others, frustration grew with every passing week.

"It's difficult conducting two pianos," said Inge Fabricus, a thirty-three-year-old former oboist from Copenhagen. "They're percussion instruments and they respond differently than an orchestra. You want to try out all the things you learn in class and there are some things—like problems of balance and of structuring sound—that you can't possibly do. So for me, the seminar was a bit too long."

Fabricus began piano at age six, clarinet at fourteen, oboe at eighteen, and decided to pursue a conducting career several years after graduating from the Royal Conservatory of Music in Copenhagen. She took a dozen lessons with the director of the Danish Royal Opera, went first to Sweden and then to London to study, but was frustrated in her wish to find a live orchestra to conduct on a regular basis. Finally, she talked to the music director of Tivoli, who agreed to let her conduct the Promenade Orchestra for one week. "If it went well," she said, "I could stay at Tivoli. If it went badly, I was out."

It went well and Fabricus was offered a debut with the Tivoli Symphony, the Radio Symphony, and other, smaller orchestras. Like most of the conductors at Tanglewood, she also entered competitions and won the competition for the Queen's Life Guards Orchestra, a 400-year-old military band. Traditionally, the winner of the competition has been awarded the conductor's position, but in Fabricus's case, the job went to a male runner-up because she did not pass a psychological "leadership" test. "That's the army," she said. "The press loved the story, and it was the only time since I began conducting that I felt any discrimination against me as a woman. When I'm on the podium, I'm not a 'female conductor'; I'm me. There's a danger in focusing on it. I've tried not to."

On the other hand, Fabricus says she does focus on the same employment problems in Denmark that American conductors face in the United States. As a free-lance conductor, she has had to supplement her income by teaching oboe and theory, and she has still not found a way to break into the charmed circuit of conductors who "do everything" in Denmark. Since she is a young native artist, her career also suffers from the fact that "they would rather engage some complete stranger from abroad than try out one of the young conductors at home." The privilege the Tanglewood Conducting Seminar offers—of writing in one's curriculum vitae, "worked with Leonard Bernstein, Seiji Ozawa, et al."—is particularly useful in that kind of climate.

As a result, Meier tells his students that their commitment to conducting must include a commitment to pursue avenues of professional life that do not only occur onstage. He does not shy away from "urging his students to improve their social skills and to make themselves visible without being obstreperous. "If you want to be a conductor," he says, "you may have to do all of it—the hanging out backstage and shaking the star conductor's hand after a concert, seeking access to him, asking for advice and help, learning how to communicate with an agent...

"One way—and probably the most successful one—is to find a mentor. It must be a first-rate conductor whom you can observe—how he rehearses, how he studies, how he functions. An apprenticeship situation. There are maybe a dozen of them around. *How do I get one?* is always the question. Either by recommendation or by going to the conductor yourself, I say. But you must not *ask* for anything such as conducting or job opportunities. You must be content to observe, to absorb the conductor's environment, his artistic life. Go to every concert and every rehearsal with a score. Travel with the conductor if you can afford it. Maybe you can sit next to him on a plane. You don't get paid for doing this—you'll have to find another way of supporting yourself during this period. But be there as much as you can and, eventually, it's very likely that the conductor will come through and give a disciple some conducting opportunities!"

Several of Meier's students have indeed followed his advice to the letter and have successfully completed such an apprenticeship which proved a springboard to their own careers—despite the fact that they might not have seemed the most talented. There is no substitute for first-rate musicianship, Meier emphasizes, but being a conductor in the twentieth century requires more than just that. "You have to understand how the game is played," he maintains to his more idealistic students. "If you aspire to a top orchestral position, do not go into academia. No C or D or E orchestras. Work with the best musicians you can. Get exposed to the best conductors and let them know you are there."

By the fifth week of the seminar, a string of brilliant guest conductors have come and gone. Their afterglow, the exhilaration of making and hearing music at a fever pitch, and sheer exhaustion have all begun to wear holes in the conductors' defenses. At concerts and rehearsals, all of them—fellows, students, auditors, Ozawa, Meier, and guests—sit beating their own time against the time of the conductor onstage, disputing his choices and motions in whispered asides: *Did you see how he did that? Can you believe it's so slow?*

In the dorms and at meals, the young conductors ask one another: *Did Ozawa talk to him after class? For how long? They had lunch? Why did Meier choose him to conduct yesterday? What did Bernstein say? What does Masur think?* They compare the remarks made about their conducting to the remarks made about the conducting of their classmates. They worry that Meier has not selected them to perform before a guest conductor for two weeks running, or that, if selected, they did not get enough time or warning, or that they did poorly, or that they were given a particularly difficult or uninteresting piece. The foreign students worry that they do not understand everything that's being said; the Americans worry that the Japanese are putting in extra practice hours with the Japanese accompanists and that they have had easier access to Ozawa. All of them are sick and tired of being unfailingly polite in the hope of being asked back to Tanglewood for another summer. Some have lost the ability to distinguish between politeness and politics. Some of them wonder whether their sexual orientation or ethnic identity will determine the course of their careers. Others worry about stories of the unfair advantages musical artists have enjoyed by becoming the lover or spouse of a prominent conductor. Every day at Tanglewood underscores the importance of personal relationships and the impact that a good connection may have on a career.

~

It is when anxiety is running at its highest that André Previn becomes an unusually welcome guest. Direct, unpretentious, unretinued, and dressed more like a college professor than a star conductor, Previn often begins his seminars as he did during the summer of 1985—by asking the students questions. *How many of you have ever played in an orchestra? How many have done orchestration? How many of you are pianists? How many of you studied at a conservatory?* Even if you dispensed with everything else and just did the traveling, being a conductor would be a difficult profession, he said. "They never tell you in conservatory what to do when you're in a town so short a time that you can't get the laundry done, so I'd like to answer any practical questions you might have."

The seminar students seemed taken aback for a moment, then one raised a hand.

"Do you carry around with you your own orchestra parts?"

"When I guest conduct, I try to take along things that would save a lot of time. But if you try to conduct the BSO in the Tchaikovsky Fifth using your parts, you'd be crazy—they'll play it their own way anyhow. If you are going to a good orchestra with standard material, it's not always necessary. I try to bring Mozart and Haydn because there are so many variations. George Szell used to take all his parts everywhere."

"Do you address American and English orchestras differently?"

Previn grinned. "Do you mean in terms of musical terminology or whether I just address them more politely?" and the students burst out laughing. "English orchestras tend to be more insular than Americans. If you say 'sixty-fourth note' to them, they won't get it immediately. Besides, it would be idiotic of me, living there for so long, *not* to use their language. As far as programming goes, I've always loved twentieth-century English music. When I went to live in England, I was able to indulge that. In Cincinnati, if you say you want to do an evening of George Butterworth, they'll say, 'Well, leave your number.' It's much easier to be adventurous in programming if you work with one orchestra. If you arrive one Sunday and leave the next, orchestras tend to be difficult about it. In Chicago, I did a Messiaen evening and it was very difficult. They didn't want to bother."

"What are some of the differences between working in England and here?"

"In England, *no* orchestra member has a yearlong contract. They get paid by the session. They always show up, but legally there is no contract. No orchestra musician on January first knows how much he will earn that year. The basic pay is less than fifty percent of any American major orchestra member or a Viennese orchestra member. They have to do *anything* that comes their way. They can play Mahler all day and then go off and do background for Duran Duran. The average number of rehearsals in London is *two*. That's absolutely hair-raising. I've seen really accomplished colleagues from other countries who don't use their rehearsal time well because they keep going back—you simply don't have the time to do that in England. British musicians are the most overworked and underpaid I know. The problems on either side of the Atlantic are so different. I have never ever forgotten that at the New York Philharmonic one time we were twelve bars before the end of a piece and a musician got up and left the stage. However, to be fair, American unions have protected musicians here from very violent things that have been done to them in the past."

"How do you feel about the extramusical activities you have to perform?"

Previn leaned back in his chair and gazed at the student through thick, black-rimmed eyeglasses. "I have a lot of babies," he said, "and I spend a lot of time with them. Boards, meetings, parties—these are things I have to do. What I *love* is playing chess with programs. Making up a season, fooling around so that the season has a shape. That's great fun. The buttering up of sponsors is anathema. I do it. And I am ashamed to tell you that I do it well. But you just must. It doesn't happen in England because contributions to the arts are not tax-deductible. The administration part of a conductor's job is, to a great extent, boring. It takes up untold hours. As soon as you're home settled down to studying a score, your management calls up about some contractual matter that has to be dealt with right then and there. I'm interested in anything that has to do with the musicians themselves or anything that has to do with what happens on stage. The rest..." He waved the rest away with a hand.

"Are famous mentors necessary?" asked a student and, suddenly, the quiet living room grew even more quiet.

Previn answered matter-of-factly, as he had all the other questions.

"Attaching to a famous conductor may temporarily open doors for you, but you need the stuff. I have a theory that there are not a great many hidden geniuses around. If you're very good, you'll make it. There's something wrong with people who say they starved in a garret for forty years. I don't care if you conduct the Ice Follies for a while. If someone says, 'Do the pit in *Hello Dolly* in Kansas City for a little while,' don't say, 'I'm sorry, if it's not Janáček, I won't do it!' You can always learn something. You may know the story about Stokowski: Once a student asked him, 'How do I get an orchestra of my own?' Some people tittered, but Stokie said that it was a very honorable question, that if you didn't want an orchestra of your own, you would not be a conductor. 'Now, this is what you do,' he said. 'Pick an orchestra—not the Philadelphia or Vienna—but a small orchestra with not so many performances a season that you can't handle it, but not so few that it is not worthwhile. Go to their city, observe them, see how they play, watch their conductor. Then—get the conductor fired!' And there is no doubt in my mind that that was what Stokie did."

~

In 1986, the American Symphony Orchestra League counted 30 orchestras in the United States that offered year-round employment and had an operating income of at least $3.4 million. These "major" orchestras include the New York and Los Angeles philharmonics, the Boston and Philadelphia symphony orchestras, and four Canadian ensembles in Vancouver, Toronto, Montreal, and Ottawa. All have music directors as well as assistant and guest conductors. Just below this tier are the 44 "regional" orchestras such as the Grand Rapids Symphony in Michigan, the Alabama Symphony, and the Hartford Symphony in Connecticut, which do not support their musicians year-round but, with an operating income of nearly $1 million, can afford to pay their conductors reasonably well. The third tier is composed of the 104 "metropolitan" orchestras such as the Akron Symphony in Ohio or the Albany Symphony in New York, and it is this group of orchestras which is most likely to hire a recent Tanglewood conducting seminar student and offer him or her between $1,500 and $3,000 to conduct a concert. There are many of them on this circuit now, working their slow way up.

Some of them set out at the end of a Tanglewood summer with confidence. Others have their doubts. "I don't want to be anyone's protegé," declare some. "Coat-tailing is just a form of prostitution!"

Others are cementing the ties that will lead to guest appearances, recommendations, lucky breaks.

"Maybe I'm not as good as I think I am. Maybe everybody back in L.A. is totally wrong about me," a twenty-seven-year-old conductor originally from Buffalo exploded one late afternoon as the seminar drew to a close. "You know, you never hear the conducting students compliment each other the way the instrumentalists do. There's no one to really *talk* to around here. How are you supposed to know whether you're any good or not? And how much do you study? How much do you live? I came here thinking that I'd put blinders on all summer and just work on the music. The biggest revelation to me is that you have to be human to play music. You have to know how to relax, to talk to people, do things with people. Look at Seiji—great at sports, a wife, two kids. Look at Bernstein—it's mind-boggling; you learn from him how much you don't know. It's intimidating almost. I don't know how I'll ever be able to get all of it together."

As the conductors return home and the living room at Seranak is emptied of the rows of metal folding chairs until next summer, it is difficult to say what, exactly, they have learned from their string of famous and impressive teachers.

"Conducting is very hard to teach," says Seiji Ozawa. "People change while they are here. There are no gestures that *have* to be. Pierre Monteux moved his eyes but not his body at all. I cannot say *this* is gesture you should learn. It's all in conductor's head and inside head of musician. It's invisible."

Leonard Bernstein conducting at Tanglewood. (*Peter Schaaf.*)

3

Listening to Lenny

The kids in the Berkshire Music Center Orchestra at Tanglewood—some of the best young musicians in the country—had suddenly forgotten how to count. The horns missed their entrance; the strings started in a fuzz. Excitement had claimed their throats and fingers and it was a while before they could calm down and accustom themselves to the fact that the impatient, intensely concentrated man with the deep tan, silver hair, and pale blue riveting eyes was really there conducting *them*.

There was not a musician under forty in the world who did not grow up with Leonard Bernstein. He was among the very few public heroes from the early 1950s who were still around, still working, thirty years later. In 1943, when he was just twenty-five, he had made the front page of the *New York Times* by stepping in for Bruno Walter as conductor of the New York Philharmonic. "He was good enough to get ill at just the right moment," Bernstein would say later. "He was kind to me. He brought Mahler into my life." In the years that followed, he composed the scores of *On the Waterfront, Fancy Free, Wonderful Town, Peter Pan, Candide*, hoping always that "out of the vernacular of American speech and music would emerge something called American opera."

In 1957, when he was thirty-nine, people on every continent began whistling the songs from *West Side Story*, and half a year later he was named music director—the first American—of the New York Philharmonic. Throughout the next decade, Bernstein's opinions and his animated podium style were the talk of New York City cab drivers as well as of the people they drove to concerts, and as his nationally televised Young

People's Concerts grew in popularity, they became the talk of culturally minded American families across the country as well.

It was that televised image of Leonard Bernstein—so handsome, so articulate, so *interesting*—that impressed itself upon the minds of millions of American children, and as they grew older, he grew ever more impressive and complicated. There he was at the White House Inaugural Gala of 1961 with the Kennedys, an artist whose claim to government attention was clear long before government support for the arts came to be taken for granted. There he was in 1967 conducting the Israel Philharmonic on Mt. Scopus shortly after the Six Day War, a Jew celebrated at Harvard, in Washington and New York, who had not abandoned or ignored the Jewish world he came from. In the Leonard Bernstein resumé that is part of his press kit, Bernstein listed not only the date and place of his *bar mitzvah* but the long-forgotten fact that he was one of the few musicians to perform for Holocaust survivors, in a displaced persons camp near Munich in 1948. The resumé noted some twenty-five years later his designation as Charles Eliot Norton Professor of Poetry at Harvard, trying to synthesize the linguistic theories of Noam Chomsky and the music of Mozart in six lectures termed brilliant by some, regarded by others as only slightly less vulgar than his fund-raiser for the Black Panthers in New York City, which the journalist Tom Wolfe had savaged as "radical chic."

Controversy had always been a Bernstein specialty. His effect on people was immediate and palpable. He had the power to horrify them, shock them, or move them so deeply that they felt and performed things otherwise far beyond their reach.

The kids in the Tanglewood orchestra were feeling that power. They played as though infused with a magic potion, as though their lives depended on it, as though hypnotized by what one of them called "his magnificent face."

It is a face that would require a Rembrandt to render its tremendous world-weariness and paradoxical curiosity, its arrogance and vulnerability, its quick intelligence and heavy, overriding sensuality. One minute Bernstein could look like the most paternal of rabbis; the next, like the most outrageously ribald rock star. "You never know which of the Lenny characters you're going to see," said a man who has watched him for years. "He doesn't have to worry about his image anymore. His wife is dead. His homosexuality is an open secret. He's no longer music director and responsible to a conservative board. He can run his own show."

That show was a three-ring circus. Unlike such artists as Vladimir Horowitz, who liked to mastermind theatrical comings and goings from the privacy of his living room, Leonard Bernstein was constantly surrounded by people and he fed on crowds. As soon as he arrived at Tanglewood, where he had been a star student himself and to which he donated all the conducting fees he received while working there ("and then some," as he said), the tail began to swing the tiger. The schedules of hundreds of other musicians were juggled, programs changed, rehearsal times rearranged because "Lenny wanted to do something else," or "Lenny changed his mind." On the evening of July 4, 1981, Tanglewood traffic was backed up six miles as thousands of people waited for the privilege of sitting in the pouring rain in order to hear Bernstein conduct a program of Bernstein. Every summer, when Bernstein conducts, available rooms in the Berkshires disappear, audience tallies at Tanglewood rise sharply, and the atmosphere becomes electric.

The other face of this electricity was less positive. The Boston Symphony had a long and complicated history with Lenny. He was the hometown boy (raised in a succession of Boston area neighborhoods) who was never invited to assume its leadership—some said because of a latent Bostonian anti-Semitism, some said because of his flamboyant style. During the first week of July, the orchestra was impatient with rehearsing new arrangements of his "show tunes," unimpressed with his new music, and furious at his loquacious, digressive rehearsal style which resulted in hours of overtime. Unlike the kids in the student orchestra, they were long familiar with Lenny's *shtick*. And Bernstein, as he told anyone within earshot, was "sick of that lousy, fucking orchestra."

The students got an earful of the kind of language commonly associated with Lenny Bruce. They and everybody else tried to assimilate a Leonard Bernstein whom they had never seen on TV. This man dominated conversations as insistently as he drew out a musician's best playing. He introduced sexual innuendo into every possible place while quoting passages from Plato, Melville, or Thomas Mann. He appeared at rehearsals dressed as everything from a beachcomber (old shorts, rubber thongs) to a punk rocker (satin motorcycle jacket, shiny black boots), talked about self-discipline, and carried on like a six-year-old.

"Everybody out of the closet, bam-bam," he began chanting one afternoon to a gathering of students, colleagues, a reporter, and waiters in a local restaurant. Members of his party looked into their drinks or out at the Berkshires, trying to ignore him without appearing rude. "It's hard not to compromise yourself around him," said a musician who has watched Bernstein reduce whole roomfuls of fellow artists to tongue-tied mutes. "Why does he behave like that?" students kept asking each other while they vied for seats in his classes, seats at his rehearsals, a chance to meet with him for a few minutes by themselves.

The composers wanted him to hear their work; the conductors, to critique their conducting and tell them what to do next; the faculty members, to respond to their ideas; the instrumentalists, to hear them play; the tourists, just to see him up close, to have the touchstone of a word, a glance, a photograph of themselves with Lenny. And I, watching him manage all these people with surprising humor and warmth, began to want something too. I had come to Tanglewood to write about the conducting seminar, but my notes on Bernstein were beginning to crowd out my notes on everyone else, including Seiji Ozawa, André Previn, Kurt Masur, and several other conductors of international stature. He affected me the way he affected the kids in the orchestra: He made me feel that the only thing that mattered in the world was art, that in practicing and performing an art, one was participating in the holiest and most exciting human experience available. He made me feel impatient with, even ashamed of, journalistic conventions, made me want to ditch them and write from my heart in the same way he inspired those music students to play. So I made a few calls and, after an initial runaround, was told by the young man who served as his assistant that Bernstein would have some time to talk. The story I would write would appear in the Sunday *New York Times* on the occasion of his sixty-third birthday. He liked that idea. I should hang around and observe him in his interactions with the students and then later we would have a formal interview.

Boston Globe music critic Richard Dyer had interviewed Bernstein a few days before and had written, "It can't have been easy being Leonard Bernstein. Everyone has always had such enormous expectations for him. His piano pedagogue, Mme. Isabella Vengerova, probably went to her grave wishing he'd *practice* a little more. The world that loved *West Side Story* wanted more of the same and wondered why the composer spent his time writing symphonies like *Kaddish*. Admirers of the astonishing promise of Bernstein's early music worried that he wasted time writing things like *West Side Story*. . . ."

At the time we talked, Bernstein was working on a piano composition titled *Moby Diptych* and on a sequel to his 1952 opera, *Trouble in Tahiti*. The first was to be published as part of a fund-raising effort by a group he called Save the Whales. He was preoccupied with a huge recording project of Wagner's *Tristan* with the Symphony Orchestra of the Bavarian Radio in Munich, and he had just announced to the Israel Philharmonic, which he had signed on to conduct in Europe and South America, that if they insisted on playing in Argentina, they could do so without him. "It smells exactly like the thirties in Germany," Bernstein said. "The Israel Philharmonic particularly wanted to go to Buenos Aires because they had three sold-out concerts there and they could have had six. The Argentine government and the Jewish community there would have been very happy to have had them. We got the same messages that we got from Jewish communities in Germany in the thirties: Stay out of our affairs, leave us alone, Yankee go home, you're only making things worse. Which is, of course, admitting that they are bad. I've been following things in Argentina for a while now. My kid brother has a close friend who's the grand rabbi of South America. Anyway, the Israel Philharmonic finally decided to cancel the Argentinian part of the tour."

That comment grew out of a question a conducting student had asked about the responsibilities of guest conducting and was typical in its candor. There is no small talk with Bernstein, little *politesse* once he is on, no off-limits. The one condition he insists upon is that he talks, everyone else listens, and only if you are brave or lucky or persistent enough in your interruptions, he may stop and consider what it is you would like to know.

"What was most difficult for you as a student?" I asked one evening after what had been billed as an informal chat with the conducting seminar students had grown into a monologue before an audience of about a hundred and he had momentarily run out of steam.

"Oh, controlling myself," he said without hesitation. He was sitting on the floor in his blue jeans and cowboy boots, his shirt unbuttoned to expose a tanned white-haired chest and a protruding pot belly. "So as not to fall into a fainting fit in the middle of the finale. The second week I was here, in 1940, I was doing *Scheherazade,* and in the middle of it, I remember having something like a heart attack. That was a big lesson to me. You are there to serve the music and you have to take care of yourself. There's a certain point beyond which you cannot let yourself go.

"I still haven't learned that lesson completely. I still go haywire and walk off the stage after a Tchaikovsky symphony so that they have to throw buckets of water at me. But the advice I have to give has to do with *not* going overboard. Your ideal situation is the complete *loss of ego*."

He paused, examining the young faces around him.

"I don't know whether any of you have experienced that but it's what everyone in the world is always searching for. When it happens in conducting, it happens because you identify so completely with the composer, you've studied him so intently, that it's as though you've written the piece yourself. You completely forget who you are or where you are and you *write the piece right there*. You just make it up as though you never heard it before. Because you have *become* that composer.

"I always know when such a thing has happened because it takes me so long to come back. It takes four or five minutes to know what city I'm in, who the orchestra is, who are the people making all that noise behind me, *who am I*? It's a very great experience and it doesn't happen often enough. Ideally it should happen every time, but it happens about as often in conducting as in any other department where you lose ego. Schopenhauer said that music was the only art in which this could happen and that art was the only area of life in which it could happen. Schopenhauer was wrong. It can happen in religious ecstasy or meditation. It can happen in orgasm when you are with someone you love."

The students received all this in silence. Then someone in the back of the room raised his hand.

"How do you train yourself to lose your ego?"

Bernstein lit another in his chain of cigarettes and regarded him politely. "If you have to *train* yourself to do that, I don't think you're in the right business. If you are an artist, you are a driven person. My father didn't want me to be a musician but he couldn't win. It was destiny. I didn't care what it cost me. My father wouldn't give me money for lessons and I had to go out and play in jazz bands at the age of twelve. But it was in the stars. If you have to *try* to concentrate, you should be in the shoe business.

"That doesn't mean you don't have your doubts every now and then," he said, more gently. "I don't know any great musician who has not had the experience of wondering whether he shouldn't have been doing something else and then saying, 'Of course not!' It's like love. What was Plato's definition of love? You desire the happiness of the beloved. You desire the best for the music. What you are interested in is the well-being of the object you love."

~

A few days later, in the living room of Seranak, where Tanglewood's conducting fellows have their seminars, Bernstein was giving me his version of an interview. He had stuck a huge dandelion behind his left ear, and the flower, combined with his faded blue jean outfit, lent him the appearance of an old hippie. He had been talking just before with a Russian Jewish emigré pianist, one of the hundreds of young musicians that are sent to him every year for a hearing, and Jews were on his mind. He made a point of telling me that he owned a copy of *Children of the Holocaust*, which I had written. He had it "in hardcover!" and he had read it with interest. He talked about his recent visit to Israel, about Menachem Begin, about "that wonderful orchestra, the Israel Philharmonic," and about his father, a lifelong Zionist, whom he had first taken to the country in 1947 when he conducted the then Palestine Symphony. At that point, like an ambulance trying to cut a wedge through midtown traffic, I managed to make enough of a commotion to effect a pause.

"You said the other day that your father hadn't wanted you to become a musician. What was the background of that?"

"What was the background?" he repeated slowly, musically. Then he gave me an answer that lasted over half an hour.

"It was the *shtetl*. Ignorance. Provinciality. I don't mean ignorance in the general sense. I just mean ignorance of what's in the world besides Talmud and the love of God. See, he came from a very strict Hassidic background. *His* grandfather was a Holy Man, did absolutely nothing. His own father was like that but also taught. My father, at the age of sixteen, left, rebelled against it for various reasons, although he was a brilliant scholar. But he ran away at sixteen to the Promised Land: Golden America. The *shtetl* is in Russia now. *Everything's* in Russia now.

"To the ghetto mind," he continued in the tone of a lecturer accustomed to a sophisticated and attentive audience, "no matter how brilliant and interesting and far-seeing, the concept of a musician was restricted to the image of a *klezmer*, and *klezmers* were little better than beggars in the eyes of people like my father and his father because they wandered from city to city with a fiddle or a clarinet or whatever it was and for a few kopecks they'd play for a wedding or a *bar mitzvah*—whatever they could pick up. They'd get fed a few crumbs and then off to the next town. The concept of a musician was of a person who could never really support himself."

Bernstein stopped to replace the dandelion which had fallen from his ear.

"My father was a self-made businessman. He was very proud of that. Stable. Determined that I was not going to suffer the way he had. He was president of the Samuel Bernstein Hair Company! Of Boston!"

Here Bernstein looked ready to sing, and, in fact, what followed came out of his mouth in a sort of chant: "In Boston is Bernsteins! Best in the beauty business! Those were the days of switches and *sheitels*. Wigs were a very big thing. He got a job in a *sheitel* place called Frankel and Smith, sweeping the floor. This was in New York City and a great step up from what he had done before, which was cleaning fish under the Brooklyn Bridge for a dollar a week. It was like Sir Joseph Porter's song in *H.M.S. Pinafore*, you know?" And here, he began to sing, "*As office boy I made such a mark, they gave me the post of a junior clerk*! First he became a salesman. Then he learned how to make the wigs. And when the Frankels decided to open a Boston branch, they delegated him to be its manager. So he moved to Boston. And that's where he married and that's where I was born and grew up. And before you could say Frankel and Smith Incorporated, he had founded the Bernstein Hair Company. His own. Which by that time was selling not only wigs but curling irons and bobby pins and hair nets. And gradually, with great reluctance because of the religious factor, he acquired cosmetics. Because half of him was still Holy Man. Half of him was Business Man. And, of course, he wanted me to take over his business because I was his son."

He paused, letting the drama of the incipient conflict between father and son make its full impact on me, then filled in the social background.

"We lived in the various obligatory suburbs. Roxbury. Dorchester. Those suburbs of Boston where Jews then lived and which are now totally black. The usual rise up the ladder was to move from Dorchester to Roxbury to—if you were lucky—Brookline, although you usually had to go through some other suburb first. And then...to Newton! There were two of us: me and my kid sister, Shirley, and in 1931, my little brother was born. This was the time of the Great Crash, remember. People were

throwing themselves out of skyscrapers. Millionaires were suddenly selling apples in Times Square. And *that* was the year my father got rich.
He got rich because there was invented in that year or shortly before
something called the Fredericks Permanent Waving machine. This was
the first permanent waving machine, and it stood about as high as the
ceiling and from it hung this big umbrellalike metal thing, and from it
dangled these cords with big curling irons on the ends. And women went
crazy because they sat under this thing and baked for a whole afternoon
and got a permanent wave, and my father for some reason got the exclusive
New England franchise. Hi! How are you?"

One of the student composers had wandered into the living room and
Bernstein got up to talk to him about a new piece that the student was
working on. I looked at my notes, then at my watch, and calculated that
if we were now talking about 1931, we had fifty more years to cover. I
suddenly felt the irritation of a Boston Symphony Orchestra musician,
aware of the constraints of time and the ground yet to be covered, yet
unable to either control the agenda myself or convince Leonard Bernstein
that there was a problem.

"Don't worry," he said as he sat back down, checking whether the
dandelion was still behind his ear.

"All right," I said. "You were talking about hair curlers."

"Don't be so *neurotic*." He smiled and leaned back in his sofa.

"I'm not being neurotic!" I said in a tight little voice. "I just know my
editors. This is a newspaper story. It's not 1931, you know. This is not
going to be a book."

"You're the one who has to *make* a story out of all this welter of material.
That's your art, right? If you're good at it, you'll figure out what the story
is."

"Do you really expect a newspaper to run a story in its arts pages about
your father's hair product business in the 1930s?"

"I see. I see." He nodded. "It's like my last experience with the *New
York Times*. A guy calls up from your paper—"

"It's not my paper," I began. "I'm a—"

"I *think* of it as your paper," he said regally. "It's like my last experience
with your paper. This guy calls the day before the Fourth of July and says,
'We're running a big feature on what great Americans think of the Fourth
of July and we have so-and-so and so-and-so. Would you please tell us
what you think about the Fourth of July?' His deadline is in fifteen

minutes and this *idiot* is sitting on the phone without a tape recorder *typing* as I talked! There's nothing more horrible. And I'd say, 'Well, the Fourth of July is...' And he'd say, 'Wait now, the Fourth? Of July?' You know, when you do it that way, you lose track of what you started to say. I had to do it over and over. He didn't understand anything I was saying so that I was on the phone for almost half an hour. Anyway, it *never appeared*."

"This will appear," I said evenly. "What I'd like to—"

"I mean, all those people appeared. It was a big feature article the next day...but...my part..."

"*Your father* is getting rich on Fredericks Permanent Waving machine," I resumed with resignation.

"That's *so* interesting. *Why* is he getting rich? And what did he do with the money? That's what's interesting. He built two—not one but two— houses. One in Newton—we skipped Brookline, don't you see? None of this is digression. Do you realize what it means to a man who's grown up in a ghetto to own his own house? That had been his lifelong dream. And then he built a second house, a summer house in Sharon, Mass. That's *that* story. Now. It was just about then that—"

"That you decided to become a musician?"

"No," Bernstein shook his head impatiently. "I decided that when I was ten, when I put my fingers on a piano for the first time. And we didn't even have a piano. Not only didn't we have a piano, I didn't know there was a world of music, that you could buy a ticket and go hear a concert. I was never told. I never knew until I was about thirteen when my father got some tickets for a benefit for the temple. Rachmaninoff, it was. And he came home with these tickets and said, 'I don't know what to do with these. Anybody wants these?' I said, 'I do.' So he and I went together and sat and listened to Rachmaninoff on a Sunday afternoon playing late Beethoven sonatas and God knows what. My father was just lost. He didn't understand what this man was doing. And I was in heaven. I discovered that this *happened*. Then we got a second pair of tickets, this time to the Pops. I was fourteen and it was the first orchestral music I'd heard except for over the radio.

"I didn't know you could *be* a musician. When I was ten, an aunt of mine in Boston decided to move to New York. She dumped some of her heavier furniture at our house and in the load was a piano, an old upright piano with a magic middle pedal that made it all sound like a mandolin. And we didn't have anywhere to put it. It sat in the hallway. I remember *touching* it. I was ten years old. And that was it. That was my contract with life, with God. From then on, that's what I knew I had to do. I had found my universe, my place where I felt safe."

I must have looked a little skeptical at his tone, for Bernstein, ever the performer, suddenly returned to earth.

"I was a very skinny, sickly little kid. I was not happy at home. I was underweight. Undersized. Pale. Sort of weak and not good at sports. Overworked. Because I had to go to Hebrew school after regular school. And this thing suddenly made me feel good. I had no problems. And it was strange. During those first two years I had a piano teacher, but I did it mostly alone. I invented my own system of harmony. I gave it funny names, which later turned out to be quite accurate when I started studying harmony. And in those two years, I grew about a foot and a half. Got strong, athletic, won all the diving prizes, all the track prizes, fell in love with a different girl each week. It was as if the *piano* had done it. Which of course it hadn't. It was just that my adolescence coincided with the discovery of this universe where I was..."

His eyes searched the room for a word, and when he finally found it, he pronounced it as though it were unfamiliar. The word was "happy."

"I was happy," he repeated. "Safe. And protected. I don't know how else to describe it. When I was at the piano, whether it was just improvising or playing a Chopin nocturne or a pop tune or a Bach prelude, I was *in-vul-ner-a-ble*. And the more serious I got about it, the more the piano teacher cost. It started with a dollar a lesson once a week. Okay. It was a neighbor, Frieda Karp, whose parents were friends of my parents. Then one year later, I realized I needed a better teacher. She said, 'You play better than I do so go to the conservatory and find somebody.' I auditioned and was taken by somebody who cost *three* dollars an hour. My father said no. So at that point I had to find a way of getting that money, which I did by playing in jazz bands at *bar mitzvahs* and weddings—by being a *klezmer*! That's the real irony of the story. You think I digress—"

"No, I just said—"

"It's a story, don't you see? I'm telling you a story which has a form. I'm forming your story for you, all right?"

Something in my face must have hardened because he was suddenly apologetic.

"I don't mean that," he said quickly. "I don't mean to tell you I'm doing your job, because you do your job and I do mine. But all the webs are connected. If there are any loose strands you just tell me and I'll try to tie them up.

"So: I had some friends who put together a jazz band and we made two bucks on a Saturday night and I'd come home with bleeding fingers from playing nineteen choruses of 'St. Louis Blues.' I attach bleeding fingers to the concept of two dollars, but I had the money to pay for my lessons. Then, by the time I was fourteen, I had to pay *six* dollars for my lessons. My teacher was Helen Coates, who later became my secretary, and she was assistant to Heinrich Gebhard, who was thought to be the best teacher in Boston at the time. I was with her for a couple of years and then I went to him. And he cost *fifteen*! So you can imagine the amount of jazz and the amount of lessons that I myself had to give to friends of mine and to younger kids."

"How did your father deal with all this?" I asked.

"Very badly. We developed an emnity, a hatred over this subject, which dates exactly from when I began to be serious and when I began to feel completely secure. There was *nothing* that could move me from my musical universe. He thought I should be a stable and successful businessman, by taking over the business that he had labored so hard to build. He would have been equally happy had I decided to become a rabbi because someone always takes care of a rabbi—nobody's going to let a rabbi starve. But a musician? A *klezmer*? He was out of his mind. He fought it tooth and nail! However, he did agree to pay for my Harvard education because that's a very Jewish thing. The education, the *book*, is still the star character in every Jewish life. So I went to Harvard and I majored in music but I took as little of it as possible, just enough to satisfy my distribution requirements. In the late thirties, at Harvard, you couldn't study the piano. There was not a note heard in the place. Just chalk scratching on the blackboards, and sometimes you could hear a phonograph being played very softly. But anyone *practicing*? There was no such thing. Because Harvard was very theoretical and snobbish about it and would not allow anything resembling a music conservatory on its premises."

"How did you get to conservatory then?" I asked.

"Oh, that's a long story," he said. "You say you don't have time. Well, I *didn't* decide to go to Curtis. I never even decided to be a conductor. It never entered my mind the whole time I was at Harvard. I'd gone to hear the Boston Symphony up in the second balcony, sharing a ticket because I couldn't afford a whole one, and I had seen Koussevitzky conduct but had never met him. I *had* by that time met two people who were absolutely and basically important in my life. One was Aaron Copland, who became my mentor, the closest I would ever come to having a composition teacher. The other person was Dimitri Mitropoulos.

"Mitropoulos sort of kept track of me. I spent the whole summer of 1939 in New York looking for a job and Copland tried to help me, Bill Schuman tried to help me, but there were no jobs in the summer of 1939. So I came home to my father's house with my tail between my legs. It was September first, 1939. Hitler walked into Poland that day. And my father said to me, 'Well, have you had it? Are you ready to come into the business?' I almost said, 'Yes, I give up.' And then suddenly Mitropoulos appeared on the scene. I saw him and asked him, 'What do I do? I can't get a job.' And he said, 'You've got to be a conductor.'"

Now Bernstein's tone had taken on the warmth of a teacher, passing on traditional lore from one generation to the next, taking pleasure in recalling the circumstances of his own initiation into a musical career. His face softened into its rabbinical mode; his eyes flashed.

"Now, to me," he continued, "a conductor was that tiny remote glamourous figure that you saw from the second balcony of Symphony Hall. You could barely make out what he looked like. He wasn't a real person: He was a god or a high priest. And here was Mitropoulos saying: *I just know you were born to be a conductor and there's a very good conducting course given at the Juilliard School.* I called Juilliard and found out that auditions had been held one month before. Nothing doing. So Mitropoulos said I should call the Curtis Institute, where Fritz Reiner was giving a course. He was a very fine teacher.

"I hadn't heard of Fritz Reiner. I didn't know anything about conducting and had little interest in it. All I cared about was writing and playing the piano. Playing *Tristan* and *Porgy and Bess* and *Of Thee I Sing* and *Carmen* and the *Lyric Suite* of Alban Berg. So I called Curtis, and indeed they were holding auditions, even though it was already September, because Reiner was late in coming back from Europe. I had to study scores from a point of view I had never studied scores from before. Beethoven's Seventh. And *Scheherazade*. I had a horrible case of hay fever. I was sneezing. My eyes were swollen and closed and I was coughing. And in that state I was ushered into the room of this lone little man with tiny green eyes. I was quaking in my boots, and he asked me, 'Did you ever conduct?' 'No,' I said. 'You play the piano?' 'Yes.' 'Go to the piano. Do you know what that is?' 'No.' 'Do you think you can play it?'

"I played it right through to the end even though I could barely see, and it turned out to be the Academic Festival Overture of Brahms, which I suddenly remembered because I had sung those tunes in grammar school. I passed the audition and I became his pupil and that was a *thrilling* year. He taught me standards I didn't know existed. You never relaxed. He was so *cruel.* You'd be in the middle of something passionate and he'd stop you and say, 'Okay, what's the second clarinet playing there?' when you didn't even know there *was* a second clarinet playing there. A lot of people fell out of that class. One boy was taken away to the nuthouse; one tried to shoot Reiner and me because he thought I was the favorite. Others just left. Reiner was a very tough man and, besides, I had this great piano teacher there, Isabella Vengerova, who turned out to be equally tyrannical and brutal and fabulous. She taught me how to listen to myself, which is the greatest gift any teacher can give to a student.

"That spring, I saw a notice that Koussevitzky was starting a school at Tanglewood and I went up to Boston armed with letters of introduction. We fell in love with each other instantly. He took me into his class without an audition, and from that day, the first day of the first season at Tanglewood, July first, 1940, we were like father and son. He needed a son. I needed a father substitute, God knows, by this time. We found what we needed in each other, and until he died exactly eleven summers later, it was very, very close."

Bernstein adjusted his dandelion and glanced up at the large oil painting of Koussevitzky that hangs in the living room of Seranak. "Tanglewood is my life," he said unabashedly. "It's the place I've spent my happiest hours musically and erotically and in terms of nature and friends and activity. I don't think I slept a night that first summer or the next or the next. Up all night and then nine o'clock rehearsal. In between you were coaching and studying. Just like now. I see kids separately, in classes, work with the composers, with the orchestra, look at scores. *I owe this place a lot.* My main feeling about it is gratitude. I guess that's my main feeling about anything I love. If you have enormous feelings of love, if you are in bed with the person you most love, what is your main emotion? You say, 'Thank God for giving me this.' I feel that way about Tanglewood. It didn't cost anything so I've never taken a penny for teaching here. In fact, I've charged the Boston Symphony very high fees and then given them back to the school in the form of fellowships.

"I feel very sentimental about this house in which we're sitting. I can hardly walk into this room without a *bang* in the heart. I suddenly had a vision of Koussy after dinner, sitting me down, saying, 'Lenushka, I have something from the most grave to discuss it with you.' It was 1942. We had entered the war, and I had been turned down by the draft board because of asthma and I was feeling very depressed about that. I was a year away from the front page of the *New York Times*, although I didn't know it, and desperate. I wasn't good enough to get into the army and I couldn't get a job. The only job I ever held in New York aside from getting a dollar an hour here and there playing for a dance class was working for a music publishing company for twenty-five dollars a week. I hated it. I had a little room. My father...helped out. Even at Curtis, which was free, you had to have a little pocket money. So I gave lessons. Country day school. Nursery classes. Terrible things..."

I had noticed from the moment I had first watched Bernstein drive up to the hilltop mansion in his white Mercedes convertible his evident pleasure in luxury items, expensive and outrageous pieces of clothing, excess in all things. It was as though he was amassing proof of his success to bring home to his father, now dead, who had never really ceased to regard his son as a mere *klezmer*, despite his television appearances and international stature and steadily growing assets.

"Anyway," Bernstein continued, "it was in this room that Koussy said to me, '*Lenushka, I have something from the most grave to discuss it with you. It vill be open to you whole the gates from the vorld. Whole.*' I sometimes hear this in a dream word for word, in that Russian accent. '*You vill nothing lack. They vill make you celebration. But it vill nothing happen ven you vill not change it, the nom.*' That's it. Exactly. In fact, he had the new name all picked out for me. It was Leonard S. Burns, S being the patronymic for my father, Samuel. Russian-style. Leonard Samuelevitch Burns. I didn't like that, but he was crying. It was the time of the worst anti-Semitism. We had just begun to hear something about concentration camps in Europe. We heard so late...which is why, by the way, I've just canceled my tour with the Israel Philharmonic. It would have made a nice show. *They* wanted to go to Argentina, that's what's so strange. It's enough to make you scream."

"Do you discuss politics with your students here?" I asked.

"I talk about it all the time."

"What do you tell them?"

"I don't *tell* them. I *ask* them. Being a real teacher, I teach by the Socratic method. I ask them questions. I try to find out what's going on in their heads, to what extent they feel like artists, citizens of the world, citizens of America, citizens of an artistic community. And eventually, we begin to compare. How it was for me when I was their age. That was the thirties, years of marching in the streets, playing the piano at benefits and concerts for progressive causes, helping miners with silicosis, Paul Robeson's committee. I mean, we were up to *here* with causes.

"They don't *have* causes," he emphasized, somewhat petulantly, then began a lecture on the postwar generation and the evils of television. "The only generation that had a cause was the Vietnam generation, which took it out in trashing and rock music. Outside of that, there have been no kids with causes, and I know. I have kids ranging from nineteen to twenty-nine. I know my three children *very* well and I know their friends. I was also at Harvard a long time writing those Norton lectures, and there's a clause in the contract that says something about accessibility to the student body. You can imagine how much accessibility there was when T. S. Eliot was there. Or Stravinsky. Or Hindemith. Well, I was running a shrink's office. I must have seen over a thousand students. They don't have causes. And the *reason* they don't have causes is that these kids are used to pushing a button and getting instant gratification. If you don't like what you see, push another button. There's always something else.

"Infants need instant gratification, and most get it. Then, little by little, they don't get it instantly, and that's called growing up. And the extent to which you can accommodate yourself to that lack of instant gratification is the degree to which you can mark your maturity. The kids here at Tanglewood are special. These are kids who have chosen a field and made a commitment and a commitment to music is...it's like..." Bernstein shook his leonine head. "It's bigger than a commitment to another human being because you can *change* that. The other one changes too. There is such a thing as an affair being over and starting a new one. There's marriage and there's divorce. That's all easy compared to music. It's not a thing to be taken lightly and it's twenty-four bloody hours a day. But anyway, these kids with all the goodwill and all the talent in the world and all the desire to succeed—alas, the latter is the main driving force in most—still don't have a *cause* the way we did, and that's too bad."

"What do you say to them about that?"

"Something different to each one. I don't have any prefabricated dime store shibboleths or rules or solutions. Advice is the easiest thing in the world to give and you can wreck someone's life with it. What's hard to say is what's really relevant to that person. You have to know a little bit about them, more than will show up in the notes they play or write.

"Because most of the time, the notes are fake. They are what the students were told to do in the composition seminar at the University of Michigan or wherever. It's a piece they had to write in order to graduate. A certain kind of serial music maybe, strict something or other, which is orchestrated to the hilt and sounds just perfect, exactly like every other piece of serial music. Then if I ask them, 'Do you like this piece?' very often they'll say, 'I've never said this before, but I *hate* it.' 'Well, what do you like?' I ask them. I like to write songs. I happen to have one here, half finished. And there's a setting of Whitman poems, a lot of arpeggios. And tonal. Tonality is the key to it.

"The abandonment of tonality was critical in our time. It had to happen, it was a historical necessity, but it created an enormous gulf between the composer and the audience. A lot of people *pretended* to like it. Boulez gave rug concerts and people used to come and sit on the rugs and listen to Stockhausen, digging it, and it turned out they were *all* stoned and they all felt really great because it was stuff they didn't really have to *listen* to. They could just let it swirl around them like the smoke from their joints. And they felt highly cultured and really in. And then they started to get over that.

"Because they realized music is a community of art. If it doesn't create that community it has no real function except to aggrandize the musician who's involved and to *bore* the audience. And the composers are trying more and more to get back to something the audience can listen to. And that's a big problem. Because how do you write music that's in some way tonal that doesn't sound like everything that's been written forever?"

Bernstein had clearly placed himself in the center of the composition students he was describing and was, in fact, asking questions he constantly asks of himself.

"How do you write a B flat major chord and not sound like Schubert? The minute you touch a B flat chord you're dead. That's what you think, anyway. But you're *not* dead. There's always a fresh way of doing it, if you have freshness in you, in your language, and in your soul. I try to encourage that in the composers I talk with. I try to get them to say what they really want to say and not what they think they should be saying. Because it's not going to do them any good as people or as artists. Or as successes—which is what most of them want to be..."

Here Bernstein took a break, and I wondered how much of what he was saying about success reflected his feelings about the public reception of his own compositions. He had not conducted during the entire year of 1980 in order to compose. The transition from one activity to the other had been difficult and the results disappointing. He had begun a collaboration on a project with Arthur Laurents, who had written the book of *West Side Story*, but the two men had given it up after six months. He had completed four pieces: a divertimento for the Boston Symphony Orchestra, a piano piece for the Van Cliburn competition, a two-minute memorial for the conductor André Kostelanetz, and a piece for flute and orchestra dedicated to an Israeli flutist killed in the Sinai desert in 1973. None has set the world on fire. None attracts one-hundredth of the attention that a program of Bernstein's early music routinely inspires.

The dandelion had fallen out of Bernstein's ear again and he looked slightly ridiculous as he tried once again to replace it: a man in his sixties whose lined face and ample belly contrasted with the sleek mane of silver hair and expensive, youthful clothes. He looked like a man who had packed several lifetimes into one and who, even now, refused to concede one inch to age.

I had talked with people who hate him, hate what they see as Bernstein's endless posturing, his dissolution, irresponsibility, boundless egotism, refusal to behave like an adult. They say that Bernstein has squandered his gifts instead of building on them; that the only works of genius that he has produced are *West Side Story* and *Candide*; that, yes, he can be a great conductor but that the best do not carry on like lunatics or antagonize the musicians they lead. They say he is an inspiring teacher but that the best teachers inspire by the lives they lead, not the rhetoric they spout.

I also talked with people who cannot say his name without an enormous well of gratitude. Yes, they say, Bernstein tries your patience, but he is almost always honest about the things that really matter. Yes, he wastes time on trivia and digressions which seem self-indulgent in the extreme, but he is one of the few artists living who move us and provoke us to question how we feel, what we see and hear, what form we give to life in art.

"I don't care who he sleeps with, how he dresses, or how he talks," said one student at Tanglewood. "When he gets up on the podium, he makes me remember why I wanted to become a musician."

He made me remember why I had wanted to become a writer.

Dorothy DeLay with Midori. (*Charles Abbott. Courtesy of Aspen Music Festival.*)

4

The Best Violin Teacher in the World

It was raining in New York City, and the thirteen-year-old Israeli boy who had spent the morning drinking ginger ale in the bar and the afternoon watching *Million Dollar Movie* in his dingy hotel room was in no mood to play the violin. He and his mother had just come from Tel Aviv to New York so that he could appear on something called *The Ed Sullivan Show*. She spoke no English. He had jet lag. He missed his friends, the sun, and his violin teacher. So when the blond lady in the black lamb coat walked in and said she was from the Juilliard School, he greeted her with a glare.

Dorothy DeLay had received a message to please audition the boy at his hotel, and when she saw him sitting at the foot of one of the twin beds, she saw why: Back in Kansas, where Miss DeLay was from, she had seen many children who had survived polio. His mother had said something in Hebrew, Miss DeLay had said something in English, the two women had bowed to one another, and the boy had taken out his violin. Then, paying no attention to what he was doing, he had ripped through the Mendelssohn Violin Concerto faster than Miss DeLay had ever heard it played before. He was in a terrible mood. He was also, Miss DeLay saw, an extraordinary violinist.

When he had finished, Miss DeLay smiled. Then she stood up and gestured and repeated, "I will do...I will do," a few times to convey to Itzhak Perlman's mother that she would do all she could to bring her son to study at the Juilliard School. It was a pantomime that the violin teacher born in a small town called Medicine Lodge would be performing with increasing frequency over the following quarter of a century with Japanese mothers, Korean mothers, Italian, French, and Russian mothers, as her "class" of students grew to include the most promising violinists any-where, all those hundreds of children and teenagers with the telltale crescent of discolored skin under the jaw whom millions of people would eventually hear. Itzhak Perlman was only the most famous name on the list of former DeLay students, which included nearly every successful young soloist on the concert circuit, the violinists of ten major string quartets (including the Juilliard, Tokyo, and Cleveland), young conduc-tors such as Christian Badea and Michael Stern, concertmasters such as Jaap Van Zweden of the Amsterdam Concertgebouw, faculty members at Juilliard, Peabody, Eastman, Yale, and the New England Conserva-tory, and orchestra violinists and private violin teachers almost every-where.

When our conversations began in 1986, Miss DeLay, sixty-nine years old and facing the prospect of hip surgery, was teaching five days a week at Juilliard, alternate Tuesdays at the New England Conservatory of Music in Boston and the University of Cincinnati (where she was Starling Professor of Violin, occupying a chair that had been endowed for a teacher "of the stature of Leopold Auer"), Sundays at Sarah Lawrence College, and all summer at the Aspen School and Music Festival in Colorado.

Most mornings, she began her day with a cup of coffee and the telephone. There were calls from students who had given concerts the previous night in Paris or Tel Aviv or Seoul ("Miss DeLay, last night I play in large hall, thirty-five hundred people. Two years ago, I receive eleven curtain calls. Last night, only nine. What I do wrong?") or from students who had arrived at Kennedy Airport for the first time and did not know how to get to the place they were supposed to go ("Miss DeLay, is here speaking winner Tokyo National Competition Japan. How I go Aspen?"). There were calls from the parents of her students ("We just wanted you to hear what they wrote about him in Germany. It went wonderfully!"). There were calls from managers who wanted to know whether it was all right to book a certain concerto or recital program for one of her students, from instrument dealers who had just the violin, from former students or their boyfriends or girlfriends who were passing through. After the telephone calls came the mail: Piled up on the kitchen table were letters, cables, newly printed records and audiocassettes—most of those audition tapes from around the world that, some months, came in at the rate of two or three a day.

By noon, Miss DeLay was driving herself across the George Washington Bridge—it was about an hour's drive between her home in Rockland County and her studio at the Juilliard School in Manhattan—where she would spend the next eleven hours. She often taught from noon to midnight without a break, flying or driving herself back and forth from her various studios, and drawing not only students but their parents, friends, managers, publicists, teachers, and other musical artists into a web of relationships that involved far more than learning how to play the violin.

"What's the most significant thing about her? When you get right down to the nitty-gritty, it's that she believed in me," said Itzhak Perlman nearly thirty years after first meeting his teacher. "There was a time when my parents and Miss DeLay were the only people in the world who believed I could have a career. The fact that I was disabled—a lot of people looked at me with distorted vision. And she never did. She was able to see."

Teachers are not represented by managers and publicists like the students they turn out. Nor do they get reviewed. Their worth is measured by the way their students develop, how well they succeed, and, more subtly, how well they live their lives. It was fear of exactly that kind of responsibility that had led Dorothy DeLay to swear, as a teenager, that she herself would never teach and that kept her honest in a world dominated by authoritarian teachers, geriatric as well as adolescent prima donnas, and insistent stage parents. She moved in that world with a gentleness that her students recalled years after they stopped visiting her studio. Miss DeLay's father, who was a school superintendent, once told her, "Before you say anything censorious about anyone, ask yourself three questions: *Is it true? Is it kind? Is it necessary?* If the answer to any one of these is even a qualified no, you'd best be quiet." And she remembered it.

Miss DeLay, as her students call her, was born on March 31, 1917, into a family where teachers and clergymen dated back to before the American Revolution. Her maternal grandfather, William Osborn, had come to the small farming community of Medicine Lodge in southern Kansas when the only houses were log cabins and he was the richest man in town by virtue of owning a few more cows and acres than other people. His daughter, Cecile, grew up wanting to be a concert violinist, a "wild and

69

gorgeous dream," the genesis of which Miss DeLay would later lament never having discovered. That dream, however, was what Cecile DeLay instilled into the first of her three daughters. Dottie DeLay could read by the time she was three and play the violin at the age of four because her mother taught her. She played her first public concert—in a local church—at the age of five. Her mother said the world was hers for the taking, and Dottie, sailing through school in an environment where most families were not academically oriented, was easily the best in the class no matter the subject, even though she was always the youngest by three or four years.

"Insufferable" is the word Miss DeLay punctuated with a laugh to describe the child she was. "Comparing myself to others from the age of four. I always wanted to be the best. I think I got that from my mother, who always respected first-class achievement. I don't think babies are born with that. Babies are born wanting to conquer the universe, with a tremendous curiosity and desire to know, and great confidence that one can know anything one wants to—because they're not afraid. You only become afraid as you start to fail. I think the competitiveness comes later, when the parent says, 'Oh, you got a ninety-two. Did anyone do better?' I don't think there's such a thing as anyone growing up in this country without feeling competitive. You play hopscotch or jacks and you try to rack up a score. It's unrealistic for a child not to be competitive, but it's a matter of degree: The trouble comes when the competitiveness is so strong that it's crippling. If a person is self-confident enough to compare and then to learn from what someone else is doing, then he can produce the results he wants."

Miss DeLay began her senior year of high school at age fourteen, stayed home for one year at her parents' insistence, and then entered Oberlin College in 1933. Although the Depression had not devastated her family, she had to support herself and worked three jobs during her freshman year. She then transferred to Michigan State, in part because her parents urged her toward a broader education than a conservatory offered, in part to study with violinist Michael Press. In 1937, she was accepted as a graduate student at Juilliard and, with thirty dollars in her pocket, no family or friends in New York, and a determination that she would not be coming back to the middle west, she headed east.

Unlike many of the students she would later teach and for whom she would help to arrange luxurious living quarters and chore-free lives, Miss DeLay began life as a Juilliard student working as a live-in baby-sitter.

She had come to New York against her parents' wishes and later said that she would have done almost any kind of work to be able to stay there, that she sometimes thought if worse came to worst she would get a job as a chauffeur since she had been driving since she was eleven. Juilliard was, for her, the first place she had ever been where it was not a snap to establish herself as best. "I'll never forget my shock," she sometimes told her students, "when I walked into Juilliard the first time and realized there were other kids who played the violin." There were even people, she had to concede, who played as well as she did.

In the late 1930s, the Juilliard School was situated on Claremont Avenue just north of Columbia University, and its student body was far less international in character than it would become after the Second World War. There were few Europeans or Asians, and DeLay's impression was that most of the students were Jewish. Certainly most of the violinists were. Louis Persinger was the reigning violin teacher at the time, and his students Isaac Stern and Yehudi Menuhin, as well as virtuosi Jascha Heifetz, Joseph Szigeti, Nathan Milstein, Efrem Zimbalist, Mischa Elman, and Fritz Kreisler, were all Jewish. One woman, Erica Morini, was highly visible on the American concert scene; she, too, was Jewish, and Miss DeLay was often told that you had to be Jewish in order to really play the violin.

This information surprised but did not dissuade Miss DeLay. "She's closer to the nineteenth century than to the twentieth and she has that midwestern sense of the possible," her husband of forty-five years would explain to people struck by her attitude. "Everyone knows that if you sit down and do things properly in a reasonable amount of time, you'd be painting as well as Leonardo da Vinci! We had this conversation when we met and we're still having it. She has a tendency to ignore real obstacles. And if you ignore them, they sometimes cease to exist."

Ed Newhouse met Miss DeLay in 1940 aboard a Missouri-Pacific railroad train bound for New York. Miss DeLay was twenty-three, still at Juilliard, and had just completed a tour of South America with Leopold Stokowski's All-American Youth Orchestra. She had worked on a recording in Los Angeles, stopped off to visit her parents in Kansas, and was on her way back home. Newhouse, who was born in Hungary, was twenty-eight years old, a writer who had just published his first book of short stories. He boarded the train in St. Louis and, in a story he liked to tell, saw the back of her head. He strolled up to the water cooler to get a look at her face and stared so intently that she took her purse, which had been sitting on the aisle side of her seat, and, very gently, moved it to the window side. Newhouse proposed in Harrisburg, Pennsylvania, and his wife-to-be, he liked to say, did not agree until Trenton, New Jersey. They were married six months later.

During her last year at Juilliard, Miss DeLay continued following up on Violinist Wanted ads of every description and signed up with a small management which began to arrange concert dates. A soloist's career had been her (and her mother's) goal since the time Dottie had given her first church concert, but, at graduation from Juilliard, it did not look as though she would have one. In her husband's view, the conditions that Miss DeLay expects and sometimes helps create for her students were unavailable to her. There was no way she could practice six hours a day and support herself, she did not have anyone to manage the daily concerns of food and laundry and bills for her, and she did not have a teacher who both believed in her and had the interest in planning her career in the way Miss DeLay does for each of her students.

Miss DeLay, on the other hand, said that the problems she faced were more psychological than material, and of her own making rather than outside in the world. "I was basically—how should I say?—not very skilled socially," she said, and former students recalled that she had often remarked on the same thing to them. "I found the process of dealing with people very difficult. I wanted to go onstage and wanted everyone to think that what I'd done was perfectly wonderful. And *I* wanted to feel that it was wonderful...and that never happened. I'd play a concert and everyone would come to the party afterward, and I'd sit there worrying about all the things I had done wrong. Everyone would be happy except me. Soon I started not answering my letters and sabotaging my dates. I'm sure I was not ready for the role of a concert artist. I did not like what I was doing. It wasn't fun. I was horribly self-critical. I think it was my competitive thing that was overly strong...maybe...I'm not sure what happened to me."

Together with her sister Nellis, a cellist who later played in the New York City Ballet Orchestra, Miss DeLay founded the Stuyvesant Trio (family myth had it that they were related to Peter Stuyvesant), and she also free-lanced around New York. But the bombing of Pearl Harbor soon changed that. Ed Newhouse volunteered for the military (he started out as a drill and gunnery instructor in the air force and wound up on the staff of General Henry H. "Hap" Arnold), and Miss DeLay became a camp follower, moving from New York to North Carolina to Virginia, during which time she played a season with the National Symphony in Washington and had her first child, a son named Jeffrey. When Newhouse was demobilized and the family had settled in Rockland County, New York, Miss DeLay was pregnant once again and thinking about maybe applying to medical school. She was twenty-eight and home with her infant daughter when a friend called in the fall of 1946 and asked her if she would like to teach once a week for a few hours at the Henry Street Settlement School in Manhattan. From the first day, she later said, she was hooked.

"They played abominably," she recalled later. "Three eleven- and twelve-year-old little girls. Screeech! But I had a lovely time. I got up at five o'clock in the morning to take the bus to New York. It took me almost three hours to get there, but I had never felt that way about work before. To watch someone become able to do something he couldn't do before—well, that is such a fabulous thing. People come in with ideas about themselves—I'm this kind of person, I can do this, I can never do that—and they're unhappy with their self-concept. If you find a way to bypass that kind of thinking, they find they're better than they thought they were. I've always felt we only use a small part of ourselves."

A few weeks later, another friend, Robert Hufstadter, then director of the precollege division at Juilliard, asked her to teach there. In 1947, another friend asked her to come out to Sarah Lawrence, and without quite knowing it, Miss DeLay had undergone a career change. The assumption one might make was that she had taken up a traditional woman's profession to accommodate her growing family, but that assumption would be wrong. Since the birth of their first child in 1943, the Newhouses had employed a full-time housekeeper, and, within a few months of embarking on her teaching career, Miss DeLay was working six days a week.

~

In 1946, the Juilliard School had engaged another violin teacher, Ivan Galamian, who soon became Miss DeLay's mentor. Galamian was fourteen years her elder. He had been born in Persia of Armenian parents, had studied violin in Moscow, and then had emigrated first to Paris, where he studied with Lucien Capet, and then, in his mid-forties, to New York, where he opened a private studio. In 1944, he had established a summer camp for string players called Meadowmount, in the Adirondack Mountains of upstate New York, where his students from Juilliard, the Curtis Institute, and elsewhere could continue their work under his supervision as well as that of cellist Leonard Rose, violinist Josef Gingold, and a staff of assistants. In 1948, he asked Miss DeLay to join him there and to assist him at Juilliard.

Miss DeLay accepted with pleasure. Galamian had succeeded Louis Persinger at the Juilliard School as the preeminent teacher in the United States, and students from the world over were already beginning to make the conservatory the thoroughly international place it would become. Galamian was known as a severe taskmaster, a man who could say proudly of his summer school, "This is a concentration camp—this is where you learn to concentrate on the violin!" or, to Miss DeLay, "You are a *veek vooman*. You vould *cry* if this happened!" But Miss DeLay would maintain until the end that she really liked him.

"One summer, I was watching Galamian work," she recalled, "and wondering why he was up in Meadowmount in an old house with the roof falling in, beating his brains out, when he could be in New York teaching and making a lot of money without moving from his apartment. So I asked him. He thought for a while—this was one of the things about him I liked—and he said, very simply, 'Because I vould be proud of it.' And I thought: *Wow*! Just, *wow*!

"He was very direct, able to speak directly about his own feelings and, you see, I don't think many people can do that. Most people have a big wall up. Galamian and his wife invited me for dinner every Monday night. I'd teach all day and then go to their apartment, where Galamian would talk and I would listen. He would talk about the kids and what kind of people they were and how their minds worked. What I saw—and many people would disagree with me, I'm sure—was a very shy man who respected good craftsmanship and respected solid work and was passing on this respect to the younger generation. I kept learning things from him. I took a few lessons from him and I didn't feel criticized. He had the capacity to make me feel comfortable, to bypass my self-critical thing.

"I learned all about how organizations work, because he was building an organization at Meadowmount, but I learned most of all how to take care of other people, how to figure out what it is they need. That's why teaching has been so wonderful for me. You see, if it's your own baby, you're so frightened, so afraid of not doing it right. If it's a child you see once a week, you think, 'Well, the responsibility rests on the parents' shoulders, but maybe I can help some.'"

The area in which Miss DeLay learned the most from Galamian, in her account, was not technique, for which the older teacher was famous, but psychology. They would discuss the progress, or lack of it, of students they taught in common, what repertoire would be appropriate to assign, whether the student could do the work. Miss DeLay would teach the students up to a certain point and, when she felt they were ready, would send them on to Galamian, but very soon after this arrangement had begun both the students and Miss DeLay began to have problems with it.

"For Galamian, I would in some ways be better prepared because I was frightened of him, plain and simple," said Itzhak Perlman. "I'd be frightened of playing out of tune, frightened of forgetting something. It was all technical. Miss DeLay made you think about the music. It wasn't like following orders. You'd think about where the phrase was going: Where was the top? Where was the bottom? She would never come out and tell me I was playing out of tune. And we could have a good fight."

"They used to say about Galamian that he could teach an armchair how to play the fiddle," said violinist Isaac Stern, who knew both teachers for decades. "What Miss DeLay does is to give an enormously solid physical base to her students but also allows them to keep a measure of their individuality instead of stamping them. She has a sense of responsibility to young psyches and an ability to arouse in them a devotion which she returns tenfold. The result is that she's the most effective violin teacher in the world."

Miss DeLay, who had minored in psychology at Michigan State, was convinced that environment had more influence on a student's potential than heredity and wanted to prove it because, as she said, "You can't *do* anything about heredity." Galamian would more than likely say, "You can't do anything about this student." All his former students recalled his insistence on one system, one set of fingerings, one set of bowings regardless of their wishes or their physiques, or the size of their hands; her students recalled Miss DeLay's intelligence in analyzing problems and finding new, individualized ways of solving them. (Martha Potter, who studied with both teachers for years, claimed that Miss DeLay had committed Gray's *Anatomy* to memory so that when a physical problem arose for a student, she could identify the specific nerve or muscle responsible and remedy it.) Galamian believed that building a career necessitated winning competitions; Miss DeLay disliked competitions and encouraged her students to avoid them. Galamian insisted on maintaining formality and distance as a teacher, sometimes saying no more than three or four words during an hourlong lesson; Miss DeLay called all her students "sugarplum" and sometimes gave an hourlong lesson without their once touching the violin, so that some of them recalled that what they had really received was psychotherapy. One of the unwitting students around whom these conflicts were played out as he grew into a mature artist was Itzhak Perlman.

Miss DeLay liked to end one lesson with a bridge to the next one, and as Perlman was leaving, she would often say, "Itzhak, I'd like you to think about this."

"I won't, Miss DeLay," he would often reply.

"No? Why not?"

"Because I don't want to."

It took a while for Miss DeLay to discover that her student understood "think about it" to mean "worry about it." She suspected that such misunderstanding between a teacher and a student was not confined to cases where the student's English was poor. "I realized a long time ago," she told interviewer Ellen Freilich in 1980, "that most of my confusions as a student came from a lack of communication between me and my teachers. They might just as well have been speaking in a language I didn't know at all. One teacher used to object, 'Oh, that doesn't sound right! Make it sound like heaven.' So I'd say to myself, 'He doesn't like what I did. I wonder what he wants me to do?' When I'd try something else, at random, he would say, 'No, that's even worse! Heavenly music! You don't understand. Make it sound heavenly!' So I'd make another attempt, but that didn't please him either. I'd go home very upset, sure that my teacher thought me stupid. It took me years to understand that he wasn't describing the music. He was describing his emotional reaction to it."

The extent to which she communicated with her students was one thing that irritated Galamian; another was the way she became involved in their personal affairs. During summers when she taught at Meadowmount, for example, both the Newhouses and the Perlmans lived in Westport, New York, a few miles away. Since Mrs. Perlman kept a kosher kitchen, she would run out of acceptable meat after a few days in the Adirondacks. Miss DeLay tried driving her across Lake Champlain by ferry to a kosher butcher in Burlington, Vermont, but the meat there was not very good. As a result, every two weeks, Miss DeLay, Mrs. Perlman, and Itzhak would make the approximately 500-mile round-trip to New York City. The three would talk and sing, and Perlman remembers the DeSoto as the car on which he learned to drive.

During the school year, Perlman saw few people during the week besides his tutor and his mother. His father was still working in Israel at first and, at the time, most handicapped children were schooled at home. Perlman would arrive at Juilliard on Saturday mornings with his mother, who carried his books and violin. She waited for him to finish his lesson, then took him to theory class, to orchestra practice, and then home. When Miss DeLay was later asked what Perlman had most clearly needed as a young violinist, she would reply without hesitating: "Friends." She first arranged for a scholarship student at Juilliard to meet Perlman's taxi every Saturday so that he could come and go without his mother, and then helped him find a way of carrying his violin while grasping his crutches so that he could manage alone. Then, too, there was the story of the picnic that had become one of the standards DeLay students told others.

One of her students had told Miss DeLay that there was a group planning a picnic and asked whether she thought they should invite Perlman. She said yes, and the next time Perlman arrived for his lesson, his face was grim.

"Miss DeLay! Guess what horrible thing has happened!"

"What?"

"I have been invited to a picnic!"

"Really?"

"Miss DeLay, what is a picnic?"

Miss DeLay explained that a picnic was a kind of outdoor party during which participants ate and had a good time.

"Well," Perlman considered. "I said no."

"Why?" asked Miss DeLay.

"Tell me one reason why they want me."

Miss DeLay thought about it for a moment, as she almost always did when asked a serious question. Then she said, "Well, I'll tell you why *I* like to spend time with you. When I'm with you I'm happy. And it's because you tell such funny stories and it's fun, and I suppose that if the kids ask you to go to a picnic, that's why."

Perlman was silent. Then he said, "You think I should go."

Miss DeLay said, "Well, you might like it."

She was later told that Perlman had bought a stack of joke books, memorized them, and spent the picnic holding forth, keeping his audience in stitches and establishing an enduring reputation as a raconteur.

A second story that is part of the folklore is Perlman's marriage to another DeLay student, Toby Friedlander. She was twenty and Perlman sixteen when things began to get serious: She would come to class and say, "I think I'm in love with him, don't you think so Miss DeLay?" And Miss DeLay would listen and say, "Well, maybe. Maybe."

"What do I do if I'm in love with him, Miss DeLay?"

"Well," Miss DeLay would say, and then pause to think. "If you're really in love with somebody, you have to try to give them the things they need."

"What do you think he needs, Miss DeLay?"

Miss DeLay and Toby Friedlander would spend much of her lesson time discussing what kinds of things Itzhak Perlman might need and, three years later, Miss DeLay was a guest at their wedding. "It's in my book a real love story," she would say after the couple had had their fifth child. "I adore traveling with them—to England, Scotland, Israel, France. I just love to watch them working as a family and remember back to when Itzhak was a little guy. The relationship I have with Itzhak has shifted: It's a friendship now. I will never forget the day when Eddie strained his back—I thought he was having a heart attack and I insisted on taking him to the hospital right away. The nearest one was Columbia-Presbyterian, where one of Toby's uncles had once worked, and I called her to ask who to ask for. She told me and we set out. Five minutes after we got there, Itzhak arrived and sat with me in the waiting room for three hours."

~

The intensity of Miss DeLay's involvement with her students was reciprocated, and many of the ones who studied with both her and Galamian began displaying a clear preference for Miss DeLay. Martha Potter, who regarded both teachers as surrogate parents, believed that Galamian simply could not comprehend that a woman as charming and feminine as Miss DeLay could also be smart and independent of him. Unlike the rest of his assistants, students would say, Miss DeLay always had her own ideas and her own style, and, after a while, it became clear that she should "assist" no one. Miss DeLay herself always told people that Galamian was a man "who listened with courtesy—so few musicians are able to do that!" but as the years passed, the two had less and less to discuss. She had been thirty when Galamian had asked her to become his assistant; at fifty-three, Miss DeLay finally decided to make the break and to spend the summer of 1971 teaching at the Aspen Music School instead of at Meadowmount.

When she called Galamian, who was then sixty-seven, to tell him of her decision, he listened in silence for a while and then hung up the telephone. He had not said another word to her at the time of his death in 1981. Their rupture, former students said, was traumatic for everyone concerned and much talked about at Juilliard. Galamian went to see the president of the conservatory, Peter Mennin, demanded that Miss DeLay be dismissed, and threatened to see to it that she would have no students if she were not dismissed. Mennin saw no reason to dismiss Miss DeLay, and the two teachers continued to serve together on committees and juries for over ten years without speaking to one another. The break was so bitter that even sixteen years after the fact, Gordon Hardy, the director of the Aspen School and Festival who hired Miss DeLay and who was concurrently dean of students at Juilliard, was loath to explain in public what had happened. What was clear, as Isaac Stern later said irreverently, was that "the branch office had taken over," that Miss DeLay had come into her own and would soon become the first American-born-and-trained as well as the first preeminent woman violin teacher in the history of western music.

~

Thirteen-year-old Cho-Liang Lin was sitting in a master class in Sydney, Australia, when he first heard the name DeLay. Someone in the audience had asked master teacher Itzhak Perlman to describe *his* teachers and Perlman had imitated both.

"*Galamian!*" Perlman had announced. "Galamian distinguishes between three kinds of vibrato. Fast (Perlman demonstrated a fast *vibrato*), slow (Perlman demonstrated an identical *vibrato*), slower (Perlman again played the same *vibrato*).

"*DeLay!*" Perlman put down his violin, smiled at the assembled students, and said in a high, cheery voice, "Hi, sugarplum!"

The entire class of Australian students had burst out laughing, and the boy from Taiwan, who happened to be exactly the same age as Perlman had been when he had first met Miss DeLay and whose English was not much more advanced, was not sure if he understood. He had never before heard the word "sugarplum" and he had never heard of a great American teacher. Jascha Heifetz had studied with Leopold Auer in St. Petersburg. Fritz Kreisler had begun in Vienna and continued in Paris with Massart, the teacher of Wieniawski. Even Yehudi Menuhin, who was American, had studied with Louis Persinger, who had studied in Brussels with the Belgian virtuoso Eugene Ysaÿe. Lin had been sent from Taiwan to live in Sydney, alone at age eleven, for the sake of a virtuoso career. Locating

Cho-Liang Lin. (*Bill King. Courtesy of CBS Records.*)

a fine and influential teacher was no casual matter, and he was careful to make inquiries. His own teacher, Robert Pikler (a Hungarian who had studied with Bartók and Kodály), urged him to go to Juilliard and to study with Miss DeLay, but it was not until another Hungarian, Gyorgy Pauk, came through Sydney on a concert tour and recommended her that Lin made up his mind.

It took him two years to get to New York. There were financial problems, visa problems, the question of where the fifteen-year-old would live once he was at Juilliard. He had to play an audition before a committee—as all Juilliard students did—before he could be accepted, and he did not know which member of the committee was Miss DeLay. Finally, he had his first lesson, during which he waited—in vain—to be called that peculiar word he had heard in Australia.

"It wasn't until two or three lessons later when I showed up with an étude that she called me that," Cho-Liang Lin would recall eleven years later. "She was very businesslike actually. Being the cautious, long-range planner that she is, Miss DeLay tried to solidify my technique first. She gave me exercises, studies, and hardly any repertoire—*one* Paganini caprice, *one* Mozart concerto. I thought I was going to get to the meaty stuff right away—Tchaikovsky, Sibelius. No. She wouldn't let me touch that stuff. Bow exercises. Scales. Basics. Every Saturday the same thing. I didn't do very well that first year."

Miss DeLay gave Lin an A−, which she had shrewdly figured would jolt her student into working harder. He had been living and attending school in Connecticut after being the equivalent of adopted by the Porter McKeevers, who were patrons of young students from Asia. He only came into New York on Saturdays, as did many Juilliard Prep students, and it was not until the following year, when he moved into the city and began spending time with other Juilliard violinists, that he began working in earnest.

Lin characterized himself as a highly observant listener who, according to Chinese custom, would, at the beginning of his studies with Miss DeLay, never disobey his teacher or dare to raise a question, and he was able to describe six years of study with her in a strikingly organized way. Miss DeLay, he said, had analyzed his playing during their first lesson and had placed strong emphasis on developing his bow arm—an emphasis that he thought came from the Galamian method. She told him he needed to enlarge his sound from the delicate English-influenced style that Australian violinists favored to one that could easily be heard "in the fiftieth and not the fifth row. More bow, more bow speed, more bow pressure." When his bow arm had become stronger, Miss DeLay began work on the left hand: "She developed the whole concept of intonation for me, emphasizing that I analyze each note in its context. That took much longer than learning the bowing. Many people, she thinks, have the ability to perceive an idea years before they're able to do it. It took me *months* to work on a certain note in a certain chord. It's not even so much what she teaches you—it's what she tells you to teach yourself. I had never had that kind of teaching before and some students have trouble accepting it. They can get away with just playing faster and faster—they say, 'Why study?' But I really trusted her and I went her way."

Cho-Liang Lin found it difficult in the extreme to follow her way on repertoire. Miss DeLay urged Paganini caprices and Bach on her student, who was wild to begin work on the big concerti. "I'd see Shlomo Mintz in the hall or Mark Kaplan. I'd ask what they were doing and they'd say, 'Oh, I just played Tchaikovsky with the Cleveland Orchestra last week,' and I'd think: *The Paganini Caprice is not going to get me anywhere with those big orchestras*. But I wouldn't dare to complain to her. She would have to ask me before I'd give her a different opinion. She wanted a give-and-take, and I was only taking then."

Miss DeLay started Lin on a Mozart concerto ("There's a basic sequence to the repertoire you start kids on," said Miss DeLay. "It's like kids learning to read in school. You're not going to give a college textbook to someone in the fourth grade—they don't have the vocabulary. But you can adjust it"), although her usual sequence of concerti began with one or two of the many Vivaldi concerti and continued through the Bach Double Concerto, the two standard Haydn, the three standard Mozart, the Mendelssohn, the Bruch, the Lalo, two Vieuxtemps and Wieniawski, one Paganini, and one Saint-Saëns before a student could sink his or her teeth into the great romantic and modern works. But right after the Mozart, she asked Lin to choose his next piece himself.

"Everyone was playing Wieniawski or Glazounov or Bruch," Lin remembered. "I picked Saint-Saëns. She said it could be a very good audition piece and it was. It became my debut piece with Pittsburgh, won a Juilliard competition for me, got me my first engagements with St. Louis and Seattle. Conductors don't want Wieniawski because, musically, it's not really substantial. And they don't want to hear a fifteen-year-old kid play Brahms. So we did Saint-Saëns and then the Tchaikovsky."

Miss DeLay believes that the first study of a concerto can bring the student to a level good enough to play in a master class. A second study is required to bring it up to performing standards, and she encouraged allowing for some time between the two so that the student could become familiar with the composer's symphonic, chamber, and recital works as well. "I did a second study of the Tchaikovsky with her," said Lin. "That's when I first realized what a great musician she was. She analyzed the structure with me, broke it down into litle bits, and then taught me how to bring it out, strictly by technical means. You often hear violinists say, 'It's got to be stronger here,' but they don't know how to make it stronger. Even some great violinists don't know *how* they're making a phrase vivid; they just do it. Miss DeLay's analysis translates the music into technical terms. We'd discuss an eight-bar phrase of the Tchaikovsky so minutely that I'd know how much bow to use on each note. Some violinists think that's too unmusical an approach. I don't."

Lin spent one month working on the Tchaikovsky Concerto, then learned the Vieuxtemps Fifth, and did a second study of the Mendelssohn.

He never worked with Miss DeLay on either the Brahms or Beethoven concerti while he was a student, but by the time he had graduated, they had managed to create a menu of offerings—enough concerti in the classical, romantic, and modern periods—that was extremely attractive to managers.

Miss DeLay did not encourage Lin to enter competitions. Although DeLay students in the 1970s began winning many of the major competitions for violin and she herself occasionally served on a judging panel, they had all heard her arguments against competitions: Almost all were political in one way or another; they would damage a violinist's morale if he or she lost; they might lead to a violinist's getting stuck on the competition circuit if he or she won; they might serve as a springboard to more concerts and more attention than the violinist was ready for. Instead, she urged Lin to study the history of art, to engage a private tutor in political science, and to develop his relationships with friends at Juilliard as well as with people he met as a result of his growing concert career. She had arranged for Sheldon Gold, the late head of International Creative Management's music division, to hear Lin, and by the time he was nineteen, she was coaching him on how to work well with a major management.

"I played in Louisville recently," Lin would later recall, "where the local orchestra manager had worked with ICM. He had a letter from Shelly Gold about me, framed, in his office. I was twenty at the time of the letter, a junior at Juilliard. Shelly had written him that I had my studies to pursue, my repertoire to develop, that he shouldn't book too many concerts for me. I think Miss DeLay had a lot to do with that letter. Then, right after I signed with my English manager, he called to ask her how she'd feel if I played Tchaikovsky with the Berlin Philharmonic under Muti. She said one day later, 'I just wanted you to know, sweetie, I turned down a date with the Berlin Philharmonic on your behalf.' I started laughing. First I couldn't believe that they wanted me; then I couldn't believe she had turned it down. Then I realized it would have been premature. It would only have been my third performance of it ever.

"She believes that you should never play your first performance of a concerto with a major symphony orchestra. *Never*. It's suicidal. I needed twenty or thirty more performances before playing with Berlin. On the same principle I later turned down a Brahms Double Concerto in the Hollywood Bowl with Erich Leinsdorf and Lynn Harrell. I had to have at least five warm-up dates and it was too short notice. It broke my heart, but I don't regret it now. I learned never to take a concert for granted. We gambled once. When I was twenty, the L.A. Philharmonic came in with an offer of Beethoven in the Hollywood Bowl six months before the concert date. I'd never played the Beethoven in my life, but we managed three warm-up dates, the L.A. *Times* gave me a rave review, and I've since played thirteen concerts with the L.A. Philharmonic. But she said, 'Don't do that too often.'"

Like most of her students, Lin continued playing for DeLay long after he had graduated from Juilliard, and, again like many of her students, he found that there were things he had learned that he only began to understand after his weekly classes were over. By 1986, at the age of twenty-six, Cho-Liang Lin was a major international artist. He had a recording contract with Columbia Records, had been interviewed by both the *New York Times* and *People* magazine, and was himself giving master classes at conservatories abroad.

"You know, it's very hard to teach!" he exclaimed one night after playing a Prelude concert at Tanglewood. "I teach a master class for two hours, I listen to four kids play—I'm exhausted! I've used up my brain power, my concentration. And she does this ten and twelve hours a day. It takes tremendous endurance. And she always has new ideas—she's always evolving. I don't really know how she does it."

~

If any DeLay student could be described as the polar opposite of Cho-Liang Lin, it would easily be Nadja Salerno-Sonnenberg. Born in Rome into a working-class family with an absentee father, eight-year-old Nadja was the reason that her maternal grandparents, her mother, and her brother moved to Cherry Hill, New Jersey, in 1969. Her mother supported the family by working in the Philadelphia public schools and Nadja was enrolled at the Curtis Institute—one of the youngest students that the school, which does not have a preparatory division, had ever accepted.

"I played for Galamian at his apartment," she said years later. "All I remember is how his cigarette ash grew as long as the cigarette itself. He would lift his arm and carefully move it over to the ashtray, over a beautiful Oriental rug—maybe to show off the strength of his bow arm. There's the Galamian Method: My little Oriental teacher said I had to hold the bow a certain way and that I had to learn things in a certain order. And for some violinists that worked perfectly. Not for me. I'd ask why. I got no answer. Then I started developing bad habits."

Salerno-Sonnenberg was fourteen and spending the summer playing the violin in France when conductor Philippe Entremont's manager, the late Eleanor Morrison, heard her and decided to take her to Miss DeLay. She accompanied the violinist and her mother to the Juilliard School, where Nadja sat clutching a violin case that was plastered with stickers of the Partridge Family, waiting for Miss DeLay to show up—one- or two-hour delays, she would discover while at Juilliard, were par for the course with her new teacher. She played part of the Bruch Violin Concerto, then Miss DeLay said, "Beautiful, sugarplum," and asked her to wait outside. Miss DeLay told her mother that she did not understand how Nadja had managed to get through the piece using the bowings she had and holding the violin in such a strange position, but she accepted the Italian girl as her student. Soon Nadja was moving in three worlds: Cherry Hill, where she lived and frequented the malls; Philadelphia, where she was one of two white girls in an inner-city school ("not the kind of school where you told anyone you had just won a violin competition"); and Juilliard, where she soon established herself as one of the more difficult students.

"I wasn't disciplined," she said, looking back at herself from a distance of twelve years. "I practiced what my mother made me practice. She knew when I was out of tune or rushing. When my grandmother wanted to know why she wasn't hearing me, I'd say, 'I'm practicing the rests.' I think discipline only comes when you want something badly. I came to Juilliard and I was stubborn. Basically, it's like I've been walking my whole life with the right shoe on my left foot and vice versa and Miss DeLay is telling me I've got to switch shoes and I don't want to because it's comfortable and, I mean, it's *hard* to switch positions. You can't just do it. It *hurts*. And I didn't do it. *I didn't do it.* 'Cause I figured: *Look, I got into Juilliard. I played my piece.* See—that's what I was like, like Rocky Balboa. I'm doin' fine. Just, you know, teach me. That's all.

"And *she*—she looked at me and sized me up and said, *Okay, now we're going to have to show a lot of patience with this one,* I imagine, because for *three* years I went into the studio once a week and she'd say, 'Why don't you use this fingering?' and I'd say, ''Cause this one feels a lot better.' Never mind that I couldn't get the passage and it was horribly out of tune. *It felt better.* She could've said, 'If you don't come into this studio next week with the position I want, you're out—you're outta my class.' And I would've done it. Because I was threatened. And I was a kid. But I would'na done it because I thought it was the best thing, and she knew this. So at the end of each lesson she'd go, 'You know, sugarplum, you've

Nadja Salerno-Sonnenberg. (*M.J. Quay.*)

gotta change that position,' and I'd go, 'Uh-huh,' and next week I'd do the same thing. She'd teach me something else and then, at the end of the lesson, 'You know, sugarplum, you've gotta change that position...'

"Well. This went on for three years. Meanwhile I got to know the kids. I started listening to the other kids play. Every week there was a recital. I'd say: Jesus what a great bow arm that guy's got. Things they did that

I couldn't do. And it started slowly seeping in: *This is because they have the right position.* So. Gradually I was going into my lessons and changing. From then on our lessons were really good.

"I said to her when I was fourteen, 'I'm no ass-kisser—I never will be!' You see the kids going into her studio—especially the foreign ones—they're so polite. Outside, they're smoking cigarettes and talking about sex, and when they get in there, they're angelic. Well, I never changed. From the beginning, I was in trouble. I never passed a theory course at Juilliard. In *college*, I was having problems. I'd come in and say to Miss DeLay, 'I'm failing theory; *I'm failing theory.*' And she'd say, 'You've got to sit down and tell him you don't understand the concept as quickly as the other kids do.' And I'd say, 'Miss DeLay, that means I'm dumber than the other kids,' and she'd say, 'Well, you want to pass, don't you?' So I'd go in there and I'd talk to him and he'd say to me, 'You're not slow, you're very smart. You're just lazy, you don't *want* to learn.' And I'd get mad and I'd say to him, 'You know, your course is *boring*. Instead of just coming out and saying, *a* and *b* equals *c*, you've gotta go this roundabout way and confuse the shit out of me.' So he failed me. Of course he failed me. If I had done what Miss DeLay wanted, I would have gotten a tutor and passed the course. Two or three years later, after I dropped out, it sank in."

Five years into her work with Miss DeLay, Salerno-Sonnenberg began appearing for lessons without her violin. For seven months, she remembered waiting outside the studio and then going in just to talk. "It was a very hard time for me," she remembered. "Finally one day she said, 'If you don't come in next week with your violin and a piece prepared, you're out of my class and I'm kicking you out of Juilliard.' I laughed. She said, 'I'm not kidding.' And then she lifted herself up out of the couch with that little sound she makes and she walked away. That scared me. The next week I came in with the entire Prokofiev Violin Concerto. I started practicing. Thirteen hours a day. It was two months before the 1981 Naumburg Competition. My goal was to reach the finals, and I won."

Since then, Salerno-Sonnenberg has appeared as a soloist with the Philadelphia and Cleveland orchestras, with the Chicago Symphony, with a string of other major orchestras, and at all the major summer festivals. Instead of striding onto the concert stage like her hero Dave Winfield, she has learned how to walk like a concert artist, and she has also learned diplomacy. "I knew I had mastered it when I was working with a conductor who used to be a violinist. He was abominable to me," she recalled. "He didn't give me an

A to tune, he didn't introduce me to the orchestra. I was livid. I was contemplating hitting him, kicking him, or just walking off the stage, but somehow I got myself through the rehearsal.

"I had already decided in the first two minutes that I would never work with this man again, but I had to figure out a way of getting through the concert. So I thought of Miss DeLay. 'You want a career? Here's your goal. Here's what you have to do to get it. Step one, two, three.' The goal here was a successful concert. How was that going to happen? 'Be logical.' I called the conductor up—we were staying at the same hotel— and I invited him out to dinner. He talked about himself and his accomplishments for three and a half hours. I told him that since he was a violinist, I'd appreciate any comments he might have about my playing. I paid the bill. By the end of three days I was his favorite violinist; he's been calling me every season to get me to play with him again.

"She always said, 'Don't get into any trouble on the road.' Well, I was playing with a very important conductor, a wonderful conductor, with whom I wanted to play again. He came to my dressing room, I played through the piece, and immediately it was 'What are you doing after rehearsal?' I knew what was going on, but his wife was around. Luckily. Then the concert came. He invited me out to dinner afterward and his wife was not at the concert and I was in the first half. We spoke at intermission and I was very warm—because I knew there was nothing he could do at intermission. This guy's gotta go out and conduct a symphony! I called the airport. I changed my flight. And I was out of there before the symphony was over. Turns out I'm working with him again, that he liked my playing more than he liked my body—which is nice. I went back and I told it all to Miss DeLay. She said, 'You're so smart, sugarplum. Lucky there was a flight, huh?'"

~

Both Cho-Liang Lin and Nadja Salerno-Sonnenberg, like almost all DeLay students, had begun discussing their private lives with their teacher initially because an emotional problem had intruded upon their playing that could not be solved by technique. Any teacher, with several years' worth of weekly one-to-one meetings with a student behind him or her, might be expected to develop an interest in the student's extramusical life, but—as many DeLay students could testify—this was not true. Such a relationship required interest and time on the part of the teacher and trust on the part of the student, and it was central to the experience of Miss

DeLay's violinists. For Lin, whose mother had lived in Australia during his student years, the teacher had served as a surrogate mother. For Salerno-Sonnenberg, whose mother and grandmother were nearby, Miss DeLay was an alternate role model, a woman who like all great teachers had, over the years, amassed a body of knowledge about human behavior on which she could draw.

Miss DeLay had been fortunate: Her students had had few of the problems—burnout, nervous breakdown, drug problems, pregnancy—that occur in a population of highly driven children and adolescents. On the other hand, almost every student would eventually present her with some form of problem involving his or her parents, and all of them would fall in love.

The parents of the violinists Miss DeLay taught ranged from the "extraordinary" and "wonderful" to the "devastatingly destructive." Some were married, some divorced, but in every case, one of the parents (usually the mother) had made it her business (and sometimes her life) to supervise the development of a concert violinist. This decision could be appropriate and healthy, Miss DeLay would emphasize; but on the other end of the spectrum, there were parents who were "foolish" or worse, parents who misled themselves about their child's talent or disregarded their child entirely, focusing instead on their own failed ambitions. She recalled one small boy who arrived in her studio for an audition and, once he was alone with her, announced that despite everybody's expectations, he did not want to be there and that the audition was not "going to work." It did not, and Miss DeLay did not accept him. Less funny are the stories Juilliard students tell of the occasional DeLay student who was idolized by the younger violinists for a time and then "disappeared"—an ostensible casualty of one or one too many competitions, of too much parental pressure, of what Miss DeLay sometimes called "mismanagement" of his or her life.

"How does a parent make a child want to work hard?" she said recently. "Well, I think it's enthusiasm for the goal. I think it's sharing happiness with the parent over it. You know, little kids want to do everything to please you. Because they love you. And they want you to love them. Now, if you become a concert artist, people will *admire* you, sometimes emulate or envy you, but *love* you for it they don't. You don't get love that way and a lot of young performers don't understand that. They go onstage hoping for something they got from their mothers—or didn't get enough of from their mothers—and, very often, they're disappointed."

Romantic problems, on the whole, were much easier for Miss DeLay to handle. Her younger students seemed to be well informed of the marital status of the older ones, and of Miss DeLay's theories about what constituted an optimal spouse for a concert artist—judging from the remarks of one teenager who said he thought that a dual-high-powered-career-marriage was not a good bet and then cited violinist Pinchas Zukerman's divorce from flautist Eugenia Zukerman as an example.

Miss DeLay suggested to her male students that they look for a woman who could tolerate the strains that a concert career put on a relationship, a woman who was able to help them have the kind of life they envisaged for themselves. Her advice to her female students was, necessarily, more complicated, both because even in 1986 it was difficult to successfully market women violinists and because Miss DeLay herself had not resolved the conflicting demands on her time.

"I have the greatest respect for my daughter Alison, and Toby Perlman, and Vera Stern, who create happy families," she said one morning before embarking on another ten-hour workday. "And it makes me furious that it's not fashionable today to respect that. Women who stay at home say, 'I'm only a housewife.' Well, that's ridiculous! The really important things happen at home. If you're *really* gifted, you can be a good mother. That's at the center. Everything else is peripheral, and poor men don't even know how outside they are! In my next life I'm going to do what my daughter and Toby Perlman are doing!"

In this life, she would tell students like twenty-six-year-old Nadja Salerno-Sonnenberg that she had to have the right timing. "For me to get married and have a child right now would be stupid," her former student said in the living room of the new condominium she had just bought herself. "Though I might be ready for that kind of responsibility, I have to wait. Miss DeLay says you have to wait until you're more established so that you can take the time off to have kids and not have your career suffer for it. She says to me, 'Never mind falling in love, huge phone bills 'cause you're on the road, okay *that's* the one you marry! No. You marry someone older. Because if he's older he'll be more established in whatever he does.' *Very important.* Because anyone my own age I've gone out with has been completely intimidated by what I do. Mutual respect. Whatever he does for a living—she urges that he shouldn't be a musician—you should respect. He should be a good father. You have to take into consideration your life-style—you can't marry someone who wants to keep you at home all the time! Try not to fall in love with a bully. Think. Be logical. And then you think how she married Eddie! She met him on a train!"

Miss DeLay, of course, believed that it was difficult but possible for a woman to have a virtuoso career and a husband and children. "What you need," she would say, "is time with the baby, time with your husband, time to plan for both, time to do your work, and money to pay for all the things you can't get done. Look at actresses who have had children—that's a good model. It's a question of how much energy you want to invest in your work and how much you want to invest in your kids. Most of the girls I teach want to play concerts but they also want a home and a family. For a woman to have to live a man's life is dreadful. It's *dreadful*. It's lonely.... So. It's got to be another style."

~

Miss DeLay's studio is a plain, carpeted room on fifth floor Juilliard's, whose large windows overlook Lincoln Center's plaza and the facades of Avery Fisher Hall, the Metropolitan Opera House, and the New York State Theater. It is decorated with a few prints of legendary violinists, a color photograph of a wheat field near Medicine Lodge, Kansas, and two souvenirs of Itzhak Perlman—an enlarged contact sheet of photographs, and a woodcut, dated 1962, that he had given Miss DeLay after starting art lessons at her suggestion.

"What makes this manager not good?" a student was asking Miss DeLay at five one afternoon during the first week of September 1986, as he leaned back on her couch.

"He's a crook," said Miss DeLay, who was sitting at the other end, without her usual pause for reflection.

"But beggars cannot be choosers. What can I do?"

"Nothing," said Miss DeLay. "Even a crook is better than nothing."

"Can you look over the bio I'm giving him? *You* wrote it; you can fix it."

Miss DeLay looked at his bio, despite the fact that an instrument dealer, about fifteen students with registration forms, and another three students with prepared lessons and their accompanists were waiting. Miss DeLay was slated to fly to Indianapolis the following day to judge a violin competition, she would be gone for two weeks, and a traffic jam was building up outside her door.

"What do you call five hundred Indian women without breasts?" interrupted her student, and she looked up from his bio. "The India-nippleless five hundred! Haha!"

Miss DeLay giggled. Although she would be having major hip surgery within the next few months and was using a cane, her face showed neither pain nor anxiety as the door to her studio opened and reopened, and yet another face peered around its edge to find out how late she was running. Instead she told a joke about a man who called home, talked to a strange man, ordered him to shoot his wife, and then realized he had the wrong number.

"I think a lot of people don't realize the moments when they are truly happy," she had said a few days before, "because they're so anxious about whether they're doing well, whether they're getting anywhere. They don't recognize and value the wonderful moments they have because the anxiety cuts across them." It was clear that Miss DeLay was having a wonderful time.

The student left and the instrument dealer came in. He and Miss DeLay had, earlier that afternoon, examined a violin that was thought to be a Stradivarius for Nadja Salerno-Sonnenberg, then Miss DeLay had seen a few students; now they were looking at another violin. Most of Miss DeLay's students did not own the violins they performed on. Some had friends of friends who bought an instrument for them; some had borrowed instruments; a few were lucky enough to have, in performing, so captivated a listener that she or he volunteered to pay for an instrument. Miss DeLay tried, she said, to teach her students about instruments in the same way she taught them about music. She asked them to read, to do research on the instrument in question, to try the instrument out in various halls and rooms, to call up instrument dealers themselves.

One of the major extramusical points Miss DeLay repeatedly made to her students was the importance of interpersonal relationships, starting in school with their classmates and continuing outside, in the world. She urged the teenagers who had started giving concerts with major orchestras not to flaunt their success in the halls of Juilliard, to keep low profiles, to avoid making enemies. She urged her graduates to keep index cards for each city in which they concertized, writing down the names of all the people whom they had met and noting those who had been particularly helpful to them—those people, she said, should receive thank-you notes and, if the artist had a recording contract, a copy of a new record.

The instrument dealer left and fourteen-year-old Midori and her mother Setsu Goto came in. Midori was, after Perlman, probaby the best known of Miss DeLay's students just then because on July 28, 1986, a front-page story about her had appeared in the *New York Times*. Two E strings in a row had broken on her violin two days earlier while she was performing at Tanglewood under the baton of Leonard Bernstein, triggering a rash of press coverage nationwide. Richard Dyer, music critic of the *Boston Globe*, wrote that she might be the "largest instrumental talent to emerge since the youthful Yo-Yo Ma," and even *Time* magazine gave her a column of space.

Miss DeLay found all this fuss about two broken E strings a bit "foolish." "Great, sweetie," Cho-Liang Lin recalled her saying after he had brought in a batch of excellent reviews. "Now let's get back to work." "She tried to get me to understand that critics are not the final word," he said, "and that *I* was the only judge of my own playing, and that I should never be satisfied with good reviews—I should look for new things. When I got *bad* reviews, she took them seriously in the sense that she always tried to figure out the critic's perspective. I would get very cross when I got bad reviews. She'd say, 'Before you get so mad, let's see if he had a point.' Maybe the review said it was bland, boring. She'd ask me, 'What were you doing? Was your bow stroke producing enough energy? Were you projecting enough to the hall? Maybe that's why he thought you were bland.' She would turn a bad review into something I could use."

Fourteen-year-old Midori bowed to Miss DeLay, then smiled as she turned to the pianist for an A. The phrase "slip of a girl" seemed invented to describe her, in the pink dress that hung on her eighty-pound frame and the shiny black patent leather shoes. Like so many DeLay students in their teens, she seemed less an adolescent than a child. Her mother, a violin teacher herself, leaned forward in her chair; Miss DeLay settled back on her couch with a smile; and Midori closed her eyes and began the Brahms Violin Sonata in G.

When Midori finished the Brahms, she opened her eyes. Miss DeLay and Midori's mother were silent; the last phrase still hung in the studio. Then Midori, shrugging a little, said, "I don't really like this...It doesn't have a very brilliant ending."

Her mother, who was used to her daughter's unorthodox and highly un-Oriental remarks, laughed. In Japan, she had taken Midori to the most highly respected teacher in the country and her daughter had said out loud, right there in front of him, "No, thank you." What Midori really liked about Miss DeLay, she would say later, was that "unless it's really strange, Miss DeLay lets me do what I want."

"That's true, it doesn't have a very brilliant ending," Miss DeLay said. Midori was slated to perform in Japan and needed to put together a recital program.

"How 'bout Franck?" said Midori.

Miss DeLay considered. "Something, Franck, intermission, something, *Carmen* Fantasy," she said. "We need something German in there to make it kosher. How about Mozart, Franck, intermission, something, *Carmen?*"

"I wanted to open with Bach," said Midori. "The one Pinky played with me."

At Aspen Miss DeLay had arranged for Midori to play for a master class given by Pinchas Zukerman; the violinist-conductor had wept and, subsequently, had invited Midori to record with him.

"You could do Bach," Miss DeLay agreed. "Bach, Franck, coffee and cigarettes, Mozart C major Rondo, Paganini, *Carmen.*"

"She needs one more program," said Midori's mother.

"Well, do you think people will buy tickets twice?"

"Management said so," said Midori's mother.

"They said so?" asked Miss DeLay.

"I wanted to do Prokofiev or Bartók, but I don't know," volunteered Midori, and the sequence of possible combinations of pieces was examined all over again, with Miss DeLay keeping track of the keys in which the pieces were written, the period, the style, and the country, with maximal contrast in mind.

"I'll write it all down and management will choose," said Midori's mother.

Miss DeLay shook her head for the first time. "Don't let them choose. *You* choose."

It was nearly eight in the evening by then. Midori and her mother left the studio and another student came in. Some of the waiting students had gone off to get something to eat. A few were still clustered outside Miss DeLay's door. There were about 150 young violinists studying with Miss DeLay and her seven associates in 1986; she expected all of them to go on to professional careers, and I asked her if she ever worried about glutting the market.

"Of course I worry about the market," she replied, "but it seems to me that something needs to be done about the market—not the violinists. People *need* music, live music, and they need the events in their lives that concerts are. Going to a concert is quite a different thing from the isolation of sitting at home watching TV. To get yourself out with your friends and have a really festive and wonderful evening! There are communities all over the United States like the place I came from where all people know about music is what they get on TV, and that's too bad...

"I'll tell you what I've been thinking: Concert managements are going to sell to communities where their artists get good fees. They have to— to support their artist and themselves. In Kansas, they'd sell to Kansas City, Wichita, and Topeka and that's it. Well, there are hundreds of towns across the state and many of them have small orchestras, college orchestras, high school orchestras like the one at the high school I went to, and if a person wanted to, he could make his way across the state playing with them. You wouldn't make a lot of money, but you could do it.

"There's got to be a way to organize that using the institutions that are already in place. You could use the YMCAs and YMHAs, for example—they're certainly found everywhere you go. I have an old friend who retired from teaching at the University of Kansas. He's in his eighties now and he started a concert series in Lawrence, in a community that didn't have a concert series before. I have some ideas of my own on that. If I had the time, if I could get going on it, I'd be really pleased."

Signpost on the way to the Marlboro Music School and Festival.

5

Chamber Music
Up in the Hills:
The History of Marlboro

It rains a lot up in the Green Mountains of Vermont, as seventy-five musicians rediscover every summer when they gather for dinner night after night in the communal dining hall of the Marlboro Music Festival. Outside, the dark hulks of the surrounding hills, the damp grass, and the fog suggest why Vermonters have one of the highest rates of alcoholism in the nation. But these musicians, most of them, do not spend much time in Vermont. The reason they are there has nothing to do with the outer landscape and everything to do with what goes on inside the white clapboard houses that look abandoned in the moonlight.

Inside the dining hall one summer in 1976, three pianists are trying to find an hour during which all of them are free to rehearse the Bach Triple Concerto, which they will perform in a few days with the Marlboro Chamber Orchestra. Mieczyslaw Horszowski, the oldest musician at Marlboro, who is over eighty, is playing one piano; Rudolf Serkin, who is in his seventies and the director of Marlboro, is playing the second; and Cynthia Raim, their twenty-four-year-old student at the Curtis Institute in Philadelphia, is playing the third.

In another corner, Luis Batlle, also a pianist and the director of the Kolischer Conservatory in Montevideo, Uruguay, is serving as relief crew captain, charged with the supervision of five other musicians now waiting on tables in the hall. All Marlboro musicians take a turn at "crewing" at Marlboro for at least two nights, prompted by an unsigned mimeographed notice placed in their mailboxes which reads: "We trust you will find it most rewarding and a giant step forward in your personal growth and development."

At the moment, one of Batlle's crew members, am ambitious young Korean violinist named Young-Uck Kim, has taken advantage of the open ice cream bar to serve a colleague a mock sundae—two scoops of cold mashed potatoes smothered in chocolate sauce and whipped cream—a favorite Marlboro prank in a repertoire that includes wrapping cottages in sheets and moving toilets from bathrooms to roofs. Another crew member, the tall, middle-aged principal flutist of the Orchestre de Paris, is trying to start clearing tables when the air suddenly fills with flying objects. Young-Uck is hit with cottage cheese; the Bach group, by a deftly aimed wet napkin ball. Throughout the dining hall, some of the most prominent musicians in America are ripping up the paper tablecloths and launching paper missiles while a rising din of voices urges them on in French, Japanese, Italian, Hungarian, Spanish, German, Russian, Hebrew, and English.

"Some of it is pure fun, some of it is boredom, but most of it is release," says Paul Tobias, a young cellist, of the nightly custom. "You play all day in these intense situations where the basic tenets of your musical beliefs are put to the test. The ideal is that no one should feel competitive, but of course there is a great deal of competition here, and there's a certain driven quality in seven weeks with a hundred and fifty people isolated on a mountaintop in the middle of nowhere. Dinner is literally the only time to let loose."

"You stick a hundred and fifty people on a mountain and what's there to do?" says concert pianist Virginia Eskin, who, like several other musicians, lost one spouse and found another at Marlboro. "There's no TV. No movies. It's hard to even get a radio station up here. The only recreation is sex and more chamber music."

Marlboro is different from other summer music festivals in several ways. It is remote, exclusive, and indifferent to the ordinary world. Unlike Wolf Trap, Ravinia, Saratoga, or Aspen, it is located neither in a popular resort area nor near a large city. The nearest air link to Marlboro is in Hartford, Connecticut, two hours away by car. The lack of any supplementary cultural attractions in the area—dance, theater, movie houses—conspires with its location in keeping the festival small. Moreover, Marlboro is not a school, with the large attendance of an Aspen or a Tanglewood: All participants, regardless of age, are considered professional musicians and no private lessons are given. Because Marlboro exists, in part, to offer the musician a respite from the tensions of professional life, there is a minimum of publicity, no published schedule of concert programs or performers, and only two public concerts per week. Marlboro tries (vainly) to discourage a star system and holds up the ideal of a "musical republic of equals" to a group of people notorious for creating both stars and dictators.

Some Marlboro participants—mostly the older ones—will speak seriously about this ideal. Others consider the seven weeks in the mountains a holiday for professionals. Still others—mostly the young, ambitious, career-minded ones—see it as a certifying agency for a chamber music career, a place to establish important contacts, and there is no doubt that Marlboro serves that function well. Over 1,000 musicians of note have summered there, and dozens of chamber groups (including the Guarneri, Cleveland, and Vermeer string quartets) were started there.

"We have to work at becoming more like the republic of equals that is described in our publicity," concedes Philipp Naegele, who has played violin and viola at Marlboro for over twenty-five years. "You don't come here, ostensibly, to make your mark. The collaborative effort is weighed more heavily than the ambition of the individual, so that the problem people find here is to strike a balance between selflessness and self-assertion."

"A place like this has an incredible number of strong egos all wanting to assert themselves and to make it in the business," says a younger musician. "But even with all the tension, it's still the most relaxing professional environment I know."

~

The Marlboro Music Festival has an unorthodox history. Old-timers trace it to 1950, when an English professor at the University of Chicago could no longer contain his ambition of becoming a university president and founded Marlboro College. Walter Hendricks was an enterprising sort who soon discovered that among his Vermont neighbors were several prominent musicians. They included the violinist Adolf Busch and his family, who had emmigrated from Germany, and the flutist Marcel Moyse and his family, who were French. Busch was an authority on string playing; Moyse had expertise in woodwinds; and Busch's son-in-law, Rudolf Serkin, was a pianist. Hendricks figured that together they would be able to run an excellent chamber music workshop, and before they could discuss the details, he announced the project to the local press.

Philipp Naegele, then a musicology student at Yale, remembers seeing the notice for a new chamber music workshop up on his department's bulletin board in the spring of 1950. "I caught names," he recalls, "that to me were sacred, so I wrote away to Marlboro and got no response. Someone had apparently lost the letters of application. But finally it got straightened out and I took the train up to Vermont on a Saturday afternoon. I remember a few cars pulling up to the top of the hill. Their passengers took one look at the cluster of modest clapboard houses set up there in the middle of nowhere and left. When everybody had made up their minds, there were four people left: two flutists, a pianist, and me. That summer, I would practice, sit in the fields and read, and drive to Guildford three times a week for lessons with Busch. After that summer, I decided not to go into active musicological work. Summers at Marlboro became a way for me to touch base with chamber music."

The following summer, the musicians broke with Hendricks, because they felt he was financially irresponsible, and organized independently of the college. But "organization" was minimal. The group decided to welcome amateurs as well as students training for professional careers. From the start, the musical environment was heterogeneous, reflecting the respective styles of musicians trained in French, German, and Russian schools of playing. Pianist Rudolf Serkin became the leader of the group when his father-in-law died in 1952, and for a time Marlboro participants included everyone from his professional colleagues to chamber music aficionados. Serkin recalls this period with nostalgia: He is a boyish man who dislikes administrative responsibilities and particularly dislikes having to tell people no. Refusing anyone with a sincere interest in chamber music to what had become, for him, a wonderful summer experiment, was especially difficult. But in 1957, violinist Isaac Stern came up to Marlboro at Serkin's invitation and, the pianist recalls, insisted that a minimal level of musical competence be required of participants. Serkin, who is thin, shy, and anxious to avoid conflict, listened as Stern reportedly said, "If one member of a quartet plays out of tune, it's ruined, even if he's the nicest person." After that summer, Serkin says, he "swallowed hard" and simply did not invite some people back.

He did, however, continue to invite colleagues with whom he particularly enjoyed playing concerts to spend their summers up in Vermont. In 1954, after playing at the Library of Congress with the Budapest Quartet, Serkin had invited the group up for a few weeks, and Alexander and Mischa Schneider and Felix Galimir had been in summer residence ever since.

The casualness with which musicians were selected to participate in Marlboro was matched by an insouciance about money. At first, Serkin himself financed the operation, with help from friends when he needed it. In 1960, for example, cellist Pablo Casals agreed to spend the first of what would become thirteen summers in Vermont. "We had no money," recalls Serkin, "so a very dear friend of mine—I won't mention her name because although she's dead she would mind—wrote a blank check for him. The first time, he stayed for two weeks. The following summer he stayed the seven weeks, and after that he came two weeks early and stayed two weeks late."

Casals's presence greatly enhanced Marlboro's growing reputation (although it established precisely the kind of personality cult that the chamber music purists wished to avoid), and at about the same time Serkin realized that Marlboro needed a financial base more solid than one based on personal contributions and makeshift projects. For a while, the festival had experimented with a plan in which wealthy patrons could sit in on rehearsals, but when the intimacy of the small groups led the patrons to contributing suggestions as to *tempi* and style, it was scrapped. Serkin attributes the reordering of the community's financial affairs to his friend, conductor George Szell. "One day he asked me how we managed with money and I told him that I and my friends did it ourselves," recalls the pianist. "He said, 'I'll send you someone.' And the former president of the Cleveland Orchestra, Frank Taplin, came to organize our finances."

Taplin began by organizing a board of trustees. One of their first achievements was to move performances from the 300-seat dining room (where they had been able to accommodate barely 200 guests) into a 660-seat concert hall built in 1962. Another was to put together an endowment fund which, together with government grants, private contributions, ticket sales, and participants' fees, met the ever-growing budget. Although both living and practice quarters at Marlboro are simple—some would say Spartan (metal cots, small rooms, shared bathrooms)—inflation continues to jack up costs. In addition to housing and

feeding the musicians for seven weeks, Marlboro employs an administrative staff, and a recording engineer who tapes all performances (Marlboro produces a series of recordings on its private label, Marlboro Recording Society, as well as by arrangement with Columbia Records).
During the concert season, selected musicians tour across the country in
a Music From Marlboro chamber music series that is consistently sold out,
and Music From Marlboro radio broadcasts have kept the festival very
much in the public ear.

While Marlboro's range of influence, its prestige, and its activities have
grown over the years, and the number of musicians wishing to attend had
multiplied, the festival had remained deliberately small—to the point of
exclusivity. Fewer than one hundred musicians each year were accepted,
through a procedure which defied analysis and reflected the community's
idiosyncratic blend of tribalism, idealism, the wish to maintain fair
standards, and the refusal to be bound by fixed rules. Since the making
of chamber music requires a balanced ratio of instruments, about twenty
violinists, ten pianists, ten violists, ten cellists, but only two or three bass
players, woodwind players, and brass players per instrument could be
accommodated. The odds of acceptance were made even more difficult by
the fact that there were several musicians who had been returning to
Marlboro for two decades.

These Marlboro veterans—the three Budapest Quartet players, pianist
Mieczyslaw Horszowsky, cellist Madeline Foley, and bassoonist Sol
Schoenbach—were booked in first. Then the young returnees—almost all
Marlboro musicians wished to return for a second or third summer—were
accepted. The two administrators said (although it is difficult to see how)
that this process left about twenty-five places free. These were in theory
reserved for young professionals between the ages of eighteen and twenty-
eight who either came to a public audition on the east or west coast, were
invited, were recommended, or applied directly to Rudolf Serkin. Virginia Eskin, a concert pianist, came back to Marlboro by writing the
pianist a letter. She enclosed some material on American composers whom
she had been researching (including a woman named Mrs. H. H. A.
Beach) and noted that she wished to satisfy her curiosity about what the
music she had discovered sounded like. Serkin responded with an invitation. Japanese violinist Yuuko Shiokawa, who lived in Salzburg, was
invited after conductor Rafael Kubelik spoke to Serkin on her behalf. Two
members of the Israel Philharmonic were invited through the intervention
of a Marlboro elder.

"Anyone extraordinary gets accepted," says a cellist who views the festival as a kind of private club. "But most come up through the major eastern conservatories where they know a Marlboro elder who will push for their admission. That's the way it is in the music profession and Marlboro epitomizes that situation."

The group that finally assembles at Marlboro is a collection of extremely diverse, egocentric, high-powered, and often difficult individuals. Some, especially the string players, are veterans of summer music camps such as Meadowmount. Others have never been to them and are put off by dorm life and nine-to-six scheduling of their time, with the nearest cigarette machine at least five miles away. For seven weeks, people for whom intercontinental jet travel is a way of life will be grounded. Their activity will be determined by The Schedule, the enormous, complicated, color-coded nerve center of Marlboro, which sorts players into four or five different chamber groups each week and lists as many as 140 different pieces of music under study at one time.

Before they arrive at Marlboro, participants are asked to list five chamber works that they are prepared to play and ten others that they would like to study during the summer. "They are not given the chance to indicate *with whom* they would like to play," says Endel Kalam, a violist who holds the difficult job of schedule director. "All-star groups—which are not hard to organize—are frowned upon. It would also be easy to just find out which people wanted to do the same piece and put them together. But the process is more complicated. A few days before the start of the summer, the senior musicians sit down and consider what repertory makes the best sense for the musician concerned. Then they put together what they hope are compatible groups from both a personal and musical standpoint—each containing one senior musician who knows the piece under study well."

This senior musician will essentially coach the chamber group. He or she will decide whether the group is doing well and should continue studying the work in question or whether it should abandon it. "Of course there are problems," Kalam concedes. "Members of a group may have to leave for various reasons: Concert appearances, doctors' appointments, siestas, illnesses. A happy group always wants to stay together as long as possible; an unhappy group wants to change as soon as possible. Some musicians are very popular and in demand. Others are not. Some participants wind up playing only sixteen hours a week while others are booked solid five days a week. Everyone wants to be chosen to perform the piece they are working on publicly over the weekend, although they are advised by letter that acceptance to Marlboro does not guarantee performing at concerts here."

Performing at Marlboro before an audience of professional peers as well as what is probably the most sophisticated chamber music audience in America is a goal for every Marlboro participant, despite the attempt to discourage "performance-oriented" work. All of the musicians at Marlboro—whether they have recently graduated from conservatory or have been performing for fifty years—are "performance-oriented," and, toward the middle of the week, speculation is rife about which chamber groups will be chosen to perform in the weekend concerts. Some groups are rumored to be working well while others are reported as having catastrophic conflicts of personality or musical style. In an enclave as small as Marlboro, few secrets remain secret for long, and although participants pay lip service to the Marlboro ideal of "study for study's sake" and try to quell competitive feelings, the fact is that the prospect of public concerts encourages them.

Choosing which of the one hundred or so works-in-progress will be performed at weekly public concerts is a procedure as arcane as selecting Marlboro participants themselves. In theory, the senior member of each group recommends to Serkin and the scheduling director whether study of a given work should continue and aim toward a performance, whether a work should be performed at an informal concert for Marlboro participants only, or whether it should be one of half a dozen performed for the public. Serkin then decides. But in practice, the decision is most strongly influenced by the senior musician himself, who, like any coach proud of his team, must make a good case for it, and by other Marlboro elders, who take into consideration balanced programming, recording needs, personal needs of the musicians in question, and what they would like to hear that weekend.

As in every community that has ever strived for "a republic of equals," some members invariably have stronger voices and personalities than others and their wishes often prevail. This is most striking within the chamber groups themselves, where, in theory, every member of the ensemble has equal say in the interpretation of a given work. Some senior musicians deliberately try to draw out the opinions of younger musicians while others behave like conductors. Similarly, some younger musicians will straightforwardly challenge an elder's concepts while others are too shy or afraid to do so.

One afternoon, four musicians were beginning to work on a Fauré Piano Quartet for the first time and Isadore Cohen, violinist of the Beaux Arts Trio, was coaching three musicians young enough to have been his children. Cohen was a veteran chamber musician who has been at Marlboro for ten years, largely because he found playing with the same two people all year "restrictive after a while" and because the festival had become a comfortable summer place for his family. "In the summer," he says, "I find I want to be exposed to different ideas, a different repertoire, and to the stimulation that comes from a mix of older and younger people."

Cohen generally liked to have the group he was working with read through a piece from start to finish in order to see which section needed the most work. "For me," he said, "clarity is very important, and after that, timbre. You have to arrive at a concept of sound: Matching sonorities, use of the bow, vibrato, and a certain similarity within the phrase. After settling these things, they have to make sense to all the people concerned, because if they are not convinced of the ideas the performance won't be good."

Cohen was a faculty member of the Mannes College of Music and skilled in engaging his students' reactions. "I have a problem here at the start," he said to the three other musicians in the rehearsal room. "What is the subject? Is it a two-bar figure?"

"I guess it could be," said the pianist, staring at the sheet music in front of her uncertainly.

"I have it first," said the violist.

Cohen, who believed in laying bare the bones of a piece because he thought young musicians had a tendency to "go from one little puddle of music to another," asked his question again.

"Do you think that's the subject? Is it possible that it's one bar viola, one bar cello?"

"I don't think so," said the violist.

"I just want to understand what we're doing," said Cohen.

"Do you hear it another way?" asked the cellist timidly.

"It's not what I hear that's important," said Cohen. "What do you think Fauré had in mind?"

Explorations like these, however, took a great deal of time. More typical as the rehearsal progressed were polite tips from Cohen, such as "Let's not be too deceptive about that entrance, Cynthia," or "Steve, do you have any impulse to hold on to your tied note a little bit longer?"

The attempt at Socratic teaching is not, however, uniformly practiced at Marlboro. A violinist like Sandor Vegh, for example, whom students describe as looking "like you'd imagine the King of the Norse Gods," feels that he comes to Marlboro to impart the tradition of playing that he himself learned from past masters. A Hungarian who was a close friend of Béla Bartók and a student of Kodaly, Vegh views Marlboro as the only place in the world where the central European tradition of chamber music can be directly transmitted to American youth. "Hubay was my teacher when I was young," he says. "And Hubay played sonatas with Brahms and Joachim. Joachim knew Mendelssohn, and through my teacher I am a part of this tradition. But in central Europe after the war, we lost this tradition. Eastern Europe is more and more provincial. Western Europe is more and more dry, intellectual, and decadent. What we had is no more. I feel like one of the last Mohicans and I come to Marlboro because I want to continue what I inherited. We want to have successors. What I received from the past cannot die if I communicate it to the younger generation, and this is the place to do so."

In a room not far from the one in which the Fauré Quartet was being played, Vegh—massively built, his lank blond-gray hair falling over his brow—took charge of his quartet. They had barely played six notes before he stopped them. "Very good what you played but a little bit nervous," he said. "You are not enough relaxed. You are more tense than the music needs."

The other three players prepared once again to launch into Beethoven's Opus 135 when Vegh put his violin on his thigh and said, "You see— *maybe*, you tell *maybe*, not yes or no. It's a little bit open, the character here, and you play that it's tragic!"

The quartet geared up once again for the first bar. They managed ten bars this time.

"Aha! Aha! Very good!" Vegh asked them to repeat it.

"No. I don't like that and I know why. You move the viola. You lose contact."

Vegh asked the musicians to play singly and worked on matching sonorities, melding the entrance of one instrument to the ending of another's phrase.

"No," he said again. "That was too well-fed."

Vegh leaned back and launched into a discourse on bow technique as he had learned it. "Not all that is old is good," he said, winding up, "but the thing they had is bow technique. Today all expression lies in the left hand." He asked them to play the first ten bars again and again he stopped them. "It was wonderful—only too slow."

After forty-five minutes, they moved on to the eleventh bar.

Vegh's style was generally acknowledged to be more dictatorial than pedagogic, yet students were quick to point out that the groups in which he was the senior member sounded like longtime ensembles in two rehearsals. They were also impressed by his passion—a characteristic of Marlboro's style of music-making and a characteristic which is not greatly encouraged in today's conservatories and competitions.

"Today we are in great danger that science will dominate music," Vegh was fond of telling his younger colleagues. "The young people, I find, do not dare to express the way they really feel. Mozart is played *this* way, they are taught, and they adopt a skillful way of playing that is easy to defend. But the *real* value in everyone is the personality. Today you have a very high level of playing but no mountains and valleys. I try to influence their fantasy, their emotions. I try to liberate them. People here have a very high technical level. You can demand anything and they respond immediately so that in a short time you can make a first-class quartet. But they must learn that they should have the courage to express what they feel. Music is not objective; it's *subjective*. I say to them, 'Play this with pathos,' and they are afraid to sound sentimental. They want to make a studiolike, objective presentation. I think all this perfection is hypo-critical. It's not human."

The fact that Marlboro consciously makes room for mistakes and encourages experimentation that would be frowned upon in other contexts is one of the reasons that musicians come back year after year. It affords them the opportunity not only to climb out on an artistic limb but to walk out on roles (soloist, orchestra player, teacher) that constrict their activity during the concert season.

Young-Uck Kim, for example, had not studied with anyone for nearly eight years and his itinerary as a soloist resulted in his being alone for most of the winter. "I played about fifty concerts this year and it was always the same," he said. "You get to an airport, sit in the airport lounge, sit in the plane, check into a hotel where you find a telephone message telling you what time to be at the hall for rehearsal. There will be one rehearsal. At the most, two. The conductor is busy, so you get to talk to him for maybe twenty minutes. 'The orchestra knows this backwards and for-wards' he tells you. You think: *The orchestra may have played this Mendelssohn concerto a hundred times but they have never played it with me.* But the conductor is already going through the score, pointing to this spot and that spot and talking about *tempi*. You never really discuss ideas. Some conductors do a piece one way and won't change it for you. It's happened to me that I didn't see the conductor *at all*.

"Here at Marlboro, what's so satisfying to me is that you have *time*. I didn't ask to do any specific piece this summer because any piece I get I enjoy. You can study and argue the piece at breakfast, at lunch, at dinner and rehearsal. I know most of the people here but I never get to see them in New York because although most of us live there, we all travel so much that we are never there at the same time. You can renew friendships here, and for me, that's a very secure feeling."

Musicians who play in the orchestras that Young-Uck Kim complained about suffer from a similar kind of regimentation and see Marlboro as a place not only to study but to recapture the enthusiasm that led them to choose musical careers in the first place. "All year I think about coming back to Marlboro," said Eli Eban, a clarinetist with the Jerusalem Symphony. "In an orchestra situation, not all one hundred members are prepared each day and your conductor is not always inspiring. Outside the orchestra, players tend to be a bit mercenary. They won't put in the effort to work on chamber music unless they have some concerts booked. In an orchestra, you can forget to listen to the music. You listen for the conductor's beat, for intonation and accuracy. You have to project into a big hall, and all kinds of things are demanded of you that you might not want to do at a given moment. You certainly can't suddenly begin to listen to every section member expressing himself.

"For me, Marlboro is a learning situation. I learn how to listen. People prod you to listen. Everybody cares about the quality of the music they make. So when I'm going through a dry period in Israel, I remember what I did here. I try to think: *How would I approach this if I were in Marlboro?*"

That question is itself evidence of the success of an institution whose purpose includes spreading its philosophy throughout the musical world. A summer at Marlboro has become the equivalent of a Good House-keeping Seal of Approval among hundreds of classical musicians, and the fact that it has not stultified as it has grown more established is ascribed to the presence of Rudolf Serkin. Musicians are awed by his career yet disarmed by his personality. They point out that the pianist is now a senior citizen, that he has been ill and should be slowing down, but instead seems to be working harder than before. He is in on the wildest pranks, knows about most details and difficulties at the festival, and negotiates potentially explosive conflicts with humor and care.

"He is unquestionably a great man," said one of his associates, "and yet he would never give a master class or conduct the orchestra here. At the same time, he is very shrewd and ambitious, and will not relinquish the slightest amount of authority, while wanting to convince others that he is perfectly self-effacing."

"Marlboro is full of so many egos that it needs a man who commands everyone's respect. Serkin does that," said another old-timer. "I'm afraid that without him, this community just won't survive. I don't know of anyone else here who could readily take over."

Serkin himself reflected a great deal about the future of Marlboro. He was described by colleagues as a man who knew "the necessity of constant change, who is always looking for ways to disturb the equilibrium so things won't stagnate."

"I *know* nothing ever remains the same," he said one night, sitting on the back steps of the white clapboard dining hall and looking out at the green expanse of hills. "Where do we go from here? I'm kind of curious. Marlboro started really by accident. Then people began coming here looking for something they had missed.

"The landscape here brings out the generosity that is in every human being, even if you have to scratch a little bit sometimes to find it. This community educates one. We once had a virtuoso violinist here who was very arrogant, who didn't even want to help in the dining room. So without any plan or agreement, no one served him. He had to serve himself, and after ten days here, he was fine."

Serkin's lined face broke into a child's grin at the memory.

"This is a place," he said, "to learn how to play second fiddle. A lot of people know how to play first. But to play second well and beautifully is a great art."

James Galway.

6

The Marketing of James Galway

It was eight-fifty-five and silent on a Thursday night in Carnegie Hall. Into the hush walked a tall conductor in tails, followed by a short, stocky, bearded Irishman wearing navy slacks, a dark blue velvet jacket, and a polka-dot bow tie. A plump silver heart and silver cross dangled from a chain around his neck. He carried his $4,500, eighteen-karat-gold flute as though it were a shotgun, and there was something in his stride, something in the way the orchestra responded to his arrival that sent a rustle of disorientation through the hall.

As the orchestra began Mozart's Second Flute Concerto, the rustle grew louder. Although James Galway was in his late thirties, and the distinguished former principal flutist of the London Symphony Orchestra and the Berlin Philharmonic, he didn't look like any other classical musician. He didn't act like one either. He stuck his left hand into his pants pocket, propped his flute against his right shoulder, and proceeded to do what everybody's elementary school teacher said *not* to do onstage in assembly. Galway grinned and frowned. He shifted from foot to foot. He inspected his audience curiously with dark blue, astigmatic, dancing eyes and then turned his back on it to wink at the first violins.

Then, firmly, he brought his flute to his lips and the rustle died. Unlike soloists who wall themselves off from the world when they play, Galway reaches out to both orchestra and audience like an enthusiastic scoutmaster rallying his troop. Like Frenchman Jean-Pierre Rampal, the first flutist to have a successful solo career, he projects joy, a strong sexuality, and the illusion that playing the flute is a snap. "Even amid the most torrential cascades of notes," wrote London's *Financial Times*, "he presumably takes breath, but with such well-concealed art that you suspect a divine dispensation from such ordinary physical necessities."

As Galway finished the first movement, whispers of "Pied Piper," "Puck," "Alan Bates," and "Pan" traveled down the velvet rows of seats. Older people recalled Irish tenor John McCormack and the charismatic violinists and pianists of another age. Then Galway began the slow second movement, and a sound so beautiful filled the hall that the *audience* seemed to stop breathing.

"The man is extraordinarily gifted," says violinist Pinchas Zukerman. "He's a natural, like Heifetz. He has amazing facility, wonderful musical insight, *and* his own unique sound. He didn't study with Rampal or Baker or anyone. It's *his* sound, and there are very few musicians about whom you can say that."

As Galway launched into the fast final movement, a few people chuckled out loud.

"For me, I hear absolute perfection when Jimmy plays," says Julius Baker, principal flute of the New York Philharmonic and acknowledged dean of American flutists. "It's an inspiration to me yet it's like a *bar mitzvah*. He makes me feel like part of his family, and it's rewarding to see someone who really deserves it get the acclaim."

The audience in Carnegie Hall gave it to him, as did the critics the next day. The process repeated itself in Chicago, Ann Arbor, Toronto, Schenectady, and Boston as his audiences fanned out beyond classical music buffs to flute freaks (people who listen to Herbie Mann's jazz flute, Jethro Tull's rock flute, the classical flute of Jean-Pierre Rampal, Ransom Wilson, and Paula Robison; people who pipe to themselves on college campuses and in public parks; people who have caused a worldwide flute boom), Irish ethnics, college students, and people who had never been to a concert hall before but who had read about Galway or seen him on TV.

This audience amalgam was no accident. It was the result of a shrewd marketing strategy that has made Galway as unconventional a performer in the marketplace as he is onstage. In record lingo, he is known as a "crossover phenomenon," an artist who appeals to several discrete audiences. In Great Britain, where a classical musician was happy to sell 5,000 LPs in one year, Galway sold 65,000 *Mozart Flute Concerti* and 60,000 of Vivaldi's *Four Seasons* transcribed for flute. Concurrently, his recording of John Denver's "Annie's Song" displaced rock singles at the top of the British pop charts and sold just short of half a million copies.

In three years during the late 1970s, Galway sold 750,000 records, won a Grand Prix du Disque, and earned £250,000 in record royalties alone. His London concerts sold out within twenty-four hours and his fans included the queen. "In England, he outsold all classical artists, including Vladimir Horowitz, who had a lead time of fifty years!" says an RCA man who works with both. "Not only does the mass audience think he's a terrific flutist, but flutists think so too. A star is a star, and one of the things that makes a star is successful marketing."

While Horowitz and others cultivated a carefully noncommercial image, Galway was unabashedly involved in marketing. He lent his name to Galway T-shirts ("I know people who'd be delirious to wear a Horowitz T-shirt. Me, for example"), Galway Tin Whistle Packs ("Great Christmas gift!"), and a line of Galway-endorsed flutes ("Kids can be sure they're getting good value for their money"). He wrote an autobiography, invested his record royalties in Galway Master Class films and videocassettes, and produced six 1-hour television specials.

"Too many musicians come out of conservatory thinking the world owes them a living," says Michael Emmerson, the British manager who in 1975 persuaded Galway to leave the world's best-paid orchestra, the venerable Berlin Philharmonic. "I don't know of any who've actually mapped out a strategy. Look at Frank Sinatra and Bing Crosby and the way they've managed their careers! There's no reason why a classical musician shouldn't do the same.

"I think a soloist needs a pension when he's sixty, or when his lip gives out or his arm gets unsteady, and that pension can be found in recordings. When you have an excellent product, you have to promote it properly. Concerts are, as far as we're concerned, a way to promote Galway records. That may sound unorthodox but it's what the pop boys have been doing all along. *We've* done it in England. Now we want to do it in the United States."

~

The chances of any classical artist becoming a pop star in the United States were virtually nil, said recording executives at all the major American companies. "We've never been able to do it," said Mike Kellman at CBS. "It would take three years, at least one million dollars for advertising and promotion, and *even then* it might not work." Although the American recording industry had burgeoned from a $600 million business in 1960 to $3.5 billion in 1977, classical sales had remained at five percent of this figure. While more than 1,500 LPs had "gone gold," selling at least half a million copies during that time, only *seven* were classical.

Marketing men explained that the classical market was not only small and elusive but fragmented into subgroups of chamber music, opera, or symphony aficionados, as well as people interested only in certain instruments (like piano) or certain epochs (like the baroque). Because the classical repertoire was fixed and a "new sound" was nowhere near as welcome as it was in the pop world, new recordings might have thirty years' worth of competitors. When RCA released Galway's Mozart LP, there were already twenty-two others on the market. His *Four Seasons* was the thirtieth in the Schwann catalogue.

Classical musicians who had become household words since the Second World War had almost invariably established their reputations outside the channels of classical recordings or concerts. Pianist Van Cliburn did so in 1958, by winning the Soviet Union's prestigious Tchaikovsky Piano Competition at a time when Americans considered any victory against the Russians an advance in the cold war. Leonard Bernstein did it by writing Broadway musicals, Arthur Fiedler by welding his name to the Boston Pops and "light classics." They, as well as Herbert von Karajan, André Previn, Beverly Sills, Luciano Pavarotti, and Vladimir Horowitz, understood that television was the key to wider audiences and high visibility.

James Galway, who had watched Karajan from behind his music stand for six years, was quick to grasp the point. "On one show like Dick Cavett," he said after appearing on it, "you can reach more Americans than in six weeks of hard touring. You can get into people's living rooms and talk to the people who don't come to concerts, to the girl who works in the supermarket and the guy who works in the garage. And anyway, I *like* playing to three million people. I feel rather like a jet-age gypsy."

~

At eight-fifteen in the drafty green room of a studio in Toronto, Galway was waiting to appear on *Canada After Dark*. Although CBC staffers joked that this imitation Johnny Carson Show was "the only program in the history of Canada to have a negative audience rating," the RCA publicity people thought it a coup that Galway had been chosen over a mass of authors, models, actors, gurus, rock stars, politicians, and sports figures all eager for free air time.

Galway and his gold flute did look out of place. On the television monitor before him, the host and Canada's leading television actor were wearing buffalo coats and straw hats, waving football pennants, and making antifeminist jokes. Across the room, seven polyester-swathed aspirants to the Grey Cup annual football queen contest were getting ready to trot onstage. On the couch beside him was a lank, wild-eyed folksinger/guitarist named Valdy and three of his entourage. The script called for Galway and Valdy to accompany the television actor as he sang the theme song from his new TV series.

Galway watched the monitor, his full, puckish face inscrutable. Within the last twenty-four hours, he had played a concert in Ann Arbor, slept a bit, flown from Detroit to Toronto, and then fielded seven hours of questions from six radio, TV, and newspaper reporters, all demanding a special angle, a scrap of gossip, a good quote. He had smiled into ten rolls of film, taken a half-hour rest, and then performed at a reception for 100 record dealers, middle-of-the-road disk jockeys, and more press, to whom he was introduced as "a shot in the arm to the classical music field."

All day he had been asked the same questions: *Did you study with Rampal? Why not? Who influenced your playing? Who do you consider your competition? Was it hard to leave the Berlin Philharmonic? Did Karajan really call you The Man from Mars? Did you anticipate this degree of success? Why are you so product-oriented? Why do you play a gold flute? Why do you live in Switzerland? Are there any questions you'd like to be asked?*

Even when the *Toronto Star* wanted an explanation of why his first marriage broke up, Galway stayed cool. He was a good interview: Unfailingly courteous, ready with anecdotes, well-informed. He grasped precisely what each questioner wanted and turned embarrassing questions to his own advantage.

"*Why did I never get a musical degree?* I was too busy practicing the flute."

"*Money?* Listen, my ideas on money are that if you want it, go into the stock market. Sell machine guns to the Middle East. Build buildings. Don't go into music."

"*Annie's Song?* You know, I was in a hospital room for four months after a motorcycle ran over me last year. (In August of 1977, he had been run over by a motorcycle which broke both his legs and his left arm. Galway was put in traction, unable to move for three months before undergoing a second operation. He did not walk much until March of 1978, and tackling stairs was still difficult for him.) One day I listened to these records of John Denver and I liked the way he talked about his wife in front of all those fans and groupies. I thought: *I'm going to do this for my Annie.* You know, people forget that some scherzos and minuets were the pop songs of their time. I recorded "Annie's Song" with the intent of bringing some happiness into a jaded classical music scene. The people who buy it will go out and buy Mozart tomorrow. I know it works that way. You have to lead people to it slowly."

"*Avant-garde music?* No, I have no sympathy for it—just for the composers who write it and the audiences who listen. Mr. Boulez and Mr. Stockhausen have never touched my heart. I commission new music and I play it. But I think we ought to encourage composers to remember where they were born and what tunes their mothers sang to them. We should encourage musicians to admit to their traditions. We should not encourage people to become robots."

Galway's interviewers would leave perplexed. Some sneered at his "Irish act." Some were disarmed by his bluntness. Few suspected the strength of a Belfast Protestant upbringing which accounted for, Galway believed, an unremitting perfectionism and a belief that "it is every man's duty to put as cheerful a face as possible on himself. We are not here to make others feel miserable."

Galway was raised in a Belfast neighborhood which, during the first four years of his life, was bombed by the German Luftwaffe, aiming for the city's railway and shipyards. "I often wonder," he liked to joke, "what Hitler would have said to Goering if he had realized that the Reichsmarschall was attempting to wipe out a future principal flutist with his beloved Berlin Philharmonic."

The men on Carnalea Street worked as stevedores, tram conductors, or lorry drivers, or constituted what Galway calls the "workless" class. The women rose at six in the tiny, identical, painted-brick row houses, made coal fires, fed their families, and hurried to the tobacco factories and linen mills. Their children quit school and began work by the time they were fourteen.

"It was not a place where you grow child prodigies," said Galway, "but it was nothing like the slums in the States. From my bedroom window I could see the Cunard liners grow up and slip down the runway. We played in the shipyard, the rubbish dump, and the railway station, which was just the greatest gift to children. There were air raid shelters up and down the block and the bombing was pretty scary for the adults, but we had a great time. They had some kind of a machine that made a hell of a lot of smoke that went straight up and hung over the city. It's a wonder I play the flute at all when you think I got my lungful of that!

"It was a terrific childhood," he maintained. "If I had to do the whole operation over again, I wouldn't change anything at all."

When Galway was nine, mechanized riveting came to the shipyards, and his father, a riveter, was out of a job. Although Galway insisted that "it was no big deal to have your dad out of work—it was part of the existence," he retained a memory of him sitting day after day playing solitaire, then drinking till it got "out of hand." He also remembers his father as "obsessed by the flute."

Music was highly regarded in Carnalea Street, and the Galways were known not only as proficient flute players but for actually owning a piano. "It hadn't been tuned since Beethoven's time," Galway said cheerfully, "but my mother played by ear and the house was so full of people you couldn't move. They'd sing sentimental tunes like 'South of the Border' or cowboy songs like 'Old Smokey.'"

Galway's father tried to interest his firstborn in a mouth organ, then a violin, without success. Instead, by age seven or eight, Jimmy Galway was picking out "The Mountains of Morne" and "Rudolph the Red-Nosed Reindeer" on a tin whistle. By age nine, he had become the youngest member of the Onward Flute Band, which met Tuesdays and Fridays over a local garage. "About thirty flute players, all men, would be there, plus drums, cymbals, and triangles. In my neighborhood alone, there were five bands—you can't imagine what kind of disease this was in Northern Ireland. Players got their flutes by public subscription, which meant that they'd walk from house to house and people gave them money. There were bands where everybody played the melody and then there were four-part and six-part bands. We had uniforms from the local transport corporation, and on Remembrance Day we'd march four abreast with hand-painted orange-and-purple banners and the whole town would turn out. It's very good for your sense of rhythm, playing in a flute band. It gets built into you. When I got to the Paris Conservatoire I was appalled: Everybody there thought they'd become a soloist and there was no need to play on time."

Galway began learning flute with his father, but both were so pig-headed that he soon moved on to his uncle. "Nobody studied anything formally where I come from," Galway said impatiently. "You learned things from your neighbors, and you didn't pay for it in money. My uncle taught me how to count, how chords worked, how to understand what was written on the page. Another man, a bookbinder, taught me theory. And I learned in the band."

Galway was thirteen when he became the pupil of Muriel Dawn, an English singer whose husband organized the Belfast Philharmonic, the Belfast Youth Orchestra, and other groups. For the first time Galway worked on breathing exercises, scales, and tone production. "In those days, I was just trying to see how fast and loud I could play: Muriel not only tried to instill in me some sense of beauty, but also told me how to behave, what to do. I used to turn up for lessons in short trousers with my socks hanging down around my feet, having just played a game of football. She changed that. I thought that if I didn't play and behave correctly it was a sin against God. Not to do something to the best of your ability was a heresy. I don't know where I got these ideas. I never saw my mother or father inside a church. But, you know, Sagittarians are born naturally religious. There's this thing: They have to find the way."

At fourteen, Galway quit school. Douglas Dawn had found him an apprenticeship at a piano factory, thinking that the proximity to musical instruments would make things easier. Instead, fed up with cleaning glue pots and buffing ivory keys, Galway began to despise pianos. By this time he was performing Mozart, Bach, and Elgar in chamber groups, in orchestras, and on radio, in addition to winning several flute band competitions. He was a moody adolescent who would probably have become a piano tuner had not the Belfast Education Committee, through the intervention of Douglas Dawn, offered Galway a special study grant. As a "gifted slum kid" Galway was sent to live and study with John Francis, who taught flute at the Royal College of Music in London. If he did well, his studies would be paid for until he graduated.

No one in his neighborhood had ever done anything like it. "I was fifteen years old. I had never been on a plane before. The farthest away I'd ever been was Dublin. And suddenly there I was in this fantastic house with a Rolls-Royce standing outside the door and the complete works of Bach, *bound*, in the library. John Francis became not only my flute teacher but my temporary father. He took me to exhibitions, took me swimming, showed me what the ballet was all about. I could stop thinking about those stupid pianos, I could cycle past Buckingham Palace, and I could just play the flute *all day*. I mean, someone had just opened the gate of heaven, you know?"

"Mr. Galway. One minute," called the production assistant for *Canada*

After Dark. On the TV monitor, the host declared: "Our next guest is one of the finest international flutists of our time. The man with the five-thousand-dollar, eighteen-karat-gold flute, a great legend, a marvelous man, and perhaps the greatest flutist in the world. I'm pleased to introduce James Galway."

~

Three days later, he was in Union College Memorial Chapel, Schenectady, New York. It was freezing cold, and most of the New Irish Chamber Orchestra as well as Galway had a stomach flu. The flutist mingled with the players, cracking jokes, ignoring his fatigue. "Unless you can go the whole fourteen rounds," he had said that afternoon, changing planes in Buffalo, "it doesn't matter how well you play."

Since taping *Canada After Dark*, Galway had played a concert, given four more interviews, partied with Toronto flutists and flute groupies, given a lesson to a girl who had badgered him for one in London, and presided over an in-store record signing, where about 150 people, free to say or do what they wished, tested his mettle.

"I thought Karajan called you a man from Mars. You don't look like a man from Mars," said a man in a business suit.

"Well, Mars is a district in Belfast, you know."

"Could you write 'Happy Birthday Tom Gallagher' here?"

"I'm sorry. Maybe next time. So many people here, you know."

"I wanted to ask you about your breathing."

"There's a great book you should read. *Zen and the Art of Archery.*"

About halfway through the signing, Galway's face froze. Someone had handed him a record cut by a good friend and former student who had killed herself without warning three weeks before. Galway had spent the morning before leaving for Schenectady with her parents, searching for reasons. "I sometimes wonder—these people who see me performing on stage, they don't have the slightest idea what kinds of things are going through my mind," he had said several times during the week. "And me up there like a monkey: I just go on as if nothing happened."

Now he wandered among the members of the New Irish Chamber Orchestra like a small boy. Its members treated him familiarly, with a mixture of affection, respect, and pride. Their conductor, André Prieur, who in 1947 in Paris played first flute while Jean-Pierre Rampal played second, indulged him. "Jimmy is never doing the same thing twice; you have to guess what will be next," he says. "With the others, it's more work. With Jimmy it's just great fun." Although a few players grumbled that Galway "plays a bit to the gallery, you know" and that the orchestra was not there "to play backup to Jimmy Galway," they seemed to enjoy him as well. He was one of theirs; they all knew where he came from and what he had done since.

Galway left the Royal College of Music, the Guildhall School, and the Paris Conservatoire without getting his degree. "I was not prepared to go through all that red tape," he says. "Writing theory examinations, doing solfège, learning music appreciation. I don't think everyone should be shoved through the same educational machine. There should be an allowance made for differences. I went and told the people who were giving me my grant that I was going to quit. They offered to let me be 'ill,' but I said I wasn't ill, I just wasn't interested anymore. If your professor sits in class regularly reading the paper and smoking Gitanes, there's no point in being there. So I left and took my first job in England."

Between the ages of twenty-two and thirty, Galway joined and then left London's five best orchestras, some more than once. At the Sadler's Wells Opera he lasted four years, but "it was driving me up the wall"; at the Royal Opera, where he worked six months, "the manager treated me like dirt, so I said, 'Right. Stick it!'" He had left the BBC orchestra, the London Symphony, and the Royal Philharmonic when in 1969 he wound up as the unlikely only English-speaking member of the Berlin Philharmonic.

"I learned a lot from Karajan. Everyone else conducts beats but, well, Karajan, he conducts tunes. You know, music is not one-two-three-four—it's only written down that way for convenience so you can get an *idea* of how it goes. Karajan loves phrases and he brings out the beauty of the line every time, in a strong clear way without undue emotion. There are musicians of whom they say, 'He knows how to make a violin cry.' Well there are some musicians who *only* know how to make a violin cry. Karajan knows more. He knows all kinds of sounds and he knows at each moment what sound he wants. I found I had to fit into it. Anybody strange coming into that orchestra has to fit into it. That's the tradition of the Berlin Philharmonic."

Galway tried to fit into it for six years, performing with the world's best instrumentalists, conductors, and singers. But while he loved his work, he hated being in Berlin. "I didn't speak any German, for one, and I felt very lonely because in the Berlin Phil and in Germany in general, I think, the people don't love each other or take care of each other the way they do in Ireland. In Berlin, I don't know how long you have to know someone to get invited to their Christmas party. My very closest friend in the orchestra, Lothar Koch, invited me to his house once in six years—and that was only because we had a rehearsal there. The other solo flutist never invited me to his house at all."

Galway drifted into Berlin's countercultural community. He lived in a quasi-commune with people who ate organic food, talked politics, smoked dope, and listened to rock music—none of which he had ever done before. "I never had the time to stop and think before," he said. "I was always too busy working. In Berlin, I listened to the Beatles for the first time. And Pink Floyd. It really knocked me sideways. I thought, gee whiz, I could really get into what they were doing artistically. I had started out at the Phil clean-shaven, with glasses, hair sort of short. Then I grew my Frank Zappa beard and started coming to rehearsals in my sheepskin coat. That was not the way *Philharmonickers* behaved. Mind you, some of them wore the same dark suits and silver ties for forty years, which I thought was even a bigger disaster than anything I was doing. But anyway, that's not why I left. I left because I wanted to make my own music, not somebody else's. Not even Herbert von Karajan's. I wanted to make my own sound."

~

The next day he was in Boston's Symphony Hall. Galway had passed up the orchestra bus and chartered a six-seat Beechcraft plane to Boston in order to catch an extra two hours of sleep. "I spend my fees on transportation," he shrugged. "This tour is costing me more than I'm earning from it. But it's an investment, you know; it's to say hello to America. It's our theory that you can only conquer one country at a time. We concentrate on the English-speaking ones where I can go on TV and talk to people in their own language. We did England that way. Then Holland. Now America. I'm coming back to the States quite a number of times in the next two years. You can't do it in less time. It takes quite a while before people get to know who you are."

Backstage at Symphony Hall, everyone seemed to know Galway. Over 200 flutists were in town attending a conference, and they streamed into the soloist's room, along with skinny, prepubescent flutists, middle-aged amateur flutists, hippies and businesspeople, former students and their families, other soloists.

"I just came back to say hello. I'm going. You must be nervous," said violinist Itzhak Perlman.

"Wait. Where you going?" Galway intercepted him, then presented him to another visitor as "My manager, Al Capone."

"I gave up dozens of girls; I'm staying in Boston just for you," announced flutist Julius Baker, giving Galway a hug.

"I got this guy a policeman's whistle, you know," Galway said to the crowd around him. "You have no idea how many cops I had to kill to get it."

When he walked onstage, there was an irrepressible pride in his stance. He was performing for his peers, some of the best flutists in the world. The first flutes of the Boston Symphony, the Boston Pops, and the New York Philharmonic were in the audience, as well as flute teachers, flute free-lancers, and the growing group of younger flute students who viewed him as a role model. "He's got a different outlook from most performers," said one. "He talks about sound but he also talks about God. He really believes that music comes from God and that he's a vessel for it."

Galway said that he had always felt this way, that, in fact, when he was a kid, he used to think that Mozart was speaking through him. But he credited his motorcycle accident for strengthening his "spiritual values" and for putting him out of commission long enough to assess, carefully, the possibilities as well as the pitfalls of a successful soloist's career.

"I was able to see what the publicity machine could do to me if I didn't watch out," he said. "And then this jealousy factor in the music business, which is something terrible. For a long time I was very jealous of other players, and this jealousy occupied part of me that I could have been using to better effect. Then one day I thought: *I'm not doing the same kind of thing as this or that guy. I shouldn't be worried about them. I'm in a different league.*

"I think the American way of thinking, of gauging everything by the amount of money someone makes, is ruining the life of the people. I can't say how much money I have, and I'm not really interested in knowing. We employ a full-time accountant just for me, so we're earning money. But how much do you need to make? After a while it becomes something of a game. You know, the only effect money has on me is that it removes certain worries. When you're poor, you worry about money and that leads to worrying about other things. I don't have to worry about money now and I feel very free. But I don't want to buy a jet or a swimming pool or any kind of junk. I mean, if you have a Rolls-Royce, you have to get someone to drive it, you know? If you have a swimming pool, you have to look after it.

"What am I doing then on TV and doing all this publicity? I'm bringing a great deal of music to the general public. You can't believe the letters I get from ordinary people who have never heard classical music before. These people would never hear Bach from one end of their lives to the next. They'd never go to the concert hall. You have to bring it into their living room. I bring people in touch with the spirit that's all the time there but that they're not in touch with. I mean, you *saw* some of these people listening. I don't have to talk about any particular philosophy or religion. It's there. In the music."

Galway fixed his astigmatic eyes on some inner light. They were bright, defiant, and full of life. "Sometimes it's very hard. To get a bit of personal space around yourself, which you really need. Because if you're giving out all the time, you really need some time to do nothing. Just to sit there. My ideal is to have eight months free. I want to hang out with the kids, with my wife. Go swimming. Maybe go to Israel for a month. Take the kids to Ireland. Or do my own thing. I might even teach some more people the flute. But meanwhile, I have to establish myself."

After the concert, Galway took a party of twenty out to dinner at one of Boston's expensive restaurants. It was morning before he got to sleep. He had a concert to play in Portland, Maine, the next day. Before that, another in-store record signing. Then, he planned to take a plane to Switzerland and get home.

Hugo Burghauser. (*Trude Fleischmann.*)

7

A European Musician in America

HUGO BURGHAUSER, 86, DIES; FOUNDED SALZBURG ENSEMBLE

Hugo Burghauser, a former bassoonist with the Vienna Philharmonic and founding director of the Salzburg Festival Players ensemble, died Thursday after a long illness. He was 86 years old...

New York Times, December 11, 1982

On the morning of his seventy-fifth birthday, as the antique *horloge* in his hallway completed its short musical fragment and began to chime nine, Hugo Burghauser eased into his slippers and walked over a trail of Persian carpets into the living room of his apartment on Central Park South. It was the room in which he spent most of his time and a room furnished so extensively with mementos of a musical life in Europe that one might think one was in Vienna and not New York. There were century-old rococo chairs in the darkened room; several cherubs mounted on the walls (one of which he had bought on behalf of the Vienna Philharmonic for Arturo Toscanini's seventieth birthday); tattered stacks of concert programs dating back to 1918; portraits of Otto Klemperer, Bruno Walter, and Toscanini; a silver *Rosenkavalier* rose which Burghauser received as an official gift from the Vienna State Opera; and the original score of Richard Strauss's Concertino for Clarinet and Bassoon, on which the composer had written, *"Hugo Burghauser, dem Getreuen, 1946."*

Burghauser's handsome face had softened since that year, and his hair had turned white, but on his seventy-fifth birthday he retained the erect carriage and courteous manner of a central European patrician. His hands had aged gracefully as well: They were firm and well-kept, with long steady fingers that could reach an octave and a half on a piano keyboard. His large hazel eyes now seemed wiser, less devilish than in his youth. But, in fact, time had altered the musician less than it had the Viennese suburb where he was born in 1896, when a horse-drawn tram linked it to Vienna, and the hammers of the blacksmith made the only music till two in the afternoon, when the hurdy-gurdy man came to the Burghausers' courtyard.

In New York, Burghauser owned a fine radio, stereo, tape recorder, and television set. But he preferred to sit in his living room with all of his appliances shut off, listening to the cooing of the pigeons on his windowsill, the soft roll of the elevator door, and the constant murmur of traffic seven floors below. When the doorbell rang, it sounded clearly through his small apartment, and Burghauser went to answer it with an expectant smile.

"G'morning, Professor." The doorman saluted him and handed over a stack of letters and telegrams. The top one was from the opera singer Lotte Lehmann, who was in her eighties and living on a ranch in Santa Barbara, California. She shared Burghauser's birth date and had been exchanging greetings with him for four decades. A second cable was postmarked New Jersey and came from Maria Jeritza, whom Puccini had once called the greatest Tosca imaginable. There were birthday greetings from the president of the Vienna Philharmonic; from Burghauser's second wife, a choreographer and stage manager at La Scala; from his daughter in Vienna; from many former colleagues at the Metropolitan Opera House and the Vienna State Opera with whom he had worked at one time or another in the fifty-seven years that he had been playing the bassoon; and from other friends.

The phone rang as he was sorting through them all and he went to it anticipating the voice of another well-wisher. Instead, he heard John Di-Janni, the manager of the Metropolitan Opera Orchestra, who had no idea it was Burghauser's birthday. One of the Met's regular bassoonists was unable to play *Elektra* that afternoon and he was hesitant to ask a young, inexperienced player to substitute. Would Burghauser be available?

"Of course," Burghauser replied genially, in his slow, attractively accented English. "I will be happy to help out."

~

During the 1970s, Hugo Burghauser would come out of retirement about twice a month to play his instrument, which looks like a wooden drain-pipe or, maybe, a customized shotgun. Burghauser himself liked to point out that while Vivaldi, Mozart, and Weber had written for the bassoon in a straightforward manner, subsequent composers viewed it as "the clown of the orchestra." Prokofiev had gone so far as to write a Scherzo Humoristique for Four Bassoons, which Burghauser thought comparable to writing for an army of frogs.

He sat on a small brocade couch in his living room to examine his bassoon, trying to remember whether or not he had oiled its keys that week. The instrument lay in three maple wood parts. Were it "unwound" to form one continuous tube, the bassoon would be over one hundred inches long; bent back on itself, it extended a mere four feet away from Burghauser's lips. He polished the metal crook, a thin tube inserted into the smallest of the wood parts, then put the instrument down as the doorbell rang once again. It was Dr. Brumberger, a Viennese dentist who often advised Burghauser on medical and other matters, wishing him a happy birthday. The bassoonist invited him to sit down, then continued inspecting his instrument.

In the seventeenth century, a bassoonist was called a *Tieftonholz-knüppelvergnügling,* that is, "a man who takes pleasures in the deep sound of a wooden bat." There has never been an excess of bassoon players, and it is one of the reasons Burghauser had been given a scholarship to study at the Vienna Academy sixty years before.

Hugo Burghauser's mother was "a very musical Italian" whose father had played flute under Verdi's direction, and his father was a Sudetenland agronomist who liked Johann Strauss waltzes for entertainment. He felt that music, especially theater music, was bad for the morals and un-suitable for a young bourgeois to make a living by. He sent Burghauser to a teachers' seminary. "It so happened, however," Burghauser recalled with obvious delight, "that a genuine Indian swami arrived in Vienna who was inadvertently responsible for granting my wish to study music. He was lecturing at the Vienna Theosophical Society, in the living room of a wealthy family, and there—through the incense—I saw Louis Thern, a former pupil of Franz Liszt and member of the board of directors at the Vienna Academy."

Burghauser had retained his hopes of a career in music despite his father—he had been playing piano since childhood and singing in a church choir with another boy, who grew up to become conductor Joseph Krips—and he inveigled an invitation to play for Thern. Thern gave him additional lessons and encouraged him to audition for the academy. When Burghauser was accepted, however, his father refused to finance any studies in music.

Fortunately, the director of the academy was also conductor of its orchestra, and the orchestra needed a bassoonist. "Wilhelm Bopp was the director's name, and he used a stick like the baton Napoleon used when he gave orders from horseback. Since we were talkative, Bopp would bang on his desk for quiet, often splitting the baton in two or three and then continuing to conduct with the smallest splinter. He adored his orchestra and the idea of being short a bassoonist made him almost desperate. Someone must have told him about the financial difficulty I was having because he approached me with the proposition that I could study anything I wanted to study—tuition free—if only I would play the bassoon. Of course I would have taken up *any* instrument to get a scholarship, and I was so grateful that I learned to play well enough to join the orchestra that first year!"

In 1915, when he was 19 and the First World War was devastating Europe, Burghauser was drafted into the 84th Vienna Horse Regiment, which was to be sent to the Balkans. Burghauser still recalls the painted letters on the freight cars that took the soldiers there: "Eight horses or forty men." But at the last minute Burghauser received orders to report instead to the regiment's orchestra. Its first bassoonist, he was later told, had overturned a cauldron of boiling glaze onto his hands while working in his *patisserie* and would not be able to play his instrument for months. Burghauser took his place and lived to hear that his original company was obliterated in the battle of the Black Mountain, in what is now Yugoslavia.

When the war finally ended in 1918, the capital of the former Austro-Hungarian empire was reduced to a dismal way station for thousands of unemployed imperial officials. Burghauser remembers communal kitchens serving soup and gray cake, and shops lit with candle stubs and acetylene gas which stank up the streets long after sunset. He remembers that there was a shortage of clothing and that musicians played concerts in their old military uniforms. But the poverty and malaise of postwar life in Vienna did not discourage him. In fact, for a young musician just beginning his career, conditions could not have been better. The Viennese musical tradition had remained intact, and despite the poor economy, concerts were sold out. Richard Strauss himself auditioned Burghauser, then twenty-two, for the Vienna State Opera Orchestra.

"*Namen sind Schall und Rauch,*" Burghauser said slowly. "That is Goethe: 'Names are like sound and smoke.' Already a generation of musicians have no idea there ever was a Golden Vienna or a Vienna Ensemble. Do they remember Leo Slezak? Elisabeth Schumann or Erich Schmedes? Chaliapin? I must say that man was excessive sometimes—you might think he was taking drugs! One time he sang a serenata accompanying himself on the lute and became dissatisfied with the tempo of the conductor. When the first strophe ended, he drew his sword from the scabbard, jumped onto the prompter's box, and he conducted us with his sword for the duration of the aria!

"And you should not think that the conductors were any less theatrical. In 1920, Artur Nikisch appeared like an Indian *fakir*. His hair always slipped over one eye and the ladies found him irresistibly romantic. Before giving us the beat, he turned to the public and fixed them with a charismatic regard. It *hypnotized* them, and even we hard-boiled musicians felt trancelike. Then the music began. People would say that if Nikisch appeared at the conductor's desk and raised his baton to an empty pit, the audience would be able to *hear* the music he coaxed from the empty chairs! At the same time we played under other great conductors like Bruno Walter, Felix Weingartner, Sir Thomas Beecham, and Erich Kleiber. These were everyday occurrences and not a great rarity like today, when a Bernstein or a von Karajan appears somewhere like a migratory bird and disappears after two weeks. These were *our* conductors."

~

Burghauser finished polishing his instrument and began to adapt his reed. He took a reed which had been soaking in a small bowl of water and began to pare down the cane with a sharp knife. The thinner a player's lips, the thinner the reed must be, so Burghauser was bent over the four-inch piece of cane for several minutes. Finally, he attached the reed to the end of the silver crook, spread his long fingers over the holes and keys of the instrument, and produced the sound that always seemed an anticlimax after this elaborate preparation.

The Viennese dentist laughed and the bassoonist did too.

"When I played the Weber bassoon concerto for my degree from the academy," said Burghauser, "they laughed before I even sat down on my chair! Maybe that's why bassoonists were so rare at the beginning of the century. You know, when Strauss hired me in 1918, he didn't have much choice!"

The Vienna Opera then played a ten-month season and offered fifty operas per year, as compared to the Metropolitan Opera or La Scala, which half a century later offered no more than twenty-five each. Burghauser was expected to know the scores of all fifty, a requirement made difficult by the fact that a ban had been declared on the performance of all Italian operas during the First World War and Burghauser had never even heard some of them.

His life in the early 1920s was extremely busy. Because the players of the Vienna State Opera Orchestra doubled as the Vienna Philharmonic, Burghauser rehearsed operas in the mornings, played performances in the evenings, gave symphony concerts on weekends, and taught a few students at the academy in between. At a time when travel was a luxury, the orchestra was invited abroad almost every summer.

In June of 1922, Burghauser recalls, the company sailed to South America. He had never before crossed the Atlantic, and even the brown coal which powdered the decks of the *Principessa Mafalda* did not dampen his spirits. The *Principessa* later sank somewhere off the shores of Brazil, but at the time she was sumptuously equipped for pleasure. "As we approached the equator," Burghauser liked to recount to friends, "the crew organized a magnificent ceremony. We men were given costumes, false moustaches, and huge beards and told to sit down on barber chairs next to the swimming pool. Then came Neptune with harpoon, leather brush, and razor to shave us, after which his assistants overturned the chairs into the pool.

"It was all harmless, but one violinist became frightened, locked himself into his cabin, and refused to come out. He was immediately discovered, forced out, and made to pay a forfeit: He had to crawl through a fifty-foot tube of fabric which looked like the mouth of a boa constrictor. After three feet he got scared and started to come back out, but one of the sailors had a fire hose and shot him brusquely through so that he reappeared, almost drowned, on the other end.

"This kind of spectacle was common on the *Principessa.*"

Between parties and practical jokes, Burghauser followed a concert and practice routine which combined elements of superstition and habit and which he followed all his life. After assembling his instrument and preparing his reed, he began his warm-up exercises.

The hallway clock chimed twelve times and the Viennese dentist stood up to leave. Burghauser showed him to the elevator, then went into his tiny kitchen to prepare the tea which, along with a bread stick or two, made up his lunch. One had to be careful about what one ate before playing a concert. String players did not have to worry, but for the woodwinds, a full stomach could prove dangerous and interfere with proper breathing. He prepared his brew as usual: A large dab of honey, half a cup of strong Earl Grey tea, enough milk to turn it a pale beige, a few drops of rum from a glass decanter. The color of the liquid was exactly that of the *ersatz* tea he had sipped in coffeehouses after the First World War. It had been owing to the foreign currency he acquired as a musician on tour that he had been able eventually to afford real tea.

After the war, Burghauser had taken a flat and married a young sculptress with whom he had had one daughter. And he had begun to take a modest part in the administration of the Vienna Philharmonic, first lending a hand with ticketing and other clerical work, later debating at the orchestra's *plenum*.

Richard Strauss was succeeded by Franz Schalk at the opera, and by the end of the twenties, Schalk was replaced by Klemens Kraus. "He was a competent but unglamourous conductor, and when the stock market crashed in 1929, we felt that a change of conductors was the only thing that would bring in the audiences." Burghauser proposed a new system of guest conductors, with fifty percent of the concerts going to Kraus and the other half divided among several other conductors. Kraus refused the plan and, largely through Burghauser's politicking, was voted out altogether. Various conductors, including Bruno Walter, Fritz Busch, and Otto Klemperer, took turns in his place, and the Philharmonic was soon playing to full houses again. In 1932, when he was thirty-six, Burghauser was elected president of the orchestra.

His first priority was to invite Arturo Toscanini to conduct a concert during the 1933–1934 season. Toscanini accepted the engagement, and when Burghauser formally announced it, it created a furor in the Austrian press. Aside from his artistic preeminence, Toscanini had already publicly criticized Hitler and was an outspoken opponent of the Italian Fascists.

He was also to play an important part in Burghauser's eventual flight from Europe and resettlement in the United States.

"He arrived by night train from Paris," Burghauser remembered. "He was sixty-six then and it had been a long trip. He looked like a priest in his black alpaca habit with a ribbon of white at the collar. When he entered the hall, the entire orchestra stood up. We felt as if we were to take part in a mystical sacrament, and for me, Toscanini always remained a musical priest. He chose Wagner's *Meistersinger Vorspiel*—the first time in fifty years that an Italian conducted such German music in Vienna. We were accustomed to play it every other week at the opera and took our interpretation completely for granted. But Toscanini gave the prelude a translucence which made us hear it as if for the first time. He didn't speak, only sang a part here or indicated dynamics, but he had what I can only call an extraordinarily powerful musical will. This was perfectly communicated to us, and we responded like one man. The critics outdid one another in accolades, and for me, it was the beginning of a friendship which ended only when he died here in 1957."

~

Burghauser finished his tea, placed his Rosenthal cup and saucer in the sink, and went into the bathroom to shave as he always did just before dressing for a performance. The face in the mirror was pleasant and expressive, qualities that had once caught the eye of a photographer from *Time* magazine who had chosen the bassoonist out of thousands of concertgoers at Tanglewood and shot his face as he listened to the music. The photographer was unaware, of course, that his subject had once been a prominent figure in the classical music world. Besides his presidency of the Vienna Philharmonic from 1932 to 1938, he had been a professor at the Vienna Academy, president of the musicians' union, and special music counsel to the high court of Austria. He was also known as the husband of prima ballerina Margherita Wallman, whom he had married after his first marriage ended.

His second, five-year marriage was "lively," Burghauser often said with a bemused smile. The couple's two careers often caused long separations, as well as theatrics when they worked together at the opera. The couple shared a bohemian life-style which took them all over Europe as well as to the United States at a time when, for the population at large, life was becoming increasingly constricted.

In 1935, the Burghausers spent five months in Hollywood, working on the opera scene for the film *Anna Karenina* in which Greta Garbo was starring. They lived in a bungalow at the Garden of Allah next door to the Charles Laughtons, bought a new Ford, learned to drive, and took long trips along the California coast. "I occasionally got a ticket," Burghauser remembered, "but it was taken care of by MGM." One trip led to a marketplace on Sunset Boulevard where a smiling Chinese merchant slipped a sweet brown paste into his hand and the musician swallowed a sizable dose of peyote. It was not until he returned to the Garden of Allah that the drug began to work and he experienced what he describes as "a tremendous sexual explosion." Although he searched the marketplace afterward for the Chinese merchant, Burghauser never found him. He was soon introduced to other intoxicants. "At parties, they consumed enormous amounts of alcohol, even though there was Prohibition. In Vienna, parties were cozy gatherings, sitting, eating, and being served a glass of wine. When I first tasted whiskey in Hollywood, I at once spat it out for I thought it was tincture for insecticide. Now I sip it purely and I find it a most significant change; it *does* give you a kind of uplift at the end of a long day. But I never learned to stand up for so long at parties. Despite all their luxuries, lawns, swimming pools, people seemed to stand for hours. They never sat down *once* during an evening at someone's house!"

When the Burghausers returned to Vienna, the Nazis were very much in evidence, but politics held as little interest for the couple as it did for the rest of their artist friends, and they remained impervious to events in Germany. Then the Austrian chancellor was summoned to meet with Hitler. Several musicians whom Burghauser knew left Austria immediately, like Bronislav Huberman, who was napping in a sanatorium when he was awakened by the commotion following the announcement on radio. Another musician alert to the implications of the meeting was Toscanini, who cabled Burghauser that same day to cancel his engagement in Salzburg that summer. Burghauser cabled back his opinion that the maestro was unduly pessimistic. Four weeks later, Nazi Germany annexed Austria.

"We were playing *Eugen Onegin*," Burghauser remembered, "and it was the kind of evening on which everyone was inclined during the interval to go for a whiff of fresh air to the arcades of the house. The moment we left the inner doors, we heard the noise and clanging; tanks and cannons were rolling over the Ringstrasse. I remember we looked at each other wordlessly. What was to be said? We went back to the orchestra pit and played to an almost empty house."

By the time Burghauser came out the stage door two hours later, he recalled, the streets were emblazoned with swastikas, and the bassoonist finally experienced the sense of emergency that others had felt so much earlier. Although Burghauser himself was a Catholic, he was married to a Jew, known to have many Jewish friends and known as an anti-Nazi. The next day, in fact, he was relieved of his duties as president of the Vienna Philharmonic and notified that his position at the academy would be terminated at the end of the year.

More serious developments followed. One day at rehearsal he found a copy of Julius Streicher's anti-Semitic publication *Der Stürmer* on his music stand, with his own face caricatured on the top page. He was accused of suppressing the careers of budding Nazi conductors and composers. His chief function as president of the Philharmonic had indeed been to negotiate contracts with conductors and he had indeed refused a great many conductors, including Eugene Ormandy and Fritz Reiner, simply because Toscanini, Walter, Weingartner, Furtwängler, and Klemperer were available. Among the men he had turned down were several able conductors who had now become politically powerful.

A second problem, even more dangerous, had evolved from a trivial— almost laughable, in ordinary times—occurrence at a rehearsal. Wilhelm Furtwängler had arrived to conduct the orchestra at a time when Burghauser was in the hospital for a tonsillectomy. He had held an afternoon rehearsal, which was a departure from Philharmonic routine, and he was said to be especially edgy because of the political situation. At that rehearsal, the cellist sitting just below the conductor's podium had apparently eaten too much for lunch and, after placing his cello between his legs, opened the buttons of his fly to accommodate his stomach. The conductor noticed nothing. Then, between movements, the cellist reached for the music stand and dramatically exposed himself to Furtwängler.

The conductor walked out on the rehearsal, and Burghauser, convalescing in the hospital, was called out of bed to get Furtwängler back. He found it an easy matter to placate the conductor, but when he suspended the cellist from the forthcoming concert, a public altercation took place. The cellist called Burghauser a "tyrant," whereupon Burghauser called the cellist an "anarchist." The cellist then sued Burghauser for slander.

They appeared before an amused judge who urged them to settle out of court and set a date for the second hearing should they fail. The cellist remained vengeful, and by the time the second hearing took place there was a new judge, who, like the cellist, displayed the Nazi insignia prominently in his lapel. It took the judge only a few minutes to sentence Burghauser to several weeks in jail for slander. Before the sentence began, however, elections were held in Austria, and a general amnesty was declared for all persons convicted of misdemeanors.

The incident convinced Burghauser that he had to leave Austria, now, while his wife was in Argentina on tour. All hopeful refugees went west, he calculated, and decided to go east to Budapest. He wrote to an impresario there of his desire to play some chamber music and soon received an official invitation which enabled him to enter Hungary without a passport. Civil defense guards were installing loudspeakers in the trees on the evening of September 12, 1938, when Burghauser left Vienna. As he reached the train station, Adolf Hitler's voice roared down from the loudspeakers, and in the excitement, the railway guards were singularly inattentive.

Burghauser, carrying his baptismal certificate, his bassoon, his invitation, and the ten marks allotted to travelers, boarded the train to Budapest without incident.

~

The clock in the hallway struck one as Burghauser reached for his overcoat, pulled the muffs of his black lamb's wool hat over his ears, picked up his bassoon case, and started off on his diagonal route through Central Park to the Metropolitan Opera House in Lincoln Center. He had been dressed in almost the same garments thirty-three years earlier when he arrived in Budapest. His ultimate destination then was Toronto, where Sir Ernest MacMillan had a bassoon vacancy and had asked Toscanini for a recommendation. The maestro, as Burghauser always called him, had put forth Burghauser's name and MacMillan had hired him sight unseen.

There would be no difficulty reaching Canada once Burghauser got to Cherbourg; the problem was trying to enter France at a time when the French government refused to cooperate in any way with German subjects. Burghauser's efforts to obtain a *laissez-passer* from the French embassy in Budapest proved fruitless, so he turned to a powerful friend, Count Esterhazy—whose ancestors had been the patrons of Josef Haydn.

The count advised him to go south to Yugoslavia (which did not require formal papers at the time) and try his luck with the French there. Burghauser did this, stayed with friends whom he had met while concertizing in Zagreb, and cabled his housekeeper in Vienna to send him necessities for a long journey. Two days later, a truck arrived filled not only with clothing but with all the awards he had received as president of the Philharmonic—among them the *Officier d'Académie* which he had received on behalf of the orchestra during the Great Exposition of Paris in 1937. When he presented this document to the French, he was readily granted a transit visa and immediately boarded a train for Italy. At the border, he was asked to show his passport and proof of military exemption, but by now Burghauser had learned the value of his collection of honors. Disregarding the official's requests, Burghauser pulled out his decoration of *Cavaliere Ufficiale dell'Ordine della Corona d'Italia*, and the man came to attention, saluted him, and murmured: "*Va!*"

Once in Italy, Burghauser hurried to Toscanini's home in Milan. Toscanini had remained adamant in his refusal to conduct for Nazi Germany or Austria. Moreover, he had established an alternative to the annual Salzburg Festival which he ingenuously named "The Salzburg Festival in Lucerne." Hitler found this an outrageous provocation and, as a result, Mussolini had placed the maestro under house arrest so that Burghauser had no difficulty in locating his friend. Two policemen met him at the door of Toscanini's home, interrogated him, and inspected his baggage. The maestro was certain that his house was an unsafe place in which to talk, so the two musicians drove out to Lake Como. Toscanini gave Burghauser a list of his personal friends who would surely lend him money for a transatlantic steamer ticket, but when the bassoonist reached Paris he visited each person without success. After the last visit, he found a *gendarme* waiting at his hotel, and was asked to show his papers. Burghauser showed him his transit visa and was informed, he said, that he had one week to get out of France or be deported back to what was now Greater Germany.

The next day Burghauser saw an American multimillionaire of his acquaintance who lived in Versailles for most of the year, since he found Americans increasingly vulgar. The man spent lavishly on the arts and patronized the Vienna Philharmonic, where Burghauser had met him. The American aesthete sent a Rolls-Royce to fetch Burghauser, thereby impressing the hotel's manager so profoundly that the bassoonist was never asked to pay his bill. When they were seated for lunch, the bassoonist explained his predicament and asked for a small loan to pay for his ocean passage. The American, Burghauser recalled sadly, then expressed in excellent German his lifelong belief that friendship should never be tarnished by finance, and turned the conversation to other matters while the bassoonist wondered how in the world he would ever reach Canada.

Later that day, he went to the Café Weber, where many refugees gathered, and was advised, in all seriousness, to join the French Foreign Legion. Burghauser had been in Africa in 1922 and was convinced that, given the certainty of deportation, it was his only alternative. He inquired at the appropriate office and even underwent a medical examination before an accident of such miraculous good fortune occurred that, even thirty years later, Burghauser would find it incredible.

Unable to sleep, the bassoonist awoke before dawn on what he thought would be his last day as a free man and walked for hours through the streets of Paris. Only janitors and maids were outside at this time, spreading water on the sidewalks and sweeping it off with their brooms. Burghauser recalled walking to the Place Vendôme for a last look at Chopin's home—a kind of symbolic farewell to Paris, Europe, and Toronto, which he had not even seen. At the corner of the square was the Schiaperelli shop window, decorated beautifully to display hats. As he stood admiring it at about eight o'clock, he heard the screech of brakes behind him and turned around to see Signora Carla Toscanini emerging from a taxi.

By a fantastic coincidence, the Toscaninis had been given exit permits from Italy the previous day and were to sail for America in the afternoon. While her husband had his breakfast, Signora Toscanini had arranged to buy herself a new hat. Burghauser told her what had happened during the nine days since he had seen the couple in Milan, concluding with the fact that he was expected to join the French Foreign Legion. The maestro's wife quickly gave him the money he needed, and the bassoonist arrived soon after the Toscaninis at the port of New York.

When he finally reached Toronto, Burghauser was met by a group of local journalists, who interviewed him about conditions in Europe and made him the best-known member of the Toronto Symphony for the two years in which he played in that city. But when England declared war on Germany, he was forced to leave once again. Legally, he was still a

German citizen and, as such, subject to internment in camps set up for that purpose. So, in 1940, with the aid of Toscanini, who was now conducting the NBC Symphony Orchestra, Burghauser came to New York. He was then in his early forties and—despite his credentials, his decorations, and influential friends—practically destitute. Nazi Europe had sent thousands of European musicians fleeing to the United States, and the American Federation of Musicians had, as a protectionist measure, established a six-month residency requirement for orchestra musicians.

Burghauser had come to take a gentle view of the situation in which he then found himself. "Naturally," he later said, "when one is fleeing the Holocaust, one believes that even dwelling under a bridge is more desirable than staying in Europe. But when you finally *arrive* at this bridge, it seems to you unfit for living—so quickly does one forget necessity. At first I lived in a rented room for three dollars a week, sharing a bathroom with ten other tenants. There was continual noise and dirt, an enormous contrast to my past standard, and for this reason I found anonymity somewhat of a blessing. It leaves you alone with your wounded pride without anyone to point a finger and is, in fact, a great protection."

Anonymity did, however, pain Hugo Burghauser as well. When a displaced persons' agency found him lodgings and a roommate, the man refused to speak with the bassoonist, believing him to be an agent of the Gestapo; it was not until several weeks had gone by that he could be persuaded otherwise. Some nights Burghauser went to parties of wealthy Americans who patronized central European aristocrats stripped of their social status, politicians without constituencies, artists without a stage. Some nights he was snubbed by musicians or music administrators who should have known better. New York was packed with refugees, and the saying was that any dachshund from Europe went around pretending to have been a St. Bernard. "You're the fifth man I've encountered who pretends to have been president of the Vienna Philharmonic," sniffed the NBC Symphony's manager after Burghauser had been in the States six months and was hired as a bassoon player. Burghauser remembers feeling too astonished to reply and too embarrassed to confront the men who were pretending to be him.

"My outlook was that I had achieved all my distinctions by mere chance," he would say when asked about this time in his career. Or, "If you have proved yourself to your own satisfaction and then are struck by a plague like Hitler,

you are entirely innocent of your downfall. For what did I need the ac-
knowledgment of strangers? *Famous* people were reduced in New York to
utterly insignificant insects like the others. It was not so bad. In Vienna I
could not take a lady to lunch without having an item appear in some gossip
column. Here, I was suddenly free and unmolested."

~

Hugo Burghauser broke his walk and rested his bassoon case on one of
the park benches which lined the path he always walked to Lincoln
Center. The case was made of soft black leather and looked like a wildly
elongated physician's bag—one of the reasons people called him "Doctor"
at the Met. The air was crisp and dabs of frozen snow streaked the ground,
but a few young men in sweatshirts were playing baseball. "It is only after
a long while that you understand the carefree nature of Americans," he
said. "In the beginning when I came here, all I saw was the care*less*ness,
the cutthroatedness, and the real lawlessness. The competition within the
musical world was terrifying when I came here. Perhaps it is so all over
the world, but never so uninhibited as in New York. A newcomer can
only be frightened and repulsed by it."

Burghauser does not like to dwell on the slights he had to contend with
as a newcomer, particularly those occasioned by the fact that he was a
German Gentile. He was often told that New York was a Jewish city,
that the music world was particularly Jewish, and that as a German, he
was considered to be an undesirable. In 1942, when his contract came up
for renewal with the NBC orchestra, it was not renewed, and Burghauser
found himself, in effect, fired by the manager. But since virtuoso bassoonists were hard to come by even in wartime New York, he was soon
engaged by the Metropolitan Opera Orchestra.

At the Met, Burghauser often found himself gazing up from the pit
into the faces of people he had known on the other side of the Atlantic.
He remembered general manager Rudolf Bing as a clerk in a Viennese
bookstore, and George Szell as a young pianist at the Vienna Academy.
His former neighbor in Vienna, Louis Rothschild, sat in the first row of
seats and would, during intermissions, relay to Burghauser the latest
gossip from Vienna. The war had scattered the stars of the Vienna State
Opera all across the world, but one by one they reappeared on the stage
of the Met. One night, the American multimillionaire who had refused
to loan Burghauser money to pay for his passage to America turned up,

but by then the bassoonist had relegated him to the back of his mind.

"Here comes the old horse one more time," Hugo Burghauser said, grimacing at the roar of trucks on Amsterdam Avenue. Richard Strauss had said that to him in London when at the age of eighty-four he had conducted his last concert. Burghauser entered the concrete underground of Lincoln Center and walked past the Met's stage door guard, who, like the house nurse, consistently called him "Maestro."

"*Servus*," he greeted one pair of musicians. "*Ciào caro*," he said to another, who took his arm as they walked down the yellow corridor to their dressing room. The backstage area was a far cry from the red velvet opulence on the other side of the stage curtain, yet Burghauser believed it exuded a peculiar hysteria that only opera can engender. "The legitimate stage is for madmen," he liked to say, as they had in Vienna, "but the opera is for incurables."

Burghauser had been appalled by American behavior at the opera since first playing at the Met. He was shocked that latecomers would be seated during Act I and often allowed to meander into the hall drunk during Act II or even Act III, after spending time in the opera bar. "They talked as if they were in a cafeteria, and—most disturbing—they invariably had seats ten or twelve places within a row. Ten people had to get up, shuffle, drop their programs, and sit down again! Gustav Mahler had forbidden this kind of behavior to *aristocrats* in Vienna at the turn of the century, and here was the bourgeois—innocent but thoroughly uneducated—taking such liberties!"

Burghauser nodded to a small group of young musicians as he sat down in the dressing room. They too were guilty, in his mind, of outrageous behavior. "When I taught at the New York College of Music, my pupils never prepared their lessons adequately," Burghauser sometimes told colleagues. "When I admonished them for their lack of diligence, they would take an offensive tactic and say, 'How much am I going to earn from this anyway?' I could only reply that first they had better learn well enough to be paid at all. With this mercantile approach it is impossible to train good musicians and, for that matter, good audiences.

"The Americans are so enthusiastic in their ignorance. The merest suggestion of a curtain unleashes the most thunderous applause, which is disastrous in any act concluding with a soft orchestral passage. It makes one think they come to the opera to look instead of to listen!"

He put his bassoon together for the second time that day, sitting on a plastic chair in the musicians' room. In Vienna, instruments were left at the opera house at a controlled temperature which, Burghauser said, gave them a timbre far finer than that of instruments transported back and forth in the cold. His bassoon was frigid and sounded almost a quarter tone lower than its customary range. It was for this reason that Burghauser always arrived early at the Met. Piccolo players often placed their instruments in their breast pockets to warm them, but since this was impossible to do with a bassoon, he played some warm-up exercises instead.

"The doctor's here," a clarinetist called, and Stephen Maxim, the Met's first bassoonist, came over to chat. A fond relationship existed between these two men who had together prepared for performances under conditions that the operagoer watching them play minutes later would have found difficult to believe. In Washington, D.C., they had put on their concert clothes in makeshift army tents while the wind howled and the canvas flapped open around them. In Houston, they had left their instruments in an auditorium overnight and the clarinetist had blown cockroaches out of his instrument the following day. In Atlanta, the train carrying sets and costumes was delayed so that the company presented the first act of *Carmen* in street clothes, the second act with soloists in costume, and the third act with everyone formally dressed. But the worst city of all in Burghauser's mind was Dallas. From the moment he saw a traffic sign shot through with bullet holes he was sure this was the most dangerous city in America.

On a sweltering Sunday afternoon in 1956, Burghauser had been trying to find a taxi to take him to the county fair grounds ten miles out of town where the Met performed. As he stopped for a streetlight, a Cadillac pulled up to the curb and the young woman behind the wheel asked him whether he needed a lift. In his telling, Burghauser claimed to have taken her for an opera lover and, since there was time before the performance, invited her to dinner. She agreed, said she knew a good place to eat, and turned off the main road. She told him, he recalled, that her family had gone off on a shooting trip and that she was unbearably lonely; then she had turned off the ignition and thrown herself into his lap. Burghauser recalled catching a whiff of French perfume before a second car pulled up behind them and four athletic young men jumped out.

"Any valuables on you?" one of them asked Burghauser.

"I beg your pardon," said Burghauser, deducing that this was a "holdup" of the kind he had seen in films, but unwilling to cooperate. "I'm on my way to the opera with this young woman."

The first man flashed a sheriff's badge at him and ordered him out of the car.

The driver was placed under arrest for soliciting.

~

Burghauser placed his long hand on Maxim's shoulder and stood up. Since his retirement seven years before, the bassoonist saw less of his colleagues than he liked. Maxim picked up his own instrument, and the two men went down the narrow stairway to the orchestra pit. From Burghauser's desk, the house looked like a giant planetarium, with thousands of tiny stars sparkling in the crowded tiers. The crystal chandeliers that were a gift from Austria rose slowly to the ceiling and a hush settled over the audience.

Dr. Karl Böhm stepped up to the podium, acknowledged the audience with a quick smile, then turned to the orchestra. Burghauser had played *Elektra* often under the direction of its composer, and knew the opera almost by heart. He kept his eyes fixed on the conductor's illuminated face until Böhm looked his way to signal a bassoon entry and, with a flicker of surprise, recognized his old friend. They had first met during the summer of 1933 when Burghauser invited Böhm to conduct the Vienna Philharmonic for the first time. The young conductor had received good reviews and Burghauser had followed his career ever since. His precision in conducting the difficult score of *Elektra* impressed the bassoonist even now; he remembered that the composer himself had been unable to conduct his work when the opera opened in Dresden in 1909.

Burghauser was intrigued by the different demands on symphonic and operatic conductors. "The concert conductor is the focal point of production," he would say. "In the concert hall, there is no interference with his leadership. In opera, however, the conductor must coordinate several groups of musicians and some which have *dramatic* as well as purely musical roles. Often the demands of the drama force the singers out of the rhythmic framework established by the conductor. He must be flexible enough to accommodate the singers, yet firm enough to steer the musicians effectively. This is an extremely trying task and cannot be escaped by all the histrionics so popular with conductors here in America."

Burghauser smiled, remembering when Leonard Bernstein conducted

Falstaff at the Met. Bernstein had declined the use of a score and had impressed the orchestra with his command of the music. But his exuberance—which had always seemed to Burghauser a peculiarly American quality—had struck the bassoonist as excessive. "Anyone who jumps that high into the air cannot possibly calculate when he will come down," Burghauser said, "and when he *did* come down a few times it was like an inadvertent entrance of the big drum and timpani, shattering the rhythm of the entire ensemble and surprising even Mr. Bernstein himself. But these sort of theatricalities are endemic to the profession. Vanity is a kind of occupational disease with conductors. That is why Wagner built the pit and podium away from the view of the audience. Toscanini used to say that in Bayreuth *the clown is never seen*, and I must say he was right."

Burghauser recalled those words whenever Dimitri Mitropoulos conducted at the Met. Mitropoulos had been a Greek Orthodox monk in his youth, and Burghauser could not fathom how such a modest, disciplined way of life could lead a man to insist on installing four spotlights around his podium to illuminate his body "like a piece of sculpture in a dark museum." Mitropoulos, like Bernstein, conducted with large, exaggerated movements. Not only had it been difficult to follow his intent but the gestures were projected onto the ceiling of the opera house tremendously enlarged, so that the audience was subject to a display of wild shadowboxing.

Burghauser said that Mitropoulos represented only one end of the spectrum, however. Fritz Reiner represented the other. A taskmaster who had fired nearly half the orchestra when he took it over, Reiner had the most unpleasant manner Burghauser had ever encountered in a conductor, and his conducting itself was microscopic. "Whenever a singer had faulty eyesight, he was at a loss," Burghauser said, "and we musicians, too, had difficulty distinguishing the movements of his baton. One night at a concert, the contrabass player (who is situated about thirty feet away from the conductor) brought along a telescope, which he applied to his eye the moment Reiner began to conduct. Reiner, who had perfectly good eyes himself, spotted the man and later dismissed him from the orchestra. But his style produced the effect he desired; we played three times as carefully for him as for any other conductor since we lived in *terror* of missing the beat."

Wilhelm Furtwängler, Burghauser remembered, had been quite different; from the bassoonist's desk, he had always appeared like a rhapsodic leaning tower of Pisa who defied gravity by conducting at a slant.

"Furtwängler was a Faustian character with an alchemist's nature," Burghauser often told his American colleagues. "He believed his ideas were telepathically communicated to his orchestra. In fact, his eyes, face, and the continual shaking of his head were a far better indication of what he was doing than his baton, which vibrated like the wings of a frightened butterfly. He was like a gyroscope: When the ensemble fell apart, he would immediately know which section was lagging and restore the balance. When once a timpanist asked for a clearer beat, Furtwängler became offended and walked out of rehearsal."

One of the only conductors Burghauser had known who was able to temper his pride with humor was Sir Thomas Beecham, who conducted at the Met during the war. "He was about sixty and very British in manner, with a gray goatee that made him look like a nineteenth-century Frenchman. He came in smoking a large, Churchillian cigar and never missed an opportunity to be entertaining." When once a chorus member sang out during an intended rest in the score of *Tales of Hoffman*, Beecham lowered his baton, raised an eyebrow, and inquired: "Where is the culprit?" When, after a moment, a small man stepped to the center of the stage and said, "Sir Thomas, it was I," Beecham waved his baton grandly and declared, "Remove this man."

The orchestra missed him keenly in the years that followed. They played under Erich Leinsdorf, whom Burghauser recalled being nicknamed "Mr. Univac," and under George Szell, who was considered even more of a martinet than Leinsdorf. "Both were perfectionists, and Szell was severe to the point of firing an orchestra member if he made more than two mistakes. Leinsdorf conducted in a semaphoric style. He was capable of leading the most difficult scores, but if you imagine that music, when written, is like burning-hot lava, the moment Leinsdorf raised his baton, the molten stream froze into place."

~

With a deep bow, Dr. Karl Böhm turned to accept a standing ovation from the audience at the Metropolitan Opera House. He asked the orchestra to rise and take a bow, then stepped down from the podium only to return again. When at last the audience began to move toward the doors, Hugo Burghauser stood up and followed Maxim up the stairs and into the musicians' room. The orchestra had assembled for a farewell party for Böhm, who was returning to his home in Bavaria. As Burghauser came into the party he was besieged by most of the Met's woodwind section.

"We have *four* surgical cases this year," one of the elderly players confided to him. "Two eye operations and two abdominal disturbances. But I must say, you yourself are looking very spruce."

Burghauser straightened his shoulders and drew in his tummy, relieved and flattered.

"And Hugo's seventy-five today," put in Lenny Hindel, who was Burghauser's successor at the Met. "I don't know what he does with all that spare time."

"My friend," Burghauser said, raising a slender finger, "if you are looking for distraction in this city, there is certainly more than one is capable of consuming. To be home and listening to the radio is sufficient: The music is better and there are no ladies snapping their pocketbooks beside you and wondering where their gloves are. The television I rather avoid. It tires the eyes, and I have never found, despite changing *all thirteen* of the channels, anything to sustain my interest."

Hindel was about to challenge him when the room brightened with the flash of photographers' bulbs and Karl Böhm opened the first bottle of Moselle wine. He toasted the musicians for their fine performance, and, as he finished, the group broke into "Happy Birthday" in honor of Burghauser. Böhm reached through the crowd for the bassoonist and, holding Burghauser's face between his hands, planted a kiss on either cheek as Burghauser blushed with pleasure.

"Now what *do* you do with your free time?" Stephen Maxim asked, when the bassoonist returned. "You must have a girlfriend. Otherwise life would be a total bore."

Burghauser waved away the notion of boredom.

"I'm never bored. That is impossible. There is Carnegie Hall, the theater, the movies. And I have so much reading I must still do. Of course, I have read Dostoyevski, Musil, Tolstoy, Gogol, von Doderer. But I have the ardent desire to read all of them again and I am afraid I will not have enough time. Then, I attend opera or symphony rehearsals at least twice a week. There if I'm bored—which *can* happen if they are rehearsing Berg or Webern—I just *walk out!* This is quite a blessing because earlier when I did not like a composition, I had to sit and endure real acoustic torture."

"Admit it, Hugo," prodded bassoonist David Manchester, "you were fed up."

"I *was* fed up," Burghauser conceded readily. "Four hours of rehearsal five days a week and then four more hours in the evening for fifty years wears one out both mentally and physically. On top, there is a real dearth of capable artistic leadership and you play for a plumber who makes everything uninteresting. No amount of singing, scenery, or acting can revitalize a boring interpretation, and then the only comfort is the material recompense."

He put his long hand on Manchester's arm.

"Forty years ago, when I was professor in Vienna, the mores were different. You had the bohemians, who were carefree and perhaps not too much washed but intensely devoted to their art. Nothing like here. When a teacher enters a classroom, they are not even obliged to stand up the way Bing made *us* do when a third-rate conductor walked in. You read in the newspapers that teachers are even raped! The young people here are like atavistic young animals, and when they take their place in the orchestra you can see the damage this lack of discipline has done. All the subtleties of music are difficult to realize if the youngster is unable to accept discipline.

"It is not good enough to play without mistakes. He must concentrate on the conductor—who is really a teacher—and try to understand what he says. A student who has always opposed his teachers cannot do this, and one hears the result, don't you agree?"

The group of men around him smiled and talked and finally drifted apart since each player had a second performance to play that evening. Burghauser walked over to a corner where Böhm was finishing a bottle of wine.

"Where do we see each other this summer?" the conductor asked, and Burghauser told him that he would be at Bad Reichenhall during August, as was his habit.

"Do you take a cure?" Böhm asked him.

"My only cure is quietness," said Burghauser. "Living in midtown Manhattan, one suffers terribly from disturbed ecology and is in great need of a yearly respite. I go for July to the Vierwaldstättersee, where the town has only two buildings, one of which is the hotel. It is like a sanatorium created by nature herself, in the middle of lawns and lakes and mountains. Only the conveniences have been put there by humans. The air is perfectly clean, and one hears almost no noise the entire day except for a small boat which approaches the shore every once in two hours and makes short, hissing whistles."

Burghauser whistled and Böhm smiled.

They remained at the table several minutes without speaking. Then

Böhm gave Burghauser the last bottle of Moselle from the six cases he had donated for the party. The two men—one seventy-five, the other seventy-seven—embraced in the now-empty room. Then Burghauser walked down the corridor to retrieve his instrument and returned home through the darkening park.

Edward Birdwell.

8

An American Free-lancer

In the mid-1960s, Edward Birdwell, a Texan who played the French horn in various New York orchestras, was touring Europe with the American Brass Quintet. The group had played at a contemporary music festival in Zagreb and had been so enthusiastically received that the city's broadcast authority had asked it to repeat the performance on radio for a handsome fee. They did this gladly, and it was not until they arrived at Zagreb's airport for the flight home that they became aware of any problem.

At the time, Yugoslav government policy required all tourists to exchange the equivalent of twenty American dollars for each day spent in Yugoslavia and to keep a record of all financial transactions in case they ended up with a surplus of Yugoslav money and wished to convert it back into foreign currency. Since the quintet's expenses had been covered by the festival, the five brass players found themselves in the uncomfortable position of having no receipts for their expenses, but thousands of Yugoslav dinars.

At the customs counter, Birdwell was last in line. As each quintet member was asked about receipts, he simply shrugged, excused himself, and passed back his dinars. By the time Birdwell—hands filled with Yugoslav currency—reached the customs official, the man was adamant. "He was a wizened old Communist functionary," the horn player would later enjoy recounting in a dry Texas drawl, "and he was wearing a uniform that must have belonged to his older brother. I told him I had no use for those dinars and that I wanted to exchange them for American money. He said no.

"Yugoslavia was going into the big-time tourist business then, and I told him, 'Now look here, Comrade, you are creating *ill will*.' I told him I was going back to New York City and that I would boycott the Yugoslav tourist office and do everything I *could* to keep people out of Yugoslavia. Nothing seemed to move him. Finally, when I saw he was indeed going to take that money away from me and give me nothing in return, I stopped pounding on his desk and I pulled out my cigarette lighter. I got down as close to him as I could, so that my lips were *in* his ear. I lit my cigarette lighter and I held up that money near it. And I said, very quietly, 'Listen, you sonofabitch, if you don't change this money for me, I'm going to burn it right here on your table.'

"He gave me my change."

~

Ed Birdwell was born and raised in Texas, and he could be seen as a prototype of the young, unionized, activist, American-born-and-trained musician who in the latter half of the twentieth century supplanted the European-born majority in American orchestras, wreaking considerable havoc upon musical life in the process. "For me, music was a hobby for which I had the good fortune to be paid" was the belief of many European musicians like Hugo Burghauser, who felt that unions made musicians untowardly materialistic and who played contemporary music out of duty rather than devotion.

Birdwell not only liked to play and listen to new music but, as a member of the American Brass Quintet, he often commissioned it. His collection of over 1,500 records included music by John Cage, Elliot Carter, Jacob Druckman, Michael Colgrass, and Charles Wuorinen—and the last four had written music at the request of Birdwell's group. He and his wife, Nancy, a professor of business administration at LaGuardia Community College, lived in a spacious upper West Side co-op filled with efficiency appliances, modern prints, new books, magazines, and other accoutrements of sophisticated city life. Violinists Pinchas Zukerman and Itzhak Perlman lived upstairs, where the view of Riverside Park and the Hudson River extended north to the George Washington Bridge. Hundreds of middle-class musicians lived in his neighborhood and they lived well. "Musicians finally got tired of eating in the kitchen the way they did in Haydn's time," Birdwell, whose kitchen had been featured in a national home improvement magazine, liked to say. "I don't see why a musician can't make as good a living as a sanitation worker. If he can't, I'd rather go home and drill for oil."

That alternative crossed his mind more than once in the fall of 1973 when musicians at the New York Philharmonic, the New York City Opera Orchestra, the New York City Ballet Orchestra, and the Radio City Music Hall Orchestra all found themselves at odds with their managements. As a member of the five-man Ballet Orchestra Committee, Birdwell had been involved in contract negotiations since Labor Day, when the agreement between the ballet orchestra and the City Center management had run out.

The City Center had for the previous six years been guaranteeing the musicians thirty-eight weeks of work, twelve of which involved playing for the Joffrey Ballet. When the Joffrey developed a financial problem, the City Center declared that it could no longer guarantee the musicians those twelve weeks. Because of inflationary pressures driving up production costs, the City Center also announced a moratorium on all labor contracts with its constituent unions (stagehands, singers, dancers, and musicians who participate in opera and dance at the New York State Theater). On September 1, the musicians at the opera struck and obtained an increase in salary, improved fringe benefits, and a guarantee of eleven weeks' work in addition to the regular twenty-one-week season. The Ballet Orchestra Committee agreed to continue working while negotiations were being held but were holding management "by the balls," as Birdwell put it, by refusing to promise that they would not walk out during the annual performances of the *Nutcracker Suite,* which are almost always sold out and highly lucrative.

On November 9, the Friday before the ballet season was to open, Birdwell and his colleagues on the committee met with the dancers backstage at the New York State Theater. About fifty dancers were stretching and moving about the room, largely indifferent to the presence of the men. Finally, they sat on the floor or leaned against the walls of their practice room and one dancer asked what demands the musicians were making.

"We're asking for forty weeks' guaranteed employment—two more than the old contract provides—and a sixty-dollar across-the-board salary increase to three-fifty a week," said Tom Kornacker, a midwestern violinist with long blond hair. "We want a one-year contract, Blue Cross coverage, instrument insurance, disability insurance, and only five shows a week."

There were hoots of laughter and a few catcalls from the dancers, nearly all of whom were young women in their late teens or early twenties.

"Why does this sound so far-out to you?" Kornacker demanded. "Why is there laughter? There's nothing that we're asking for that's not the norm for musicians elsewhere. We're trying to bargain the way everybody bargains. We've been offered a thirty-six percent reduction from the contract we had last year. People *outside* the arts don't believe it, it's so incredible."

A few dancers walked out. A couple stretched their long wool-wrapped legs. "They aren't really interested in the details," Birdwell said later. "Their whole life is dancing, and they're as afraid as management is that we'll strike the *Nutcracker* and they won't be able to dance. The trouble is they're kids. What sixteen-year-old is going to think about striking? They think we should all be happy for the *privilege of playing* at Lincoln Center!"

It was as much a surprise to Birdwell as to the public when the dancers announced their own strike the following Monday, explaining that they were striking against the musicians. "It's not in anyone's interest to strike," he said then. "But it's like war: You try to solve a problem diplomatically, and when you can't talk any longer, you beat the hell out of each other. The only weapon we have is to withhold our services. The dancers work for nothing because they're so young and poorly advised and because of the paternalistic nature of the company. They've allowed themselves to be exploited and they're angry at us because we won't stand for that kind of treatment. If management cancels this season as they have been threatening to do, they'll have to think hard about whether they're closing down for good."

As it happened, the musicians had to think hard too. Exactly three weeks after their meeting with the dancers, the Ballet Orchestra Committee agreed to a new contract which provided for a basic salary increase of forty dollars over the next four years, a one percent increase in vacation pay, and an instrument insurance plan. They received no written guarantee of the weeks they had lost with the Joffrey Ballet, no pension plan, and no shorter work week. It would be some time before the ballet musicians made up in salary what they had lost by not working, but Birdwell maintained that the principle counted more than the lost income. He saw the episode as one more step in a continuing struggle of the musician who, bound for so long by the niceties of tradition, had finally adopted the tactics of collective bargaining.

~

The revolution in the classical music business began in the early 1960s when Birdwell was beginning his career as a horn player. In 1960, musicians earned an average $4,757 yearly while the median for all professionals was $6,778 and that of all experienced male labor $4,750. Disgruntled with their union, the American Federation of Musicians (which includes musicians who play in rock bands and *bar mitzvah* combos as well as retired Sunday clarinetists), symphony orchestra players formed committees to negotiate with their managements and, by 1961, had united in a loose confederation called ICSOM, the International Conference of Symphony and Orchestra Musicians. Over the next twenty years—Birdwell believes largely due to their efforts—symphony orchestra salaries doubled, their guaranteed work periods were extended, and fringe benefits that were nonexistent before were institutionalized. Birdwell was an ICSOM activist in Texas, where he helped to organize the Houston Symphony's first orchestra committee, and he sees himself as an activist today.

"Why should a musician subsidize his own art?" he asks. "New York City spends millions on rebuilding Yankee Stadium for the Yankees, a profit-making organization. Lincoln Center does more for business on the West Side than Shea Stadium does for Queens. Why is it that government has no money for the arts?"

Birdwell is a man of medium height whose scraggly blond hair and drowsy eyes bring to mind the milieu of James Dean's motorcycle gangs even when he is dressed for a formal concert. His easy manner and softly inflected speech distinguished him from other New Yorkers hurrying through Manhattan, but since his arrival in the city in 1963, Birdwell had become one of the busiest free-lance musicians in a rapidly shrinking arena.

When he arrived in New York, at least fifteen Broadway shows were employing full orchestras eight times each week, and television was using more orchestras on regular favorites like the *Firestone Hour* and the *Bell Telephone Hour*. By the 1970s, no one was writing American musicals for full orchestra anymore because union costs had driven the price up so high, and whatever television specials had survived were being made in California. At the same time, more foreign orchestras were touring the United States than ever before, diluting the concert market and stealing the record market away from the Americans. The unions in America had made the cost of recording here so high that record companies preferred to work with European orchestras. Only three U.S. orchestras held recording contracts in 1973: The Boston Symphony, the Philadelphia Orchestra, and the New York Philharmonic—whose total membership represented a tiny fraction of all classical musicians. And each year, the nation's conservatories graduated thousands of new string, brass, percussion, and woodwind players. The musicians' union in New York alone reported 200 new members each month.

Mindful of this inhospitable environment, Birdwell had put together a patchwork of "jobs." He played second horn at the New York City Ballet most nights; he was assistant to the dean of the Aspen Music School and Festival most days; and he maintained a priority commitment to the American Brass Quintet. Whenever he had a free time slot, he filled it with "pickup" work, which included recording advertising jingles for toothpaste or hamburgers and sound tracks for pop recordings, or playing "one-night stands" with part-time orchestras like the American Symphony, or substituting for a regular at the Philharmonic.

His schedule was tight and tension-filled. It often called for him to practice late at night after concerts, or early in the morning before rehearsals. It involved careful juggling of commitments, the cultivation of good relationships with conductors and contractors, and even more careful bookkeeping. "My daddy hasn't understood how I make my living since I played in the Pasadena High School Brass Band," Birdwell was apt to say with a grin. "And the IRS is so doubtful, they've audited me the last five years running." In 1972, Birdwell earned about $30,000, of which about a third came from the ballet job and the remainder from his other activities. There were some musicians who made more money and a great many (nearly all female orchestra musicians, for example) who made less. "The guys who aren't working would say it's politics," Birdwell said, "and the guys who are would say it's ability. It's like any other business: It's who you know, it's luck, and it's hard work."

~

Like many brass players, Birdwell was born in the southwest of the United States, where music is integral to the public school curriculum: "The reason for that is they're committed to football and good bands are a necessity. They *play* football in Texas; they don't fool around. It's a multimillion-dollar business and some of those bands would knock your eyes out." The Pasadena High School Brass Band in which Birdwell played had 140 players—34 *more* than the New York Philharmonic. The repertoire included Sousa marches, transcriptions of symphonic works by Tchaikovsky, Wagner, and Liszt, and popular American songs. Once a year, the band would compete in a statewide contest, and if the band director did not return with a Class 1 rating, Birdwell said, he was fired.

The Birdwells lived on a thirty-acre piece of land outside Houston with room enough for their son to raise a small herd of sheep and grow clover and alfalfa for school projects. "But my parents weren't ignorant, black-dirt people like so many New Yorkers think Texans have to be," he said. "They were urban people. My father was an investment banker. My mother made me take piano lessons."

Birdwell remembers always wanting to play trumpet, which was the melody instrument in his school band. There was always a surplus of potential trumpeters around, though, and the band director asked Birdwell to learn French horn instead. Since membership in the band was second in social status only to membership on the football team, he quickly agreed: "We had great uniforms and all the girls that the football team didn't get. About the only class I *attended* my last two years of high school was band. I thought I'd go on to college, get my degree, and become a high school band director in Muleshoe, Texas."

He majored in music at the University of Houston and was working on a master's degree at the University of Texas when he was drafted. His friends advised him to audition for the West Point band, a move which proved to be the most significant in his professional life. While there, he found not only that his musicianship and musical proficiency compared favorably with those of east coast conservatory graduates but that he liked the east coast and that he enjoyed competing for occasional professional jobs in New York. He took advantage of the various festivals and concerts that were held within driving distance of West Point, and it was at Tanglewood that he heard about his first job.

The position, oddly enough, was at the Houston Symphony. He was not anxious to return to Texas but, in the absence of another offer, auditioned, won the job, moved back to Texas, and became embroiled in musical politics. ICSOM had yet to make an impact on wages: Houston Symphony musicians were playing eight services (concerts and rehearsals) each week; they were paid $100 per week for twenty-five weeks and then had to fend for themselves for the rest of the year. This did not constitute an unbearable burden for the older members of the orchestra, who had long ago staked their claims to all the teaching jobs within 100 miles of

Houston, but made it difficult for the younger, newer orchestra members to live well. They formed a committee, precipitated a crisis, and brought down on themselves the wrath of union and management alike.

"There was no way to stay alive down there," Birdwell recalled with anger. "I had to work as a salesman in a clothing store. I had to work in a gas station. Hell—all the young guys did it. Who can live on twenty-five hundred dollars a year? Well, I did it for two years. Finally I decided that if I was going to stay in the business, I had to go where the business was."

He watched for openings in eastern orchestras, but there were none. He tapped the musical grapevine for rumors, but no one seemed to be moving in the early sixties. Openings at symphony orchestras usually occur in cycles, starting at the top. When a player at the Philharmonic or the Boston Symphony retires, musicians nationwide audition for the job, and when one of them is accepted from another orchestra, a chain reaction is often set into motion, with players all over the country moving up the orchestral hierarchy. Then, everything is quiet again until another chair falls vacant. With the situation static, Birdwell began to consider alternatives to a regular orchestra position. He reasoned that he did not really like playing with the same people night after night and that his own musical interests were broader than those of Houston audiences. While his colleagues in the wind and brass sections were not as status-conscious as the strings (many orchestras now provide for string players to rotate seating periodically in the manner of a volleyball team), Birdwell was tired of the petty quarrels that arise when one hundred people work together intensively over long stretches of time. He knew that a free-lancer's life in New York would be risky, but he took a chance and arrived in 1963 with no job and no prospects.

On arrival, he began to call contractors, the men who are the vital links between a musician and a job. The contractor serves as a kind of bordello madam for anyone who wants to stage a concert: He maintains lists of available musicians and is able to assemble a complete symphony orchestra in a matter of hours. Since Birdwell was on no one's list, he was obliged to call every contractor in town, introduce himself, and offer his services. By chance, he reached Morris Stonzek (David Merrick's contractor) minutes after the horn player at *Stop the World, I Want to Get Off* quit. "It was sheer luck," he said. "I could've fainted. Two weeks in New York, barely unpacked, and there I was with a job. I was delighted to be out of Houston and all that hassle, and I thought Broadway was a wonderful place. I practiced all day. Worked evenings. I even got into a woodwind quintet with some friends."

When *Stop the World* closed, Birdwell began to branch out into what union officials call "the long-hair business." He found a gig replacing the horn player in the American Brass Quintet on a tour, played with the Brooklyn Philharmonia and the American Symphony, was an extra at the Metropolitan Opera, performed at the Jones Beach Summer Theater and the 1964 World's Fair's Texas pavilion, and recorded advertising jingles for Eastern Airlines, Canada Dry Ginger Ale, Timex watches, and Metropolitan Life Insurance.

It was through these varied jobs that he built up his free-lance contacts and met hundreds of other musicians, some of whom doubled as contractors. The horn players in New York were a very close-knit group, according to Birdwell. There were about 350 of them listed in the union book, but only about 70 were active enough to regard as competition, and those fell into two groups. The "commercial guys" gathered at the Spotlight, a bar which has since closed. The "symphony guys" met at the old Carnegie Tavern. Birdwell was at the Carnegie Tavern one night when he heard that one of the Ballet Orchestra's horn players had taken a teaching job in Illinois. At the time, he considered the ballet "strictly another show," but he auditioned for the conductor, Robert Irving, and got the job.

The New York City Ballet had just moved to Lincoln Center from the City Center, and his work there began to provide the first steady income he'd had since coming to New York. Shortly afterward, the horn player of the American Brass Quintet quit to join the Pittsburgh Symphony and Birdwell was invited to replace him. Then the quintet applied for and was granted a summer residency at the Aspen Music Festival in Colorado, and Birdwell began to work in an administrative capacity there. But like most musicians—free-lancers, regular orchestra players, and some soloists—he found that when it came to his personal enjoyment rather than livelihood, he preferred his work in chamber music over any other.

The brass quintet became his major artistic outlet, offering the opportunity for individual expression, an absence of authoritarianism, and the camaraderie of four other men. "We chose our own programs and we voted on everything, which is important to any orchestra player. There's no orchestra in the world where the conductor is not the boss. He steps on the podium and all questions of right and wrong stop."

The brass quintet, drawing as it did on prebaroque composers like the

Gabrielis, Heinrich Isaac, and Thomas Stolzer, or contemporary composers like Ingolf Dahl, Ulysses Kay, and Virgil Thomson, neatly avoided the symphonic repertoire and provided Birdwell with a much-needed respite from the classical-romantic diet. The informal university settings in which the quintet most often performed provided a nice change from the straitlaced concert hall. At chamber concerts, members of the quintet made a practice of chatting with their audience before performing, inviting questions, and sometimes telling the kinds of old jokes or anecdotes that their own friends had tired of hearing. All the men in the group were free-lance orchestra musicians, and going on tour gave them a chance not only to talk but also to shake free of other people's rules and timetables. The quintet usually arrived at a concert site in two small rented airplanes (which two of its members piloted themselves) and spent most of its fees on lodging, food, attire, instrument insurance, and souvenirs. Birdwell has played to convicts in state prisons, old people in golden-age clubs, and fourth-graders in their elementary schools as part of various private and government-funded programs which contributed to the quintet's income. The public school circuit was an integral part of these programs, and one Friday morning, Birdwell packed up his horn to play at P.S. 187 in Queens.

~

He was braving the wind sweeping up from the Hudson River a few minutes after eight in the morning when a weathered Ambassador pulled up to the curb. The driver was Bob Biddlecome, the eldest of the five brass players, who greeted Birdwell with several choice words for President Nixon and those responsible for proposing higher tolls on the George Washington Bridge. Biddlecome lived in New Jersey. Although he worked in almost the same kinds of jobs as Birdwell (at the Aspen Music Festival, in the quintet, at the ballet orchestra, as a free-lancer) and made almost the same salary, six children and a mortgage made his life considerably more complicated. He had moved his family from Long Island to Teaneck so that he could be within twenty minutes of Lincoln Center, but he worried about the effects of his career on his family life.

"Many musicians like myself are family men," he said. "They have the problems of anyone else raising a family. At night, when my kids are home, I'm out playing at the ballet. I'm not there to attend PTA meetings. My wife begins to think she'll never see me again. She has to deal with all the family problems alone, because if I'm not at the ballet,

I'm on tour or at rehearsal or at the Aspen office. If I get sick, everybody's out of luck. A free-lance musician has none of the benefits that an auto worker has: No pension, no sick leave, no vacation, no health coverage."

He stopped the car to pick up trombonist Herb Rankin, who had for ten years enjoyed many of these benefits at the Kansas City Philharmonic, where he had played first trombone and taught at the University of Missouri and the University of Kansas. At thirty-five, Rankin had tired of the orchestra musician's routine of rehearsals and concerts, packed his bags, and come to New York, where he was now a free-lancer. Waiting with him was Ray Mace, at twenty-two the youngest quintet member and the idealist of the group. Mace had only recently graduated from conservatory and sometimes irritated the others with his observations. "This is a whole different thing," he said as the others checked their watches. "At school, all we had to do was take out our instruments and play. Now I have to be concerned about the way I look, whether I offend people by the way I talk, whether I'm punctual. I had hair halfway down my back when I was a student. It took me a long time to grow it, but since I didn't want to jeopardize the quintet in any way, I decided to cut it. As long as I'm going to do this, I thought I'd play along completely. I try to be mellow."

Mace, dark-eyed, dark-haired, and attractive, enjoyed the attentions that women concertgoers have traditionally bestowed upon trumpeters. He was the quintet member delegated to make polite conversation with socialites in Dallas or Beverly Hills at the parties which often followed concerts, and he was also the one who soothed the volatile tempers of his colleagues. Mace had no trouble living on the $10,000 or so that he earned in 1973. His reservations about working as a free-lance musician in new York were musical: "In school, we'd play a piece of music till it sounded right and until the group was tight. Here, you get a call for a free-lance job, have two rehearsals, and then play a concert. All a musician has to do is sit quietly and play the right notes at the right time. Seventy-five percent of the people do just that and the other twenty-five percent are frustrated. The economics of it are impossible, and the whole thing is run by business people."

At eight-twenty-five, Louis Ranger appeared at the door of the Ambassador, setting off a chorus of complaint from the other four brass players. He had played several dates the day before and his eyes were tired behind dark glasses. The tall twenty-four-year-old graduate of Juilliard could get testy when he had the inclination, and just then he was in no mood to be criticized. After a few traded insults, Ranger put his instrument beside the others in the trunk and got into the crowded car.

"It's a very personal setup," he said later. "When we go on tour we sometimes spend literally every hour of the day together—in buses and trains, in hotel rooms. If you play music with someone for a while you get to know them real well without even having to talk anything through. They can also get on your nerves without saying a word."

Ranger taught privately to supplement his income. He lived with his girlfriend, a free-lance violinist who supported herself, but like Biddlecome he worried about his life-style: "There's no security in this kind of life whatsoever. I don't have a family like Bob, but I find myself at a point in life where I have to take stock of things, and it's a bit disconcerting not to know what kind of money I'll be making from year to year. When I sign a two-year lease, I have to think hard. I have to put money in the bank. And it affects personal relationships too. Every time I go home my family asks me when I'm going to get married. How can you make a commitment to another person if you may get a gig in Toronto next week?"

A little after nine, the children of P.S. 187 in Queens trooped into their green auditorium. After they had settled down, their principal announced, "Boys and girls, we are very fortunate to have with us today ...the American Brass Quintet."

Instruments agleam under the stage lights, the quintet played an English fanfare while the children bounced up and down in their seats, copying the two trombone players or simply staring, wide-eyed, at the stage. One by one the quintet members explained their instruments and introduced each piece of music with a brief story. "This one was written by a friend of ours who lives in Paris," Birdwell told them. "There's not going to be any tune or rhythm, so why don't you just listen hard and tell me when we're done what the music made you think of."

"A monster," shouted one girl.

"A lot of cars," said a little boy.

The quintet went on to play a selection by "Mr. Bach." After forty-five minutes, they packed their instruments and music, got back into the Ambassador, and repeated the whole program at another elementary school. By noon, they were back in Manhattan. Biddlecome and Birdwell went to the Aspen Festival office; Mace, Ranger, and Rankin to various professional engagements. They planned to meet late in the afternoon to catch a private plane for Albany, where they were to play a college concert.

With any luck, Ed Birdwell told his wife over the telephone, he'd be back in New York by midnight.

~

Postscript: Edward Birdwell played his last season with the American Brass Quintet in 1976 and then retired from the French horn to become a music administrator. First he served as Deputy Director of Carnegie Hall, then as Executive Director of the Los Angeles Chamber Orchestra, and then as Orchestra Manager of the Boston Symphony Orchestra. In October 1983, he began work as Director of the Music Program of the National Endowment for the Arts. He now resides in Washington, D.C.

The Juilliard String Quartet: (*Left to right*) Robert Mann, Earl Carlyss, Joel Krosnick, and Samuel Rhodes. (*Jack Mitchell.*)

~ 9 ~

The Juilliard Quartet: Scenes from a Marriage

Violin I: Did you see the *New Yorker?* Evidently he hated our Bartók.

Cello: Which Bartók?

Viola: He just criticizes our sound. He said, 'lean and not sensual.'

Cello: Send that one to the *New York Times* and send the *New York Times* one to the *New Yorker!* The *New York Times* said we were much too nice...

Violin I: I know, I know...

Violin II: Who cares?

Cello: Did you see the Alan Rich?

Violin I: Well. *That* was the rave of the year!

If a string quartet, as many players say, is a paradigm of human relationships, then the Juilliard String Quartet in 1981 was the most modern of marriages. Although it was now celebrating its thirty-fifth anniversary and seemed well past the tumult of its first decades, the Juilliard still thrived on the kind of emotional intensity that frightened most other people and had, despite five divorces, three residences, and a workaholic's schedule, lasted longer and been praised more lavishly than any other quartet in the United States.

Except for summers, when they went their separate ways, first violinist Robert Mann, second violinist Earl Carlyss, violist Samuel Rhodes, and cellist Joel Krosnick spent more time with each other than they did with their families. They rehearsed and performed programs selected from the 500 chamber works that constituted their repertoire; they gave solo recitals and performed with other artists; they taught twenty-four student quartets at the Juilliard School and, sometimes, caught appearances of the Concord, the LaSalle, the American, the Emerson, the New York, or the Tokyo string quartets—all of whom were their graduates. Three times a year they flew to Michigan State, where they performed and held chamber music workshops, and, since 1961, they had spent an annual month in Washington as quartet-in-residence of the Library of Congress. They had made over one hundred recordings, and their tours took them from Las Cruces, New Mexico, to Toronto, Ontario, to Zurich, Switzerland. "The physical and emotional reality of being in this quartet is considerable," said Joel Krosnick, the only member who at the time was not married. "It's very hard to lead a normal life but I can't imagine being without it."

~

Although the first string quartet in America, the Kneisel, was established in Boston in 1885, it was not until the late 1930s that a group as revered as the Budapest could earn a living here, and not until the 1960s that chamber music became truly popular. American audiences preferred the big sound of orchestras or the charisma of soloists to four staid men who sat on a bare stage communing with each other.

But the Second World War brought to the United States thousands of central European chamber music devotees as well as practitioners like the Budapest Quartet, and the postwar baby boom brought great numbers of musically sophisticated conservatory and college graduates into the fold. At the same time, as orchestra musicians unionized and soloists became media figures, opera houses and symphony societies became million-dollar institutions. Orchestra musicians found their work depersonalized; audiences found ticket prices exorbitant. For both, chamber music seemed an attractive alternative. Dozens of top-notch groups—the Guarneri, the Amadeus, the Borodin, the Janáček, the Smetana, the Vermeer, the Quartetto Italiano, the Tokyo, and the Cleveland—attracted strong followings, and by the 1980s an estimated one thousand professional or semiprofessional quartets (many attached to colleges and universities) were playing for eight million people.

They, like the Juilliard, were drawn to a form which "engenders an atmosphere of warmth and a degree of psychological rapport that are unknown to most virtuosos, prima donnas, or members of large orchestras," according to the late journalist and chamber player Joseph Wechsberg. "It is based on give-and-take; it is civilized and egalitarian; it is a garden of musical fellowship from which the law of the jungle has been banished."

Such effusions and the conviction that they are playing a music superior to all others is typical of quartet players, and Juilliard members were no exception. From the beginning, they took an almost moral stand about their repertoire and the way they performed it; in later years, they had become sponsors of the contemporary composer. They counted 150 contemporary works in their repertoire and liked to commission at least one new piece every year. Robert Mann had composed over 80 works himself, violist Sam Rhodes had studied composition as a graduate student at Princeton, and cellist Joel Krosnick had cofounded the Group for Contemporary Music at Columbia. This exposure to, and interest in, composition had influenced the quartet's style as well as its programming and distinguished them from all other major quartets. "The listener could have been led into the hall blindfolded and would have had no hesitation in identifying the group," *Times* critic Donal Henahan once wrote. "All the Juilliard characteristics over the years could be heard: The biting rhythms, the scrupulous attention to the score's directions, the phenomenal tautness of line, the concentrated energy." A quartet player who had studied with Mann could add, "Unlike the Tokyo or Guarneri, they're not concerned with homogeneity of sound or beauty of sound for its own sake. They don't think of music as music but as life. It's not beautiful all the time. It's not coquettish. It's more like a person speaking. Each line has a personality of its own."

Violin II: I thought it sounded anemic and precious.

Violin I: I thought it sounded beautiful.

Cello: It should be rich but *innig*.

Viola: Can we play it beautiful but not pressed?

Violin II: When we play at two, we get a certain richness that should be there right at the beginning.

Cello: But I'm playing exactly the same way.

The Juilliard Quartet was born in 1945 to a Coast Artillery jazz band when Mann, then twenty-five, began talking to his army buddies about performing chamber music. He had started studying violin at the age of nine (which was late by virtuoso standards), had studied with a teacher who directed him toward ensemble playing, and then attended Juilliard. He had a reputation at the Juilliard School for disliking facile young violinists and could say without hesitation, "I was not a *wunderkind*; I could not play Paganini before I could read Shakespeare. Today the kids come in and they've practiced their concerti with great care—they want to emulate Perlman and Pavarotti—but they don't practice chamber music for a class, they read it." Mann had, as a student, done the opposite. "I could not conceive of myself playing those chestnuts and getting pleasure from it over and over again. The virtuoso looks for two things: Those vehicles that allow him or her to display wizardry or mastery, and capturing the psychology of communication that knocks an audience dead. Like Frank Sinatra. Wow! The chamber musician is not a star and doesn't make as much money. There's nothing to show off. He plays music into which the composer has put his most intimate, subtle, and complicated thoughts. In chamber music, the composer was not interested in knocking an audience dead but searching for expression. And there's nothing more satisfying to me than making music among equals."

Mann, whose level of energy often startled people who first met him, persuaded fellow violinist Robert Koff and cellist Arthur Winograd to form a quartet, and then went to William Schuman, who had just been appointed president of the Juilliard School, to ask about a possible residency there. The new president had, in fact, been thinking about that very thing because, in his view, there had never been an "authentic" American quartet of international stature. He had made a list of candidates for the position but found none of them appealing. "I wanted to find people who would play *and* teach," he emphasized, "and who wanted to do that as their *life work*. They would really be in residence—I wanted to make chamber music an important part of the curriculum, and I wanted Juilliard students to get to know the chamber music literature because I thought it basic to the educational process. When Bobby came to see me, we talked. I heard him play, and I thought that he was an extraordinary man. He was always—and I will not apologize for my purple prose—a moral force."

Schuman told the group to come back when they found a violist and suggested that they speak to Eugene Lehner, the former violist of Vienna's Kolisch Quartet who was then with the Boston Symphony. Lehner, however, advised them to find an American their own age and recommended one of his colleagues at the BSO, Raphael Hillyer. The violist traded his own and his wife's positions for a one-year $2,500 contract with the quartet. "If you're a person with a deep, abiding love of chamber music and if you are a string player in an orchestra," Mann later noted, "you will do it." Hillyer was soon divorced, the Juilliard Quartet was never formally tenured at the conservatory, but, by the early 1970s, they were earning $2,500 and more for one concert.

That first summer of 1946, however, was spent studying with Eugene Lehner, who was a champion of new music and who pushed the Juilliard toward contemporary works, teaching them the habit of relying on the text of the work before them rather than on the performance tradition that had grown up around it. They looked for the "authenticity" of the Beethoven quartets, reexamining markings for *tempi* and dynamics and coming up with interpretations that were faster, more incisive, and less mellow than those of the European quartets whose interpretations had become the standard.

Their first concert that fall drew mixed reactions. "The chamber music authorities of the day as well as the board deplored the fact that I could have permitted this to happen," William Schuman later recalled with great delight. "There were choreographic excesses similar to Leonard Bernstein's podium behavior. They played like angels and looked like pigs. They did not shine their shoes. Sometimes they wore colored socks. And the Beethoven! They played Beethoven *differently* from the way Beethoven had been played before! They had none of the subdued mannerisms that people associated with chamber music. They dug into the strings. They cared about total honesty of approach. They didn't think everything had to be beautiful. And they were such purists that they didn't even play quintets!"

Immediately, they had plunged into the unknown (in America) area of contemporary works. In 1948, at Tanglewood, they played the first complete cycle of Bartók quartets to be heard in the United States and, in 1949, performed Schoenberg. They introduced to a reluctant chamber music audience works by Elliott Carter, Roger Sessions, John Cage, and a host of other Americans. Until that time, the Budapest Quartet—stable, elegant, and aristocratic—had set the tone for string quartets.

They had addressed one another as "Mr. Kroyt" and "Mr. Schneider" for decades and exuded European charm and subtlety. The Juilliard, in contrast, appeared wildly experimental, unpredictable, and emotionally explosive; its playing was often called "muscular," "urban," and "hard-edged." Some of the explosiveness may have derived from the fact that three of its members were in psychoanalysis during the quartet's first few years. They immersed themselves in the theories of psychiatrist Wilhelm Reich and certainly were the only quartet in history to have invested in one of Reich's orgone boxes.

"We created a tremendous excitement, an atmosphere of constant fermentation," recalled Arthur Winograd. "We were more interested in doing justice to the music than in getting along with each other. Our relationships were terribly complex. It's difficult to talk about—even twenty-five years later. It's like digging into an old marriage. You have to read between the lines of what people say."

None of the quartet's members liked to say much publicly about subsequent events, but as the Juilliard's reputation soared, its personal problems grew. In 1955, Winograd left the group to start a career as a conductor (he became music director of the Hartford Symphony) and was replaced by cellist Claus Adam. Three years later, second violinist Robert Koff left to become a professor of music at Brandeis and was replaced by Isadore Cohen. In 1966, Cohen left (he became the violinist of the Beaux Arts Trio) and Earl Carlyss, the pleasant, equable son of a Swedish minister, became the first of a new generation of Juilliard players. He was twenty-six, one year out of Juilliard, and working eight shows a week as concertmaster of the New York City Ballet when Raphael Hillyer asked him to audition. "I'd studied with all three of them at Juilliard, and in my wildest imagination I never thought I had a chance at the job," Carlyss recalled. "But I thought it would be fun—there are definitely worse ways of spending the day—so I went in loose as a goose. It all worked out very well and all of a sudden I thought: *Hey, they're really serious about this*. To my complete astonishment, they asked me to join a few weeks later."

The new second violinist was to have spent the first half of 1965 learning the repertoire, but relations between Cohen and the rest of the quartet had deteriorated to the point where it was safer to risk integrating Carlyss three weeks after hiring him than to continue the season as planned. "I don't know how I did it," recalled Carlyss. "I remember one of the Chicago critics wrote that I must know how it feels to be in an airplane, given a parachute, and pushed out the door. Not only did I come in in the middle of the season but I was in the strange and rather awkward position of playing with three men, all twenty years older than me, who had been my teachers. They made it very clear to me that it was no longer a teacher-student relationship, that I had a twenty-five percent share in the organization, and that I was supposed to contribute my ideas. That they wouldn't have picked me unless they thought I had ideas. But we didn't have time for long, leisurely discussions about music and I didn't have time to think about *anything.* We were to do most of Bartók, all of Beethoven, and several Schubert quartets. I had to cram for sixty concerts in less than five months."

Carlyss was described by the other quartet members as the most stable, peaceful man in the group, and, until the spring of 1985, when he decided to become a faculty member of the Peabody Institute in Baltimore, he found that quartet life suited him. Playing second fiddle presents an ego problem to many violinists, and Carlyss often was obliged to point out to his students that a quartet was like a chair—one leg was no less important than the other three; you had to have all four. Being in close contact with three other people all the time was not too difficult for him either, in his recollection. "I think a quartet is a concentrated version— a microcosm—of life itself, and I think people who can't get along in a quartet can't get along in life. The only time you have problems is when somebody says, 'Be reasonable—do it *my* way.' That's when trouble starts."

By the late 1960s, the Juilliard was performing 150 concerts per year, touring the Orient as well as Europe and South America. Problems— personal, family, business, and, ultimately, musical—mounted. First there was a falling out between Claus Adam and the rest of the quartet. Then, Mann and Hillyer, who had been buddies for over twenty years, had a blowup, triggered by the use of the quartet's contacts by the violist's wife. "When there's trouble, people start feeling left out," said Carlyss, who was sometimes the only player speaking to the three others. "Then when something goes wrong in a performance they take it personally. One person thinks the other is deliberately playing loud in order to drown him out. Another doesn't say a word for days. It's very stupid. But small things tend to become greatly magnified and pushed out of pro-portion to reality." In 1969, Raphael Hillyer was succeeded by Samuel Rhodes.

Cello:	Has the White House program been approved?
Violin I:	You know it's for the Japanese premier—it's not Helmut Schmidt.
Cello:	(*laughter*) It *changed?*
Violin II:	And I understand there's a dinner afterwards which we are invited to but the wives are not so I said . . .
Viola:	(*dismayed*) The wives are not?
Cello:	So they changed it from the Germans to the Japanese?
Viola:	Because I don't want to . . .
Violin I:	I've got news for you: It's going to be the king of Saudi Arabia!

The new violist, who was as introspective as Carlyss was extroverted, was twenty-eight years old, looked like a Talmudic scholar, and had gone to Queens College instead of Juilliard. Samuel Rhodes found adapting to life with three strangers difficult. "I was very apprehensive at first, not knowing whether the group would take to me or what I'd think of them," he recalled later. "I had tried to find out about them from friends. I listened to their records. I went to more of their concerts in that half year than I had been to in all my life. The assumption I had was that the three of them would be very solid in what they wanted to do musically and say to me: 'This is the way we do it,' but that was never the case. Somebody would say, 'Didn't we do it this way?' and somebody else would say, 'Absolutely not.' And the third person would remember a third way, and I had no idea what any of them were talking about so we had to decide right then and there how to do it.

"I felt really free right from the beginning to say whatever I wanted to. I had been in the Galimir Quartet, where there were far fewer concerts and far less pressure. But it wasn't the kind of quartet where anyone participated equally. Most of the ideas came from Galimir. Sometimes he was actually teaching us the music. The Juilliard also tended to be much more vigorous and extreme than many of the groups I had worked with before. My bowing became a lot more vigorous, the attacks more prominent and sharp. I developed a lot more variety and so did they."

That first year, Rhodes remembered, he also learned timing, "when to bring up certain ideas and when not to, when to get involved in a deep discussion and when not to." He discovered that what kept the group working well was the ability of each member to use the others' qualities to their best advantage. "There's a quartet by Elliott Carter," he said, "where the main idea is to show the personality of each instrument, and his characterization of each instrument is not dissimilar to our group. The first violin has the most variety and is always changing, running the whole gamut of emotion very quickly. The second violin is, in a way, the timekeeper of the group. It has the most special effects. It's virtuoso and steady. The viola is the most emotional in a very brooding way. The cello is very virtuoso and florid. There's a difference in the personality of the instruments, and then the difference in the personality of the players. If you hear your colleague play a phrase in a certain way, when it comes your turn to play it, you can't pretend you never heard it before but you add something to it of your own. The extent to which a quartet is able to do this, to add to each other and grow from each other, determines in large part its value."

Both Carlyss and Rhodes agreed that the traveling was the worst part of their new lives. "It's insane," the second violinist said. "My brother is an orchestra musician—he puts his suitcase outside his hotel room door, gets on a bus and then on a waiting plane; we have to carry our instruments and our baggage, stand in line, put up with all the security precautions, and then find our plane overbooked or fogged in or not flying because of mechanical difficulties." The travel became such a strain for Claus Adam that it became the reason that, in 1974, he left the quartet, and they looked for a new cellist.

Joel Krosnick was living in Los Angeles where he was artist-in-residence at the California Institute of the Arts. "It was really light up, turn on, and tune out," said the cellist, who looked like an emotion-wracked poet when performing and a madcap hippie when not. "I was feeling a need to get out of L.A. I had no idea of what I was going to do next when the telephone rang and this voice said, 'Hello, this is Bob Mann.'"

The cellist—who grew up in New Haven, graduated from Columbia, and had studied privately with Juilliard cellist Claus Adam—ran a hand through his mop of dark hair and grinned. "Well, I didn't know anyone in the quartet more than to say hello to, but what they stood for was without question something that one could believe in. I wanted the kind of high-powered musical life I knew they had. The day I auditioned, my body woke up at four in the morning and I started practicing. I probably had never wanted anything so much. There was a lot of intense communication at rehearsal, and if you're not used to it it's very intense and intimate and I was overwhelmed. I spent the afternoon walking in a park thinking: *I don't know what happened.* I had a splitting headache."

Ten months later, he played with the group again. "That time, I thought: *They can't do it with three people. They have to find someone, and if it's meant to be me, it'll be me.* The first moment I had a spasm of nerves but after that I played regular. The next day, we played again, and then Bobby said, 'Look, we'd better talk.' And Sammy, who is very shy, looked at the floor and then at his music and said, 'I guess this is over.' And then there was a silence.

"And I'm wondering again: *What's happening?* I mean, it was nearly a year since I first played with them. And then Earl, in his wonderful, round, smiling way, says, 'I think what he means is, well, welcome if you want to join,' and Bobby says, 'Are you going to say yes or are you going to play hard to get?' And I thought to myself: *It ain't going to work to try to do this slowly*, and I said 'Yeah, well, of course I want to join.' And we stood up and I hugged these people that I really didn't know well enough to hug. The intimacy between men is a very delicate sort of thing anyway, and it was an unforgettable moment for me, very shy and touching and beginning."

~

Seven years later, on a Friday, the four assembled noisily in their Juilliard studio: Earl Carlyss came in from Westchester, Sam Rhodes from New Jersey, Bob Mann from the upper West Side, Joel Krosnick from Chelsea. Some critics had written that they were the best incarnation of the Juilliard Quartet, and they themselves said it was certainly the happiest.

The group had had the week partly off and there was business to settle: Their press agent needed two hours of interviews to be used in an all-day festival of Juilliard recordings to be broadcast on radio station WNCN. The Juilliard School wished to know what they would play at a memorial service for Ivan Galamian, the celebrated violinist and teacher.

"Well," said Sam Rhodes thoughtfully, "what's more appropriate? One thirty-five or fifty-nine, two?"

"I think one thirty-five is more—" began Earl Carlyss.

"We played fifty-nine, two, the slow movement," said Joel Krosnick, "for—"

"Didn't we play one twenty-seven for Jennie Tourel?" said Bob Mann.

"Yes, Jennie Tourel," confirmed Sam Rhodes, who remembered every detail of every concert the quartet played.

"We're the greatest memorial quartet!" crowed Mann.

"Forest Lawn!" exclaimed Krosnick. "We'll take out an ad for the west coast. Hire the Juilliard Quartet!"

All four of them broke up, laughing wildly.

"Do you want to hear a bizarre story," said Earl Carlyss to a visitor watching. "We were once hired to play a concert in Miami by someone we'd never heard of and..."

"Oh, yes!" exclaimed Mann. "This is fan*tas*tic!"

"...and this man had committed suicide and put in his will—*in his will*—that he wanted us to play for an invited audience of his friends..."

"In a big downtown Miami hotel!" exclaimed Mann.

"...and he specifically wanted the third Elliott Carter string quartet," continued Earl Carlyss imperturbably. "Now we went down there and the women were in full gowns, the men in tuxedos. They weren't musicians. We were convinced that this man was getting back at them because they were forced to sit there and listen to us play such difficult music."

The door to the studio opened, a woman hurried in, handed each man a white envelope, and left. The envelopes, which contained the group's itinerary for the next two weeks, provoked a set of four variations—simultaneous—on the details of hotels, stopover times, and travel arrangements between Detroit and Findlay, Michigan. The violist wanted to drive, the second violinist to fly; the cellist didn't care as long as he could spend two nights in the same hotel; and the first violinist kept changing his mind.

"We don't all have to do the same thing," Rhodes finally silenced the rest. "Everybody does what he wants. Just get to the concert on time."

Because quartet members spend so much time with each other on tour, some quartets stay in different hotels and take different planes. The Juilliard took the same plane but sat far apart; they checked into the same hotel but asked for rooms on different floors. "We don't want to hear each other practicing or calling wives or friends on the telephone," said Rhodes. "You need the time alone. You're living with three other people and you have to learn to do that in a mature way. It's *that* more than any musical disagreements that lead to difficulties in quartets."

"When you first meet someone and they blow their nose in a certain way, you think it's darling," said Mann. "Fifteen years later, you can't stand to look at it."

Other quartets that they have coached have benefited from the Juilliard's experience in more than musical matters. "They get involved with everything: Solo as well as group technique, interpretation, but also questions of commitment," says a student in one such group. "The reason there aren't that many young quartets is that it's difficult to make the commitment. One of our members was married and didn't know whether she could handle that and be in our quartet. Bobby asked her, would she be happy playing quartets in the backwaters of New Jersey for the rest of her life? She said no and Bobby counseled her to leave. Then he counseled us."

~

About an hour into their rehearsal, the group finally began to play. The piece was Bartók's Third Quartet and the studio resounded with the group's four distinct musical voices. "When we cook a stew," said Mann, "we like you to hear all the elements."

After two minutes, the group lurched to a stop.

"Sammy, don't you think that sometimes gets a little loud?" said Mann, taking one of the stock issues of interpretation by the horns.

"Well," said Rhodes.

"I just worry if we all pile in, it's going to be very loud."

"What do you mean?" said Rhodes. "You *don't* all pile in."

"You play," said Mann, playing the line on his instrument. "Then Joel plays—"

"No," said Krosnick, pointing to the score with his bow. "I come in *pianissimo* and—"

"What I'm saying," said Mann, "is that the first four bars usually seem too loud to me. *In concert.*"

All four began talking at once.

Although many people assumed that Mann, the first violinist, the oldest, and the founder of the quartet, ran the show, just a few minutes with the quartet demonstrated otherwise. Each, in his own way, found the means to get his point across and each struggled to remain open to suggestion.

"When Joel joined the quartet," said Bob Mann, "I realized I was twenty years older than everybody else. I had played some pieces in a certain way for years in ways that were very meaningful to me, and I didn't want to change. I found out it wasn't enough to say, 'It works for me; it'll work for you.' I had to put my ideas out on the marketplace and sell them to the others. It's been a very difficult thing for me."

The quartet resumed the Bartók.

"How's the tempo?" asked Krosnick.

"Tempo's perfect," said Mann.

"I find this tempo lumbering," said the cellist.

"Well, it *is* a little slow," said Carlyss.

Sam Rhodes stared at his score. Disagreements over tempo were, if anything, more frequent than over dynamics.

"Bobby and I once couldn't agree on the tempo of a Mozart quintet," said Carlyss. "He wanted a fast speed which sounded to me like Doberman pinschers barking. I wanted a slow speed which sounded to him like we were dragging our feet in the mud. We were playing it two nights in a row, so we figured one night we'd do it my way and one night his way. The first night, as we were playing it my way, I listened and thought: *Hey, maybe Bobby's right. It doesn't feel quite as special as I thought it would.* We get off the stage and I'm about to tell him this when Bobby says to me, 'You know, this is not so bad after all.'"

"You learn timing," said Rhodes. "When to bring up certain ideas and when not to. The most dangerous time is right before a concert, when people are feeling tense. That's when arguments tend to become most personal and involved with irrational feelings. In a marriage you don't discuss big problems when you've just gotten home dead tired after work."

The quartet played on, stopping every now and then for a quick, animated interchange that gathered strength, reached a peak, and then ended, like the music itself. Three hours after they had come into the studio, they prepared to disperse. The visitor to their studio was still mulling over their last exchange, but for the four Juilliard players it was already old history.

"This is the most efficient way we can work," said Joel Krosnick. "It's very straight. There's no deviousness and things don't build up. We've been through a lot together. All of us want to be here. And when we get up to take a bow after a concert, we're proud as hell."

~

Postscript: In the spring of 1986, Earl Carlyss left the Juilliard Quartet and was replaced by Joel Smirnoff.

Yo-Yo Ma. (*Dorothea V. Haeften.*)

~ 10 ~

Yo-Yo Ma

The group is small, hermetic, a curious blend of sophistication and naïveté. Its members are young American, European, and Asian virtuoso musicians who jet from continent to continent, performing for more people during a single televised concert than their predecessors reached in a lifetime. They are living out a life for which they have been coached since the age of three or four. When they were toddlers, their parents placed a violin in their hands or sat them down before a piano keyboard and told them they had an extraordinary gift, something that other children did not possess. Since that time, they—and often their families—built their lives around this gift, nurturing it like a rare flower in a greenhouse, transporting it great distances to specialists who would help it grow. While other kids played baseball, these children practiced, four, five, six hours a day. On Saturdays, instead of hanging out or staying in to watch TV, they commuted to music lessons at the special extension schools of conservatories like Curtis in Philadelphia, New England in Boston, Peabody in Baltimore, or Juilliard or Manhattan or Mannes in New York. When summer came, they were sent to music camps like Meadowmount or music festivals like Aspen or Tanglewood, where their playing and practice could be supervised by the best teachers and performers. Several times each year they were dressed up and taken to play for significant people: Influential musicians, prominent teachers, managers, wealthy patrons of the arts, who, like their counterparts in the eighteenth and nineteenth centuries, might secure an introduction for the young prodigy, or a concert engagement, or raise the funds to buy him a finer instrument. All year long, too, there were auditions: For new teachers, for admission to schools or camps or special classes for contests and competitions where one's performance established one's standing in the ever smaller, ever more competitive world of the aspiring soloist.

For it was clear that the market could not employ all the thousands of soloists-in-training who were pouring out of the conservatories and colleges in the sixties and seventies, but only the very cream of the cream. By age fourteen, whether or not a young musician was of that standing was public knowledge. By age fourteen, the teenager in question was identified by fellow students as "a genius" and by teachers as "an extraordinary talent," or else he or she was merely one of the crowd of brilliant, accomplished young people who did not have that degree of talent, drive, discipline, charm, charisma, luck, connections—or the winning combination of all these things—to become, as the media had begun to hype it, a "musical superstar."

By the time cellist Yo-Yo Ma was fourteen, most people in the music business in New York knew that he had it. What was surprising was that his instrument was not piano or violin—the two instruments for which most of the dazzling virtuoso music literature is written—but cello. Few cellists—Pablo Casals most notably—had become international celebrities. Mstislav Rostropovich had made headlines by defecting from Russia to the United States; Jacqueline du Pré, by capturing the public imagination as a tall, dreamy-eyed woman whose musical intensity matched any man's. Other cellists like Gregor Piatigorsky or Janos Starker or Leonard Rose or Pierre Fournier were accorded deep respect within the music world but their names did not resonate outside its bounds. The cello literature wasn't flashy or large enough; the cellists themselves did not have the flamboyance associated with violinists or pianists. No cellist had ever electrified an audience in the manner of a Horowitz or a Heifetz.

Yo-Yo's instrument was only the first surprise. The second was that he did not enter competitions. The third was that, as he was growing up, he gave few concerts and hardly talked about them. Although the formidable Sol Hurok had taken Yo-Yo on as one of his artists (at the suggestion of Leonard Bernstein) when the cellist was only fifteen, nothing much happened. The Hurok organization would line up concert engagements only to be interrupted by a call from Hiao-Tsiun Ma, the boy's father, demanding that the dates be canceled, his son's schedule lightened so as not to interfere with his education. Unlike other kids at Juilliard Prep who never actually finished high school or who finessed their way to a diploma, Yo-Yo was educated in part at the École Française and Trinity, then earned an undergraduate degree at Harvard. His evolution into a virtuoso was unusual, even in the context of a group whose every member is unusual. It was the story of an Old World Chinese father and an enormously gifted Franco-American son, who grew up to realize his father's most ambitious dreams.

~

It was getting dark, pouring rain, and Yo-Yo Ma and I were hopelessly lost somewhere in the vicinity of the Brooklyn Academy of Music. No one in the slum we found ourselves in had even heard of BAM, and the young man whom Isaac Stern called "the greatest cellist alive" was hopping in and out of the Toyota querying gas station attendants, liquor store owners, and pedestrians with unfailing courtesy but to no avail. His cello, a Matteo Goffriller made in Venice in 1722 and valued at $200,000, lay across the back seat. Its previous owner was Pierre Fournier, who had probably never set foot or instrument in such a car or neighborhood. Beside it was the bow with which Leonard Rose had made his career, an irreplaceable present from teacher to student. In five minutes, he was due to rehearse at BAM.

Yo-Yo smiled one of the quick, boyish smiles that regularly illumined his face. At twenty-six, he was a slim, graceful man with thick, shiny black hair, gold-rimmed glasses, and an even, low-key manner which belied both his status in the music world and the hectic life he led.

"There may be a few cellists who can approach his expressive lyricism," wrote the *Globe and Mail* after one of his performances of Dvořák's Cello Concerto, "but they are not of his generation."

"Mr. Ma has what in vocal circles would be called a perfectly smooth and regulated scale, with no breaks from top to bottom," wrote the *New York Times* after a performance of the Saint-Saëns Cello Concerto. "He produces a big enough sound but it is never a thick one. It also is a sound that is constantly varied thanks to an infallible bow arm. Within one bow, Mr. Ma manages to get five varieties of pianissimo when he so desires."

In addition to receiving excellent reviews, Yo-Yo regularly received more concrete proofs of his ability in the invitations prominent conductors extended to him. "He's terrific," Zubin Mehta, music director of the New York Philharmonic, said after a performance with the cellist. "He's a person I'm going to be working with all my life." He had recorded with conductor Herbert von Karajan, at the conductor's request, on Deutsche Grammophon; with Lorin Maazel on CBS Masterworks; and with the English Chamber

Orchestra on the same label. "The only problem I have with Yo-Yo," said his manager, "is finding enough days of the year."

In 1981, he had played 125 concerts, including about 60 solo engagements with major orchestras, a lot of chamber music, and some recitals, shuttling between his home in Massachusetts (he was artist-in-residence at Harvard) and Europe and across the United States. He was accustomed to hassles: Cancellations at the last minute, planes that did not fly, officials who thought he was smuggling contraband in his cello. Getting lost in Brooklyn or arriving late ranked low on the list of possible catastrophes. "Cellists need to be flexible," he said, as we chased after a police car. "I tend to think of cellists as *nice people*. There's less of a demand for us than for violinists or pianists. We're not that sought after so the image is different. Most of us have played in orchestras, we play a lot of chamber music, we have to work with other people all the time..."

He hopped out of the car again and this time returned with instructions to BAM, where violinist Daniel Phillips and keyboard player Kenneth Cooper were waiting. Phillips, a small puckish man who had been playing with Yo-Yo since they were kids at Juilliard, and Cooper, a very tall, gangling man whom Yo-Yo regarded as a musicological authority, were ready to rehearse. Within five minutes, the trio was playing.

Like every other extraordinary artist, Yo-Yo Ma had long seemed so connected to his instrument that it appeared like an extension of his body. His movements on and around it looked effortless; his bow arm seemed to require no muscle. He was an expressive performer in the extreme, swaying, shaking his head, and allowing his face to reflect everything from beatific joy to impossible sorrow. It was not what one expected from an Oriental face. But then again, Yo-Yo is a Chinese who has never seen China.

He was born in Paris on October 7, 1955, and named Ernest, according to Yo-Yo, because in the Chinese village south of Shanghai where his father was born children were not given Chinese names until a month had passed and the family was reasonably certain that they would live. His father had been the eldest of four surviving children in China. He had gravitated toward the arts against the will of his parents and in 1936 went to Paris, eventually earning a doctorate in musicology from the Sorbonne. Yo-Yo's mother, Marina, came to Paris in 1949 to study singing. The Communist takeover in China precluded return, and the couple settled in Paris.

In 1951, their first child was born and they named her Marie-Thérèse and Yeou-Cheng. She has attributed the double name to her father's annoyance at the inability of the French to pronounce his name properly (they called him "Ah-choo," she says dryly). Hiao-Tsiun Ma did not have an easy time in Paris. The French refused to give him citizenship, and the tall, elegant musician retained his student status for twenty-five years. He supported his family by working a variety of jobs: As a guard in the Museum of Oriental Arts and as a clerk in the Library of Oriental Languages, among others. The Mas lived in a fourth-floor walk-up in the Quartier Latin, where the children learned to tell time by the Sorbonne clock, played in the Jardin du Luxembourg, but had relatively little contact with the French-speaking world.

At home, they spoke Chinese. They ate *baguettes* with *café au lait* for breakfast but Chinese food at other meals. They did not go to school but were taught by their father, at home. Hiao-Tsiun Ma supervised their participation in the state school correspondence course, testing them in French, history ("We are descendants of the Gauls"), math, and Bible. He also taught them the Chinese language, Chinese calligraphy, and proverbs such as "The rivers are made of little drops of water" and "Honored guests travel in the rain"—proverbs that contained in them the essence of the culture he had left behind forever. And, somehow, there was enough time to teach the children music and enough money to buy an upright piano and a succession of stringed instruments.

Yeou-Cheng began playing the piano and violin at age two and a half, and she was already eight years old when her brother got started. "He had broken some keys on our piano and had broken a violin, I think," she said in the quiet, understated way in which both Ma children spoke. "My parents were beginning to believe he was not interested in music."

"My father played the violin and it seemed that violin and piano 'belonged' to my sister," recalled Yo-Yo. "She was always four years older than me, a fantastic musician, and I probably thought I could never play as well. Then, when I was four, my father took me to the Paris Conservatory. There, in a corner, was this humongous double bass, which is *twice* the size of any ordinary bass and looked huge to me. The strings had broken on it and instead of strings there were ropes. I immediately took to it, but since I obviously couldn't play a double bass at that age, I settled for a cello."

Half a year later, Yo-Yo was playing Bach suites. His father had secured a teacher, Madame Michelle Le Pinte, and a one-sixteenth-size cello which Yo-Yo played sitting on three Paris telephone directories. Although both children had private teachers, their father supervised practice and laid down a set of inviolate rules: They were not to disturb one another while practicing and they were not to play, hum, whistle, or sing the other's pieces. They were not to practice long hours but to follow a special system of scales, then études, then Bach, and, later, concerti.

Hiao-Tsiun Ma had developed a system for doing very little at a time but doing it *perfectly* before continuing work on a given piece. "His emphasis was on technique: On learning the notes, making them perfect, learning the instrument, developing memory," recalled his son. "I learned two measures of a Bach suite every day. No more. No less. I got them right, I got to recognize all the patterns in the music, I developed my memory. It also made me think about what I was doing. By practicing only half an hour a day, I learned three Bach suites by heart by the time I was seven. Every night, I'd play through what I knew just to refresh my memory."

He played his first public concert at the Institut d'Art et d'Archéologie in Paris at age five and shortly afterward left France to visit relatives in the United States. Through a series of fortunate introductions Hiao-Tsiun Ma was engaged as a music teacher at the Trent School in New York City, his children were enrolled there, and they were taken to play for important people. They played for violinists Isaac Stern and Alexander Schneider, for cellists Pablo Casals and Leonard Rose, for conductor Leonard Bernstein. They appeared on the Johnny Carson show and on the first fund-raising telecast for the Kennedy Center in Washington, D.C., where Robert Frost read poetry, Marian Anderson sang, and Danny Kaye conducted. The Mas were a great success; their father decided to remain in America.

~

An hour before concert time at BAM, Yo-Yo, Danny Phillips, and Ken Cooper were still rehearsing, working out knots in the performance of the works on the stands before them. If anything, Yo-Yo appeared to be the junior partner in the enterprise.

"What happens here?" he would ask. "How do you think this should sound?"

Ken Cooper answered in detail; Danny Phillips didn't say much. He had been playing with Yo-Yo since childhood and was familiar with the cellist's every motion. "He'll always ask something like 'How do you think I should play this phrase?'" Phillips said, "although he knows *exactly* what to do with it. He always asks. He's always deferential. I've heard him deliberately make *mistakes* to make people feel better. And it works. He makes me play my best. He brings out the best in whoever he's playing with."

When Yo-Yo was nine, he began studying with Leonard Rose. He talked in whispers, terrified by his teacher and awed by the enormous lush sound Rose drew from his instrument at a time when he, Yo-Yo, could barely elicit a squeak. "He had so much patience with me," Yo-Yo exclaimed now. "Boy, to me, he's integrity itself. He's such an honest man; it's very rare. My whole growing-up process was under him. He's mostly responsible for what I can do on the instrument."

Rose remembered Yo-Yo as "a very small, very shy little boy, perhaps the youngest student I had ever accepted. I was very taken with him. He had an incredible memory and wonderful coordination. By age twelve he could play some of the most difficult études and could remember everything he played by heart. There was no visible emotional content at the time, and he didn't have much sound, but he was obviously very gifted. He ate things up, and as he grew older he began to develop tremendous expressive qualities and musical intelligence. I love the boy; he has the ability to move me very much."

Although it was clear that Yo-Yo was virtuoso material, Hiao-Tsiun Ma insisted on keeping his son "normal." In the Ma family, that meant continuing a bicultural education in the best schools as well as maintaining a high musical standard. "We'd get up at six-thirty and wouldn't get breakfast until we had completed our calligraphy and practiced," recalled Yeou-Cheng, who was attending the Brearley School then. "My father wanted us to be educated, good people first and musicians second." But while his older sister acquiesced to her father's regimen (study hard, home right after school, no sleep-over dates, no allowance—"We used to tell our parents that we needed to use the library just to be able to get out of the house and *watch* people"), Yo-Yo, by the time he was eight or nine, began to subvert it. He was transferred from the Trinity School to the Professional Children's School, where his classmates were child actors, models, ice skaters, and other kids whose schedules precluded a classical education. Even there, Yo-Yo preferred to cut classes, bicycle in Central Park, or go down to Times Square to browse or take in the movies.

The high point of his week was Saturday, when he was at Juilliard. "I *loved* going there," he said. "I'd cut classes just to *be* with other people. Because I was so insulated at home, I was always curious what other people were like. So I'd cut ear training and go sit in the cafeteria. Of course I flunked ear training. I played first cello in the orchestra and I was in a chamber group. Danny would fly in from Pittsburgh and the pianist flew in from Washington, so whenever the weather was bad, I got to sit in that cafeteria some more."

Danny Phillips recalled that Yo-Yo was so shy that "he didn't say a word when we first began to play together," and that "he was a consummate cellist by age twelve." Yo-Yo himself realized at Juilliard that, as he put it, "I was fairly good compared to other people," and that realization sobered and confused him. Hiao-Tsiun Ma had taught his children to embrace humility, to distrust compliments and other forms of flattery. "If someone tells you you're good, they're lying, they want something from you," Yeou-Cheng remembered as the essence of his message to them.

"It was much later before I was able to accept that people really liked something I did," said Yo-Yo. "I was afraid people would like me only because I played well, and also, I was bothered by the comparisons that go on in a place like Juilliard. I knew nice people who didn't play as well as I did and I didn't like the way they were talked about. You'd play with someone who'd say, 'I'm great, you're great, but *these* people—they're nothing,' and then the someone who's nothing turns out to be a great companion."

Companionship was a discovery for Yo-Yo. He reveled in it. At fifteen, his shyness began to ebb and he outdid himself to be "one of the guys." That summer he left home for the first time to attend music camp and went "completely wild." He claimed that he never did a laundry and that, freed from his father's discipline, he did things such as leaving his cello out in the rain. He forgot rehearsals and did not bathe. "Mr. Galamian must have been horrified," he recalled. "It was total freedom."

When he came back that fall, Yo-Yo enrolled as a full-time student at Juilliard and tried to continue his new life-style while living at home. He took to drinking with all the enthusiasm of a kid let loose in a candy store. Once he drank six gin and tonics before a recital. Another time he was found unconscious in a practice room and had to be taken to Roosevelt Hospital. School administrators thought he had overdosed on drugs when in fact he had drunk a fifth of Scotch. "My parents came to get me. I was underage," he said. "I wish they had gotten mad. Instead, my father gave up wine because he thought he had been setting me a bad example."

That year, it became clear that Yo-Yo could not go on living at home. Yeou-Cheng, who, he said, had always been a role model for him, was at Radcliffe. She had, after much painful reflection, decided to pursue a career in science rather than music. Yo-Yo went up to Cambridge, liked it, and applied to Harvard, where he was accepted for the following year.

"At Juilliard, I could do all these crazy things on my instrument although I really didn't know why or what I was doing, and people thought it was great," he said. "At Harvard, people said, 'Listen, you've got to cut this out. There's more to music. You've got to try to do other things.'"

He chose a liberal arts major that allowed him to take all the music courses he wanted as well as science, literature, and history and, although he performed and played on campus, accepted only one concert engagement outside of college per month. He began to read and think about the world of the composer and the qualities of the language used. "I began to separate from being just a cellist to being a musician interested in communicating and sharing with people," he says. "Harvard gave me a different perspective on life. I realized that there were many other things that were as important to other people as music was to me. At the same time, my commitment to music deepened. I spent a summer at Marlboro working with Casals and Serkin and Sascha Schneider and Izzy Cohen. On details, always details. You could *see* their commitment. That's when I knew for sure that music was what I wanted to do."

~

A little after eight that evening the concert hall at BAM was full and the cellist was pulling on his concert clothes. His movements were graceful, his grin as relaxed as it had been a few hours earlier when he was trying to ascertain the whereabouts of the hall. The trio walked out onto a small stage to the sound of applause. They bowed, smiled, and waited for total silence.

When Yo-Yo performed, his sound and face exuded a serenity rare in anyone, but particularly surprising in a young man not yet thirty. One sensed that many important battles were already behind him: He began his adolescence early, spent his teenage years in rebellion, and entered his twenties with a clear sense of priorities. When he was twenty-three, two weeks after he was awarded the Avery Fisher Prize, he married an American girl he had met at Marlboro. Hiao-Tsiun Ma, who continued to speak Chinese with his son and had remained as much of an Old World patriarch as ever, was not pleased with the match but was prevailed upon to attend the wedding.

At twenty-five, Yo-Yo underwent surgery to correct a congenital curvature of the spine, and the long recovery period which followed offered him an opportunity for reflection. Like other great musicians who have been through periods of enforced inactivity, the cellist emerged with a stronger sense of his art. At the same time, he has retained his father's belief in the importance of a rounded, normal life. "Music is a really tough profession on the family," he says. "Jill and I go to Europe together over the summer and, during the year when she's teaching, I try to travel intelligently. I love to travel. But I like to spend enough time at home to feel normal."

11

The Leventritt Competition

Half an hour into the finals of the 29th Leventritt International Competition, a young man wearing a purple beret appeared at the stage door of Carnegie Hall and announced that he was just in from Paris for the piano contest.

"Please go around front," he was told.

"But I'm a contestant," he insisted, and argued with the stage door guard until other guards arrived and forced him to leave.

The incident provided a rare bit of comic relief in an otherwise grave, exhausting, tension-filled ordeal. All contests—from the local raffle to the Olympic Games—engender excitement, and some provide their winners with a springboard for lifelong careers. But the Leventritt was *the* most prestigious and lucrative music competition in the United States. The winner of the 1976 Leventritt would receive not only a $10,000 cash award but an RCA recording contract and a roster of solo engagements with a dozen major American symphony orchestras, including the New York Philharmonic. It was for this reason that eighty-five young pianists from eighteen countries had spent most of their time and invested a great deal of money preparing for this competition. Their experiences during the two-week selection process provided an unusual glimpse of the behind-the-scenes workings of the music business and would demonstrate the degree to which sheer nerve and stamina—as well as talent—were required to succeed as a concert artist.

The Leventritt was first held in 1940, in memory of Edgar Leventritt, a prominent New York lawyer and amateur musician. Leventritt was fond of young artists and spent much of his leisure time in their company. When he died, his daughter Rosalie Berner says, the idea of an international competition for musicians held in the United States was new: "Our purpose was to launch young artists, to set a standard for both teachers and performers, and to make it truly international, so that a musician from any part of the world would have a chance to be heard."

Conditions in the world of classical music had changed dramatically since then of course. By the 1970s, hundreds of highly proficient pianists, string players, and vocalists were entering the concert market each year hoping to build careers as soloists. The number of international competitions had also mushroomed, so that together they now resembled a worldwide steeplechase which only the hardiest would finish. "Back in the fifties, you were guaranteed a reputation if you won just one competition like the Queen Elisabeth in Brussels or the Tchaikovsky in Moscow," said one contestant. "Now there are so many contests and contestants that a few years later, everyone's forgotten you."

But, at the same time, *because* there were so many hopeful soloists, winning a competition had, in the opinion of many, become almost indispensable. A prize brought publicity, both in the small world of music students, teachers, and performers and in the concertgoing world where people bought tickets. A prize attracted the attention of managers who imagined that they might have another Horowitz or Heifetz on their hands. A prize also was tangible proof of accomplishment, a standard of undisputed excellence in a field riddled with ambiguities. Although music competitions were disparaged by musicians as encouraging mechanical playing and politics, by teachers as causing needless demoralization, and by critics as producing technical wizards producing soulless notes, they were nonetheless a phenomenon that few could afford to ignore.

As a result, young musicians typically entered many competitions, traveling a well-worn circuit from New York to Montreal to Leeds, Geneva, Brussels, Munich, Warsaw, Moscow, and even through Texas, trying to get an edge over their peers. The contests had created a new breed, the *competition artist*, as well as a hierarchy among the competitions themselves. The Leventritt figured very near the top of the pyramid. Unrestricted by a regular annual or biannual schedule, the competition was held and opened to pianists or string players whenever Mrs. Berner and her panel of judges decided there was a substantial body of new talent. The Leventritt judges themselves were generally considered to be among the most distinguished and equitable musicians to be assembled in one place. They were not compelled to award a first prize and, in the past, they had sometimes decided to forgo awarding one in the belief that only an artist ready to launch a major career should receive one.

Six months before the Leventritt was held, notices were sent to schools, teachers, foreign consulates, and former contestants around the world. "But you can't just apply out of the blue," said a Juilliard student. "You need to have played with a number of orchestras, or won some other competitions already, or at least given a New York recital. Just to enter requires a great deal of courage."

While applications trickled in, Mrs. Berner set about finding a group of judges who would make themselves available for ten days running. She also needed to book a hall with adequate practice facilities, good acoustics, comfortable seating, and room for both contestants and judges. Then she had to hire sympathetic and competent accompanists who would play the orchestral parts of up to fifty concerti with people they had never before met.

In 1976, the competition was held for pianists. Judges Gary Graffman (Leventritt winner 1949) and Claude Frank (Leventritt participant 1954) screened a hundred applications and rejected only eleven. It was the highest number of applications that either man recalled seeing at the Leventritt and yet another indication of the rise in the level of piano proficiency. Since the Second World War, Graffman said, more and more people were seriously studying the piano. "It's due to the rise of the middle class here in the United States, and the wealth of teachers that emigrated from Europe after the Russian Revolution and the events in Nazi Germany. And there's also a blossoming of talent in places like Japan and South Korea."

Many of the judges also cited the effect of radio and recordings on young pianists. "Through the recording industry, people have become highly conscious of technical excellence," said conductor Max Rudolf. "There are simply no mistakes on a recording and *they* have become the new standard. In the old days we didn't mind a wrong note here and there. Now, young pianists have to play perfectly because a wrong note sticks out like a sore thumb."

Graffman and Frank looked first at the contestants' birth dates and compared their ages with the number of concerts they had given. "If someone is eighteen and has only played locally, that's fine," said Graffman, "but if they're twenty-six and have only played locally, it's not. Then we look at repertory. Contestants must present three full concerti: One must be Mozart, Beethoven, or Brahms. In addition, they must be ready to play between ninety and a hundred and ten minutes of solo repertoire, which is about one and a half times the length of an average solo recital.

"*Then* we look at the teachers with whom the contestant has studied and what kind of chamber music he or she has played. But once we accept the applicant, the application has nothing whatsoever to do with what happens onstage."

~

Before a note had been played at the WQXR auditorium in Manhattan, sudden attacks of mononucleosis, unexpected concert engagements, and last-minute jitters had shrunk the number of contestants from the eighty-nine who had been accepted to the sixty-five who played in the preliminaries. Each of these sixty-five players was allotted twenty minutes—a long time for preliminaries but a short time for the contestant. "They choose the first piece and after four minutes we usually know whether they will make it to the semifinals," said Claude Frank. "If they're not going to qualify, we try to make the rest as easy as possible. If they are promising, we ask for a different style or period. We always listen to part of a concerto and part of a solo piece."

At nine-thirty on the morning of the opening day, a tall, slim pianist from Port Jefferson, New York, arrived at the WQXR auditorium and walked into the glare of three 2,000-watt quartz lights belonging to the crew of *60 Minutes*. The Leventritt people had engaged the services of a publicist, and the firm had persuaded CBS's top-rated news weekly to televise the proceedings. The contestants had not been told that they would be televised, and as each one walked into the quartz lights, their faces registered first surprise, then swift accommodation to the unexpected conditions. The lights bathed the stage in white, cast shadows from the black to the white keys of the piano, and completely hid the judges sitting in the hall.

"Mr. Gemmel will start with the Brahms D minor," announced Mrs. Rosalie Berner in a carefully modulated voice. There was a pause while the pianist geared up. Then, for the next nine minutes, he played uninterrupted.

When he finished the first movement, there was silence. The judges—pianists Sidney Foster, Leon Fleisher, Gary Graffman, Richard Goode, Claude Frank, Nadia Reisenberg, and Gitta Gradova, and conductor Max Rudolf whispered together as Gemmel stared into the white light.

"Would you please play some of the Mozart sonata for us?" Fleisher called, referring to the program that Mr. Gemmel had submitted to the judges.

At nine-forty, the contestant began Mozart's Sonata No. 9.

"Thank you. Thank you very much," Fleisher interrupted at nine-forty-three. "Would you now play some of the Chopin ballade?"

Four minutes later he was stopped again.

"Thank you," Fleisher called out again, and at nine-forty-nine a young man from Kansas opened with a Chopin prelude.

For the next seven hours—counting lunch and a coffee break—contestants walked bravely onto the stage of the auditorium, accustomed themselves to the white light, and played as if their lives depended on it. Some shot out into the wings on a wave of adrenalin, convinced they had put in the best twenty minutes of their lives at the keyboard. Others sank into the nearest chair, certain that muddy playing in the second piece had cost them the semifinals.

"I'd rather put my money on a horse than on a contestant in one of these competitions," said one participant after playing. "Every jury's going to pick a different winner because there are so many different schools of playing, because they may be tired or hungry or bored by the time it's your turn, or because you yourself don't happen to be in good form. You have to have nerves of steel and not crack under pressure. In other words, you can't afford to be human, which is *exactly what you should be* in order to be a great musician. I couldn't afford to practice eight hours a day before this because I have a job. But those are the breaks."

The inequalities of a competition like the Leventritt are staggering. Some contestants spend up to $1,000 just to get to New York and stay at a decent hotel; others simply take the bus from their apartments. One applicant squeezed the contest in between a recording date, a doctoral recital, and a concert appearance, while another spent four weeks doing nothing but practicing her Leventritt repertoire with her teacher. A few contestants were accompanied by pianists who were friends or whom they paid but with whom they had worked for years; others performed with one of the Leventritt accompanists with whom they had not rehearsed even once.

The judges—all seasoned performers themselves—tried to see beyond these discrepancies. They sat impassively through the twenty-minute sequences, speaking to one another only to determine what to ask the contestant to play next, making occasional notes on the pads in their laps: *Distinguished . . . undistinguished . . . moving . . . overpedaled . . . no phrasing . . . interesting . . . highly gifted . . . poor.*

During the preliminaries, about one-fifth of the players had major memory lapses, played a phrase or a section in the wrong key, or omitted it altogether. As a group, the judges found, they played everything faster than was customary, used more pedal, and banged.

"Almost never do they play more softly," said Claude Frank. "Like any member of a concert audience, we respond to a musical and artistic experience as we listen. But as judges, our ears fasten on the components of this experience. We listen for the quality of technical equipment, for tone, for accuracy, for intensity, for the level of concentration, for musical integrity. We look at how each of them use the equipment they have."

By the time all sixty contestants—another five had dropped out in the interim—had played, the judges had drawn up two lists. The first list comprised the pianists who, they felt, were definitely semifinalists. There was general agreement on five of the people who had performed. Another eight players were added as possible semifinalists. The names of these thirteen pianists were made available to the participants on the last evening of the preliminaries and were published in the New York press the following day.

~

Pianist Marian Hahn had been the fifth contestant to play in the preliminaries and had had to wait four days before finding out whether she had made the semifinals. A slim, dark-haired New Yorker with a pleasant manner, she had appeared very much at ease onstage. Marian Hahn had graduated Phi Beta Kappa from Oberlin and was twenty-seven years old; she had entered many other competitions before and had learned to make the best of strained conditions.

"I started practicing again the day after I played in the preliminaries," she said. "No matter what has actually happened, you have to pretend that you're going on to the next round. I try to avoid speaking to other contestants during this period. I go to bed early and I try to practice six hours a day. Both I and my accompanist have endurance problems. No matter what people tell you, there *is* a difference between the endurance of a hundred-and-ten-pound woman and a two-hundred-pound man. We have to conserve our energy and it's a fairly rigid, austere life for a while.

"I was all right the first four days of the week, but the fifth day was terrible. We had been told to call the Leventritt office at four-thirty to find out who made the semifinals. When I called, the lines were busy for almost an hour before I got through. When they told me I had made it, I asked my roommate to hide the newspapers all weekend. I didn't want to know who I was competing against."

The following Monday, Marian Hahn was the first semifinalist scheduled to play before the judges. The auditorium had been changed to Carnegie Hall and the CBS television lights were now dwarfed by the circles of red velvet and gold-leafed tiers. The judges sat in a row of seats about halfway between the stage and the auditorium doors. Each semifinalist was allotted thirty minutes this time, and as they came into the wings, their faces were even more grim than the week before.

"I've never had to go through pressure like this," said Lydia Artymiw, who was competing in a major contest for the first time. She was twenty-one years old, with white-blond hair and blue eyes, and she exuded an air of determination characteristic of most of the contestants. Her parents were Ukrainian immigrants displaced by the Second World War, just as Marian Hahn's parents were German Jewish refugees. Both women were excellent students and disciplined performers, and both enjoyed the full support of their families, who had come with them to Carnegie Hall.

Lydia Artymiw looked as if she had not slept in several days. "In a concert, if you miss a note, you don't worry," she said. "Here, you immediately feel that it's fifty points against you. These judges know the repertoire inside out and each has his or her own idea of what the piece should sound like. You have to play what you play with the utmost conviction and not get distracted and not worry about the fact that you're getting no feedback. They don't applaud. They don't in any way let you know what they thought. There are all these question marks in your mind as you're sitting up there. If you make it to the finals it's wonderful, but there's a price that you pay. You have to go out and do it all over again."

Lydia Artymiw twisted her head slowly from side to side. "The worst part is the exhaustion. You practice all day; you're under stress all the time. My neck and back feel like a solid knot. But I wanted to find out how I was going to cope with it, and I've learned a lot. At this point, winning or losing doesn't matter to me. I wanted to see how I got through it."

At four o'clock, after the last semifinalist had finished, the judges retired to choose the finalists. Each judge prepared one list of the players he thought were finalists. Any name that appeared on five or more lists would be considered a finalist. As it turned out, there were five such names: Lydia Artymiw and Marian Hahn; Steven De Groot, a South African who lived in Philadelphia; Santiago Rodriguez, a Cuban who lived in New York; and Mitsuko Uchida, a Japanese who lived in London.

The night before the finals, Mitsuko Uchida was in her room at the Taft Hotel, where she did not have access to a piano. She was twenty-seven, dark-haired, dark-eyed, lithe, and composed. She had projected such a strong sense of sophistication onstage that several in the audience had dubbed her "Miss Dragon Lady."

Mitsuko Uchida did not appear to be worried or tired. "I don't practice until the very last moment," she said. "Sometimes I knit because it takes my mind off the competition. This week I've visited several museums—the Frick, the Metropolitan, the Guggenheim. If I practiced eight hours a day, I'd be too tired to play. I must have weak brain cells because my capacity for concentration is not terribly long. It's better for me to practice two or three hours and then go to a museum.

"I do certain relaxation exercises and try not to think about the competition at all. You cannot see into the minds of the judges. My attitude is to view the competition as if it were a concert. Whether I play to ten musicians in an empty hall or to two thousand people, who would certainly include at least ten musicians, is the same. If they like you or not is nothing that you can predict."

For the finals, Mitsuko Uchida arrived at Carnegie Hall in blue jeans, silver shoes, and an olive-green trench coat, but then changed to a formal evening dress. All the finalists were wearing formal concert attire, and the judges as well as some of the CBS crew had dressed up too. A live audience had been invited to the finals, at which each finalist would perform forty-five minutes of uninterrupted repertoire. The prospect of having friends, teachers, and relatives listening to them seemed to relax the five considerably, and the mood backstage became almost festive.

"I *wanted* to play," said Santiago Rodriguez. "Having an audience there makes a great deal of difference to me. When you walk out and see all those faces, they turn you on so that being nervous isn't a problem anymore."

"I definitely felt a sense of lineage," said Marian Hahn. "I thought: *Rubinstein has played this Chopin here and Horowitz has played my Haydn sonata.* The very first concert I attended, Rudolf Serkin was playing the *Emperor* Concerto and I sat all the way up in the balcony."

This time Hahn was at the piano playing the *Emperor* and Serkin was among the judges sitting in the hall. He, Mieczyslaw Horszowski, Rudolf Firkusny, William Masselos, and conductor William Steinberg had joined the original jury for the finals. They listened to four hours of playing and at three-thirty adjourned to the conductor's room backstage at Carnegie Hall to deliberate. The CBS crew had set up more lights there, and, as the contestants and audience waited for the judges to decide the winner, Rudolf Serkin refused to participate in the deliberations as long as the television cameras remained. He and the producer argued over the propriety of televising the proceedings. Finally, the producer of *60 Minutes* agreed to turn off the quartz lights, Serkin was seated, and Claude Frank brought the meeting to order.

"We shall first determine the prize or prizes," he said. "There can be one first prize or two first prizes or three—in theory. Or there can be no prize and just finalists. There also in the past has been an award of distinction, meaning that the person who gets it will be on a preferred list of finalists."

The other twelve judges looked confused. Then all began to talk at once.

"My instinct is I would like to give the prize to all of them," said Mr. Horszowski, an octogenarian whose gentle, soft voice was barely audible in the room.

"I am the only person here who does not play the piano, and I would have refused to conduct these people," said Mr. Steinberg emphatically.

"May I make a point?" asked Mr. Fleisher several times without eliciting a response.

"I would like to raise a very important issue," said Mr. Frank in a resonant tone. "Do we give a first prize? Who votes for giving a first prize?"

There was confusion again as the judges all began talking at once, and Mr. Horszowski, by far the oldest person present, asked for clarification.

Then two judges voted to give a first prize while eleven voted against giving one.

"The five finalists are the winners then," someone said.

"Rudi, will you please go out and tell them?" Rosalie Berner pleaded, knowing that the decision would be met with hisses and catcalls. But none of the judges was willing to go onstage and announce the jury's decision.

Five minutes later Mrs. Berner had taken the stage.

"The judges' decision this year is not to award a principal prize," she said. "Each of the finalists will receive one thousand dollars and a three-year management contract, with orchestra and recital appearances scheduled throughout the country."

The audience booed loudly, and speculation began immediately as to why no winner had been chosen.

"They must not have the money," said one New Yorker.

"Those judges are all senile," said another. "The ones who won it twenty years ago have forgotten how badly they actually played."

Backstage, Mitsuko Uchida did her best not to appear disappointed; Lydia Artymiw smiled for the first time in two weeks; Marian Hahn, Steven De Groot, and Santiago Rodriguez graciously acknowledged compliments. Family members and friends crowded the backstage area, and a few reporters and photographers moved into CBS territory.

Later that evening, at a party for the judges and finalists, Rudolf Serkin tried to explain why no first prize had been awarded. "The general level of playing was amazingly high," he said. "Nothing was missing technically. I learned a lot today. I was very often moved. Each of the finalists is absolutely equipped to perform in public and the booing of the audience was perhaps justified. But we felt that none of the finalists was quite ready for this prize, that each one had something but not one had everything."

Steven De Groot sipped his glass of champagne and claimed no regrets. "I don't feel discouraged," he said. "The jury's decision shows a responsibility for the integrity of future musical performance. You don't want to launch a career before it's ready to be launched. The competition did a lot for me. Everybody needs to be told that they're worth putting in the finals of the Leventritt.

"But I might add that competitions give me a feeling of nausea and general unhappiness. I'm going on vacation tomorrow. I think I deserve it."

Andrew Kazdin. (*Don Hunstein.*)

12

Andrew Kazdin

"It's Saturday night and Mr. X has just scored a triumph at Carnegie Hall," postulates audio producer Andrew Kazdin. "Thirteen curtain calls! Flowers! It takes him ten minutes to get from the stage door to his limousine!

"Monday morning, he shows up at the studio, where some guy he may or may not know has to point out his mistakes—a potentially threatening and demoralizing experience. Sometimes a composer has written something no one can play. Sometimes the performer is tired. Sometimes it's not the right day."

Kazdin is Audio Consultant to the New York Philharmonic, which pays him to supervise all broadcasts, recordings, and parks concerts; he is the audio producer for all *Live from Lincoln Center* telecasts; and he is the producer of *AT&T Presents Carnegie Hall Tonight*. As a record producer, he works with pianist Murray Perahia and conductor Pierre Boulez and, in fifteen years with Columbia Masterworks, he has been responsible for the recordings of the pianists Glenn Gould and Ruth Laredo, the organist E. Power Biggs, and members of various major orchestras.

"As producer," he continues, "I have to provide a psychological and physical atmosphere in which the artist feels free and relaxed. There's got to be *trust*. My job is to get the best possible performance out of the artist and capture it sonically in the best possible way."

Although the increasing complexity of recording technology has made the producer an artist in his own right, his work remains largely unknown to the public. There are less than forty full-time classical producers in the United States and fewer than one hundred in the world.

Kazdin lives with the knowledge that his profession and great love may eventually disappear from the United States. "No major orchestra has an exclusive recording contract with any company anymore," he says, "and not that many recordings are being done in this country, because it's cheaper to record in Europe." When he worked at Columbia he had to live with a depressing bottom line: Classical *releases* accounted for twenty percent of the total produced by all labels within the company but only five percent of total sales, a ratio that made it difficult to defend the costs that Kazdin's yen for perfection often incurred.

"He has to have a good pair of ears, infinite patience, imagination, authority, and steadiness," said the late E. Power Biggs, who admired Kazdin's musicianship. "He can't let the artist run things. He has to be a tower of strength."

"He needs a supreme knowledge of recording technology and a sense of acoustic propriety—of what a hall can be coaxed to do," said the late Glenn Gould, with whom Kazdin recorded in Toronto in the small hours of the night that the pianist preferred.

"He is like a photographer: He has to be as faithful or as unfaithful as possible," said Pierre Boulez. "When I am with the orchestra, I can't imagine the recorded sound. Someone else has to reproduce it, and he must either reproduce what he hears in the hall or create his own reality."

His artistic goals will invariably conflict with financial ones. Before a record was cut in the mid-1970s, a solo album would cost about $6,000; a chamber group, $8,000; an orchestra, about $50,000; and a full-length opera, close to $100,000. Inflation, the cost of new equipment, and the cost of musicians have more than doubled those figures. "A full orchestra in the studio costs over two dollars per second. If the conductor says, 'We'll start at letter G,' and a violist asks, 'Where?' he's just bought lunch!"

Money is a constant worry for Kazdin because of the meticulous manner in which he records. While there exists a "hands-off" school of producers that hangs three microphones before a regularly seated orchestra and gets a curtain of sound similar to that in a concert hall, Kazdin belongs to the "hands-on" school that seats the orchestra in irregular ways and uses many microphones, which give the producer better control in the final mix. Musicians familiar with the results Kazdin obtains in this way regard him as the best producer in the business, and he is the only one with a formal education in both music (the New England Conservatory) and engineering (the Massachusetts Institute of Technology).

"All through childhood, I had the dual interest," he recalls. "When I was seven, I was fascinated by a hospital paging system synchronizing sound with a flashing light. My father built me something that would do this, and by my early teens, I was building amplifiers and reproducing music. I began college at MIT, but as I got further into engineering, it became clear that the craft as a whole contained a lot of things that didn't interest me and that music did. At the time I graduated from New England, I knew I wanted to do record production, so I went back to MIT, took acoustics courses, and got a master's in industrial management.

"Almost anyone can pick up the training to be a recording engineer, while music is a talent not everyone has. But what really counts is a lucky break. When I came to New York, there were no job openings, and even though I had all this training, I couldn't do anything with it until Columbia hired me in 1964—just before I turned thirty."

Since then, Kazdin has produced about 350 records, with an input into nearly every phase of the process from a recording idea to the illustration and liner notes that appear on an album jacket.

The idea for a new recording may come from the artist under contract, it may constitute the terms of the contract, or it may come from the producer, as was the case for Kazdin's lunatic *Everything You Always Wanted to Hear on the Moog But Were Afraid to Ask For*, created with Thomas Z. Shepard, now head of classical music at MCA.

"It gets harder all the time to come up with viable projects," says Kazdin. "The Schwann catalogue lists forty-five *Moonlight Sonatas* and thirty-seven *1812 Overtures*. If you want to do a thirty-eighth, you'd better have a good reason. Now digital recordings are getting spectacular sales just because of the sound. Cannons that'll blow your speakers apart— orchestras you've never heard of selling records because they use the technology. You can also remix old recordings for compact discs. Listening to a master tape that was made into a vinyl disc is so much better than the record, that at CBS now we're putting some of those tapes on CDs. You have to find a hole in the repertoire, or some other way of making a recording that says, 'Hey! Look at me!'"

When such an idea—like the antiphonal brass music of Giovanni Gabrieli, for instance—comes to Kazdin, he writes a proposal specifying artists and repertoire, and all musical and engineering costs. A marketing expert then makes a sales projection based on previous experience with the artist and music, the success of competitive records, and overall market trends. If it is favorable, a recording authorization and project number are issued and the producer takes charge.

He begins by scheduling a recording time and place convenient to all concerned. "For the Gabrieli recording I had to fly the first-desk brass players of the Chicago and Cleveland orchestras to Philadelphia on a day that they and the Philadelphia brass players all had free. With Biggsy, we had to go where the organ was—to Harvard, Germany, or Holland. With Glenn, I went to Toronto. In New York, there are a number of recording sites; the problem is finding the quality I need.

"A fine concert location is not necessarily a fine recording location," explains Kazdin. "The function of a good concert hall is to take the sound produced onstage and bark it out into the house with clarity, good distribution of frequencies, and no unpleasant echoes. In a recording situation, I have microphones in front of the players. I don't care if the instruments are well distributed in the hall or whether there are echoes from the ceiling. But I do need a balance between direct and reverberant sound."

Kazdin will record up to sixty musicians in Columbia facilities but has shopped around for larger spaces in gymnasiums, armories, and churches—all of which have their drawbacks. His favorite orchestral recording site is the ballroom of Manhattan Center, where he negotiates with the Holy Spirit Association for the Unification of World Christianity (popularly known as the "Moonies"). The demands of his work have brought him into contact with so many forms of eccentricity that he barely acknowledges the peculiarities of that organization.

In addition to arranging for space and time, the producer must prepare his music as thoroughly as a diligent conductor. "Generally speaking, the preparation is in direct proportion to the size of the forces. If it's solo piano, I'll take a couple of hours. If it's *Carmina Burana*, I'll work on the score for over a year."

At first, Kazdin duplicates the work of a conductor, noting important phrases, entrances, and difficult spots. Then, he listens to other recordings and marks hidden passages, canons, or responses between instruments that he sees in the score but cannot hear on the record.

"Once I know what I want to get on tape, I think about the number and position of microphones and tracks. For Ruth Laredo's Rachmaninoff series of solo piano literature ten years ago, we used five mikes and four tracks. Now I'm using two mikes and two tracks for Murray Perahia. An orchestra I recorded ten years ago would use twenty-five mikes and eight tracks. Now I use the same number of mikes, but if it's digital I'd use a 24- or 32-track machine. I go through the score for a second time, thinking of how the sound will come out of your speakers at home. It's traditional to put first violins on the left speaker and cellos and basses on the right. But beyond that, I'm looking to make interesting placements of sound. Also, I have to think how I'll squeeze twenty-five mikes onto eight tracks and retain enough flexibility to position various instruments in the mix. If I raise the volume of a track, I raise all the instruments on it and strange bedfellows can develop."

The producer then goes through the score for a third time to mark cues, opportunities to shut off mikes, and other reminders that will save expensive studio time. He gives the track layout to his engineer, consults with the artist or conductor on last-minute problems, checks on the studio, and steels himself for a recording session.

~

When the New York Philharmonic assembled to record Ravel's Scheherazade Overture, Kazdin was edgy. At the time, the orchestra was routinely described as a rowdy group of prima donnas or, sometimes, "mafiosi." Zubin Mehta had once, before he became its music director, told an interviewer, "A lot of us think: *Why not send our worst enemy to the Philharmonic and finish him off once and for all?*"

Kazdin himself found the Philharmonic an "enormously flexible" orchestra with excellent soloists, very solid percussion, good strings, strong brass and woodwinds, with only occasional exceptions. But, he said, "I'm not sure the sections listen to one another. In Cleveland, neat is the natural state. In New York, the natural state is sloppy. Cleveland has no attitude problem. In New York, it's as if they say to the conductor: *We'll do you the favor of letting you conduct, but you'll have to drag it out of us every inch of the way.*"

American orchestras get paid special rates for recordings, so recording sessions are scheduled as closely as possible to concert performances and reflect whatever condition a given piece was in when performed onstage. At the same time the orchestra had been rehearsing the Ravel, it had been busy learning John Cage's *Renga With Apartment House 1776*, a piece that had unleashed yet another battle between Boulez and orchestra members who opposed his predilection for contemporary music, and Kazdin did not know how much recording time would be needed to correct problems that had slipped in earlier. Ten minutes before ten, as the orchestra players drifted into the studio, the producer synchronized watches with the orchestra's personnel manager. He consulted with Pierre Boulez, a man with whom he loved to work, and then went up to his control room one floor above the ballroom.

At precisely ten o'clock, with the orchestra enclosing his podium like a human doughnut, necessitating the use of two desks and scores, Boulez clapped his hands.

"Quiet, please! Please, quiet now!"

There was a slight decline in the noise level. There were many members of the Philharmonic who did not much like Boulez. They had nicknamed him "Buzz" and "The French Correction," mimicked his deadpan, dispassionate style, and tried to ignore him as much as they could.

"I have a correction to give the strings," Boulez said calmly over the din. "At one before twenty-three, you should play *pizzicato*. And two after twenty-three, *arco*. We will record in three sections. I would like everyone to tune properly. Strings?"

As the orchestra tuned, Kazdin checked the quality of sound coming from the four speakers around him, and fiddled with his score, a stopwatch, and a two-way telephone that was connected to a similar one on the conductor's stand. His eyes were on the closed-circuit television set before him which was featuring Boulez trying to quiet the orchestra.

"Andy?" the conductor asked finally. "What would you like to hear?"

"I'd like something loud. Maybe eighteen into nineteen."

"This is for level," he told the man on his left.

The orchestra supplied a burst of sound, and Bud Graham, the engineer with whom Kazdin frequently works, adjusted knobs on his console.

"Thank you," said Kazdin into his mike. "May I hear the celeste, please?"

After setting individual volume levels for a dozen instruments sharing tracks, the producer waited for a police siren outside to die down. Then he said, "This is Ravel, Scheherazade, take one."

Eleven minutes and over $1,300 had gone by.

~

The procedure was less nerve-racking when Ruth Laredo recorded with Kazdin. The pianist arrived at the control room twenty minutes early with a box of chocolates for the producer and a high-energy lunch for herself. Unlike the orchestra, she had spent the last week concentrating exclusively on the repertoire she was to record and had taken pains to be well rested and emotionally prepared. "In a recording session you're after perfection," she explained. "You're up against posterity."

Laredo filled out a musician's contract form to be filed with the American Federation of Musicians and entered the studio to test the piano. At exactly two o'clock, she played a loud passage so that the engineer could check volume level, and a few minutes later she was playing Rachmaninoff's *Variations on a Theme by Chopin* as Kazdin conducted along, breaking only to circle notes in the score with the air of a careful dentist marking a probable cavity.

"Well, chief?" Laredo asked, returning to the control room half an hour later.

"We had some technical problems in the beginning."

"So did I," laughed Laredo.

"So whether you're happy with the take or not, I need the first four variations again," said Kazdin, and waited until she returned to the piano. "Stand by. This is take two."

Four and a half hours later, there were a total of forty takes and inserts for a piece which runs thirty minutes. The pianist was visibly drained by the effort of returning to problematic phrases; the producer, by the effort of tactfully persuading her to do so.

"I'm not sure we're covered on the first bar of the seventh variation," he had said earlier.

"I'm certain," Laredo replied tiredly.

"I'm not. Maybe we should hear it."

"Look—I'm sure I didn't play any wrong notes."

"I'm not talking about wrong notes. I'm talking about notes that didn't speak. Can we do it again?"

Kazdin has no qualms about the morality of splicing various takes into the illusion of one start-to-finish performance, and although Laredo admitted to a fear that "a spliced performance will sound contrived," she was delighted with the note-perfect yet seamless quality of the final product. "If you have two takes of a piece and line them up measure for measure," says the producer, "one will always be better than the other.

Sore spots in a recording get louder every time you hear them. Why shouldn't notes be played correctly? Splicing has become an art—not a mechanical process."

For a solo album like Laredo's, the producer and the artist listen for several hours to the various takes, painstakingly choosing the best they have recorded and marking promising places to splice. For an orchestral recording, where the conductor is unavailable to contribute to the splicing plan, Kazdin devises one alone. An engineer then does the actual cutting and joining of tapes, and the multitrack master is returned to the producer to be mixed down to two or four tracks suitable for playing on stereo or quadrophonic sets.

"This is the hardest, most technical, and most creative part of the producer's duties," says Kazdin. "I work alone and never delegate this part of the process to anyone else. Mixing often takes much longer than splicing. Getting the right balance, making adjustments, equalizing frequencies, creating the sound I want—*that's* the really important statement I make as a producer."

When the master tape is completed, Kazdin authorizes an acetate cut, sends this prototype of the eventual record to the artist or conductor, and waits for their approval. "Most of the time it comes," he says, "and then the music is out of my hands. I'm busy discussing the title and cover. The art people will sometimes ask me to play the tape for them, but usually that doesn't help. I just cross my fingers and, after I spin a story about the background of a piece, hope I don't get a cartoon when I wanted a photograph of a forest."

Recordings, unlike newspaper articles, are not governed by deadline pressure. Months may elapse between a recording session and the formulation of a splicing plan; a tape may languish for years in Columbia's vault before it is made into a record. As it happened, Kazdin's recording of Boulez conducting Ravel's Scheherazade Overture was never released in the United States. It was made available only in Europe and, when it arrived in the mail one day three years later, he did what he always does when he receives a new release.

"The first thing I do is pull out the record, read the label, and count the bands," he says. "And even if it says 'Scheherazade,' I'll play it to make sure I don't have Blood, Sweat and Tears instead of Boulez and the Philharmonic. I play it once at home, where I have a setup equal to any professional facility in the city, and then I'll file it with about six thousand of the other records I own.

"And one day I'll be out driving and the radio will put on Ravel. And I'll say: *Hey, I know this piece—I've recorded it*! I'll think: *That sounds better than my record; I don't know who they are but they sound fantastic*! And then the announcer comes on and I discover it's my record and I can go out and buy myself a celebratory pizza!"

Cecylia Arzewski in the first violin section of the Boston Symphony
Orchestra. (©*Lincoln Russell.*)

13

The Life of Sin: Profile of an Orchestra Musician

There is a photograph in the hall of Cecylia Arzewski's Cambridge apartment that she passes every morning on her way to work in Symphony Hall. In it, she is five or six years old, her expression is serious, her party dress is pressed, and her hands are holding a child-sized violin and bow in a pose that recalls generations of child prodigies. It was taken in Krakow, Poland, where she was born and where her parents and teachers expected she would grow up to be a virtuoso violinist. She would complete the state music school, go to Moscow to study with David Oistrakh, and embark on a concert career in eastern Europe. If she were very good and very lucky, she might even have the opportunity to tour in the west.

Like many child prodigies throughout the world, Cecylia had been born into a musical family. Her paternal grandfather had been concertmaster of an orchestra in Warsaw. Her father, the pianist of the Krakow Philharmonic was one of twelve brothers and sisters whose home was called "the music factory" and where, it was said, whenever a door squeaked open, a debate would begin over whether the squeak was pitched at a perfect A, A flat, or A sharp. Cecylia was born with perfect pitch. At four she could improvise on the piano and was so much in love with the instrument that she built a nest out of blankets and toys to take naps underneath it. By five she was playing the violin and beginning the regimen of three hours of practice a day that would continue into her thirties. All the education she had ever received had been geared toward a life as a soloist; at thirty-eight, after sixteen years with the Boston Symphony Orchestra, she only rarely identified herself as an orchestra musician. She was a violinist, she would say in 1986 when she was one of the BSO's two assistant concertmasters. No, giving up the ambition of a solo career had not been painful—until the age of fourteen or fifteen one could never be sure anyway whose ambition, one's own or one's parents', was at issue. But working in an orchestra in the United States in the 1980s had its frustrations—her former teacher, Joseph Silverstein, had once called it "a life of sin." She thought of her position at the BSO not as who she was but rather as what she did for a living. At the same time, Cecylia Arzewski would say that she never felt as connected to the world as when she was playing a Mahler symphony with a great conductor. Once, when asked to find the theme which linked the little girl with the violin at age five or six and the temperamental woman whom *Boston Globe* critic Richard Dyer called "one of the most colorful, outspoken, dedicated and gifted members of the BSO," she answered, unhesitatingly, "Conflict. Conflict from the moment I first began to play the violin."

~

Cecylia Arzewski was born in 1948 into a family of Jewish Holocaust survivors. Her maternal grandmother had hidden the family—Cecylia's mother, father, and brother, who had been born in 1938—in Krakow for the duration of the war, and Cecylia, the only family member who had not been there with them, often said that she felt like a privileged outsider as a result. Despite the postwar housing shortage, the Arzewskis found a small apartment into which they crammed two pianos, a grand and a Steinway upright. Stanislaw Arzewski, his daughter would remember years later, loved the piano more than he loved anything else in his life. "When he was dying," she said, "he was going in and out of coma. One hand was hooked up to the IV and the other would suddenly start to play the piano and he would get this unbelievable smile on his face. He was playing some great concerto."

Piano became Cecylia's brother's instrument. He had gotten a late start on it because of the war, and when Cecylia told her parents that she, too, wanted to be a pianist, they discouraged her. One day after she turned five, she came home to find a violin and a violin teacher waiting. Eugene Kawalla, she later recalled, knew she did not want to play the violin, but he specialized in teaching such children and soon turned lessons into "a fairy tale." The E string, Arzewski recalled, was given the name Ellen, and when it was out of tune, Mr. Kawalla would say, "Ellen's not behaving again today." He invented stories about every piece she played and every musical marking—a *sforzando* in a Prokofiev march became a tree falling down in the woods after the elves had passed by. Arzewski would await his arrival twice a week and throw herself into his arms when he came through the door. She would remember the short, attractive, gentle Mr. Kawalla for the rest of her life, in part because her relationship with her teacher was one of the few relationships she then had.

"My parents never thought it was a good idea for me to play with the kids in our neighborhood," Arzewski recalled. "They looked at me as though I were an alien and asked questions about my mother's pierced ears. They told me what their mothers had said: That we had to be either Jews or gypsies because no one else would pierce their ears. My parents never trusted the Poles after the war. They were poised to run as long as I can remember, always afraid. They were never sure when the Poles would finish off the small number of Jews who survived the war."

In 1957, when the Arzewskis finally left Poland to live, as they told Cecilia, "as Jews in a Jewish country," their daughter was crushed. She loved Krakow and was frightened of going elsewhere; for weeks, she walked around the small city, knowing she would lose it and trying her hardest to commit everything to memory. The family took a plane to Warsaw, then a train to Munich and then to Genoa, where they stayed for nearly a year. In Italy, she learned Italian and had marathon lessons with her father, who, having left his position as concert pianist in Poland, now poured all his musical energy into his daughter. By the time the Arzewskis had found a small apartment in Bat Yam, just south of Tel Aviv, and their two pianos stuffed with pillowcases full of dried Polish mushrooms had arrived in Haifa, Cecilia was nine. She was enrolled at the Tel Aviv Conservatory and soon became part of a group of preteen violinists that included Itzhak Perlman, Pinchas Zukerman, and Miriam Fried. Prime Minister Golda Meir herself once handed out the scholarships from the American-Israel Cultural Foundation to the group that would, within a few years, emigrate to the United States. Arzewski hated Pinchas Zukerman on sight—"he was rough, rude, and conceited and once told me he was going to have a career even if it meant walking over dead bodies." She remembered Miriam Fried as an extraordinarily hard worker who was two years older and already maturing into adolescence. But she was awed and permanently charmed by the plump boy in shorts

(*Left to right*) Pinchas Zukerman, Josef Gingold, Cecylia Arzewski, Ivan Galamian, and Itzhak Perlman at Meadowmount in the early 1960s.

named Itzhak who used crutches and played the violin "so organically that I thought I might as well stop. What's the use?" Itzhak Perlman's mother was Polish and became one of Arzewski's favorite people, at first because she spoke the same language as the ten-year-old. Israel was then in the throes of developing a new Jewish prototype: *Sabras*, or native-born Israelis, were held up as heroes by everyone from the national media to neighborhood children, while refugees like the Arzewskis were put down. "I felt almost more accepted in Poland than I did in Israel," Arzewski would later say with vehemence. "It took a very long time for me to adjust. I learned the language in six months and made a point of speaking Hebrew without an accent so that by the time we were there a year, no one could tell I wasn't a *sabra*." Stanislaw Arzewski had his adjustment problems too. Israel was swamped with musicians, and, instead of re-suming a career in concert music, he did free-lance piano work in Tel Aviv cafés and accompanied singers. His son had been sent off to New York to study at Juilliard (he would later quit piano and become a high school teacher), and the father's ambition as well as frustration focused on his daughter's music training.

In 1960, the Arzewskis decided to move once again, this time to New York. Their son was there, and violinist Michael Rabin, who had heard Cecilia play in Tel Aviv, had recommended that she continue studies with his teacher, Ivan Galamian, who taught at the Juilliard School. At twelve, Cecilia was put in the Professional Children's School in Manhattan and thrown into her fourth language, which she soon learned to speak—like the others—with no trace of an accent. The photographs of this time show a smiling if slightly stiff teenager who bears a resemblance to Annette Funicello on the *Mickey Mouse Club*, a program Cecilia Arzewski never saw because she was always too busy practicing. She made friends at school and at Juilliard on Saturdays but recalled that she had been a rather solitary girl who, after reading some Freud at fifteen, had asked her parents if she could go for psychotherapy. Her parents had refused and Cecilia had not pursued the idea. At Performing Arts, where she attended high school, and at Juilliard there were many other unhappy adolescents and she had lots of classmates who were caught in a mélange of ambivalent feelings toward their primary violin teacher, Ivan Galamian.

In the early 1960s, the Arzewskis were sure that their daughter would have a career as a solo violinist—just like Itzhak Perlman and Pinchas Zukerman and Miriam Fried. The four of them all spent summers at Meadowmount, Galamian's music camp in the Adirondacks, and during the year all except Fried would take lessons with Galamian himself. Sunday mornings at seven-thirty, Cecilia would arrive at 170 West 73rd Street and warm up in a small room "surrounded by pictures of dead violinists" for a dreaded lesson. Unlike her teacher in Israel, Odeon Partos, and most unlike Eugene Kawalla in Krakow, Galamian was, to her, cold, formal, authoritarian, and sarcastic, when what she needed was a surrogate parent like his assistant, Dorothy DeLay, who might have countered the pressures she was under at home. Galamian insisted on the importance of winning competitions, insisted on the impossibility of marriage and family for a woman with serious ambition, and was, in Arzewski's recollection and that of several other students, offensive to Jews. "You'd play a piece for him," she said. "You'd get to the slow movement, and finally, after all those instructions about how much bow to use on each note, you'd think you could relax and put in a few slides, a little *shmaltz*. I mean, after all, this is the Tchaikovsky Violin Concerto! And he'd turn to you and say, 'You know, this is not Jewish music you are playing.'" Although Perlman, Zukerman, and Fried all found something good to say about Galamian's discipline, Arzewski would later say, bitterly, that she had never had occasion to use anything he had taught her. By the time she was seventeen, she had had it with Galamian, with her parents, and with New York. On the advice of Itzhak Perlman, whom she told she had to leave the city, Arzewski sought out Joseph Silverstein, the concertmaster of the BSO.

"I first met her when she walked into Tanglewood and played for me, and I said to her, 'I don't know what you want to study with me for,'" recalled Silverstein. "She was a finished player, in a style that was her own and different from mine. I told her that if she studied with me there would be things I'd want her to change, and she said that she was anxious to study with me nonetheless. So she came to Boston and did extraordinary work. She had gone through all those years with Galamian, she was used to a very formalized relationship with a teacher, and although my whole manner of teaching is very different—I try to have a more collegial relationship with my students—she was very quiet in the lessons. We didn't talk much about what else was going on in her life. I was pre-occupied with her playing."

What was going on in her life at the time seems, from the vantage point of the 1980s, an enactment of a sixties script written for the child of overprotective and authoritarian Jewish parents. Just before beginning her work with Silverstein, Arzewski had married a black chemistry major at MIT. She categorically refused to discuss this marriage or her other involvements later, insisting that they had nothing to do with her career as a musician. In fact, her personal life had determined the course of her musical life. She wanted to have a child, and, although Silverstein tried to dissuade her from having one right away, he proved to be "right there" for Arzewski when, in the fall of 1968, she informed her teacher that she was pregnant. "Pregnancy has had an extremely salutory effect on her violin playing," he wrote in a note appended to her grade at the end of that semester at the New England Conservatory; she carried the note around with her, in her handbag, for years. Silverstein later would say that he had had a hard time understanding the "volatile events of the late 1960s" as much as the explosive personality of the student whose work was so disciplined. "Her playing was on such a high level that I thought for sure she would be the first violinist of a string quartet or the con-certmaster of an important orchestra. But for the first few years I knew her, she made it clear to me that what she really wanted was to play the piano, that she was a piano freak. She had a very close, very special relationship with her father, and she has made an unerringly disastrous choice of men in her own life. She is extremely bright, but her capacity for self-evaluation outside of violin playing is not very good. I'm not a psychiatrist—I don't understand why. We're very fond of her. We've watched her with a great deal of pride and pain."

Joseph Silverstein and his wife, Adrienne, became Arzewski's surrogate parents—liberal, supportive American Jews, just close enough and far enough away from her real parents to suit her needs. As a violin teacher Silverstein was, in Arzewski's words, "truly the best." He had studied with Efrem Zimbalist and Josef Gingold (the violinist with whom she had wished to study during summers at Meadowmount). Despite winning prizes at two international violin competitions, he had not made a career as a soloist. He had joined the BSO in 1955 and had become its concertmaster in 1962. Unlike Galamian, he was interested in a world of options outside a concert career and, if anything, tried to emphasize to his students the difficulties of achieving success as a soloist: "You need a lot of luck. You need to win competitions. And you need to sign with a management by the time you're twenty or it's not going to happen," Cecylia, who was sure she wanted children and a stable place in a community instead of a succession of hotel rooms, did not question what her teacher said. There was nothing about the violin that Silverstein did not know, she would say later, and although she was "quite obnoxious" during their first year of working together and was continually "testing him," she soon began to change her style of playing and to listen to herself for the first time.

Her daughter, Ilana, was born in January of 1969, when Arzewski was a few months under twenty-one. That spring, she continued at the conservatory, practiced, taught at the Newton Free Music School for five dollars and fifty cents an hour, did some free-lance work, cooked dinner every night, and breast-fed her child. This lasted two semesters. During the second, Arzewski called up Silverstein one day and told her startled teacher that she was leaving her husband and needed a job to support herself and Ilana. Silverstein told her that the Buffalo Philharmonic was hiring violinists, and when she auditioned, she was offered the position of principal second. In February of 1970, she began life as an orchestra musician.

As one of Galamian's students at Juilliard, Arzewski had often been excused from playing in the school's orchestra since participation took time away from practice. As a New England Conservatory student, she had played in three orchestra concerts each year. As a result she knew little about the orchestral repertoire, hated Mahler and Bruckner at first sight, and found playing Mozart "terribly boring." All the training she had received as a soloist, she said, was suddenly irrelevant, and at first she was simply lost. "The dynamics were different: The lows much lower, the highs much higher. You have eighteen gangsters all playing the same thing, and if you all play a soloist's *piano*, it's going to be too loud. And you don't initiate anything in an orchestra. That's the conductor's job. You wait. As a soloist, you attack or phrase the way you want to; in an orchestra, the only choice you have is using different fingerings if you want and, at times, you can't even do that because a conductor may ask for a passage to be played a certain way—on one string, for example, or in a specific position. You're very much imprisoned."

In Buffalo, she would later recall, she really had no idea what orchestra playing was about, what was going on around her, or how to fit into it. "Everything I played I was playing for the first time in my life. If I played a piece that wasn't Mozart or Beethoven or Brahms, I really had to stare at the music—which is very hard if you're trying to watch the conductor at the same time. And it's all mental work unless you have somebody conducting that you're responding to. If you can feel his emotions— providing that person has emotions—and you can get into those emotions, *then* you can make music. But it takes a really great maestro whom you believe in, whom you almost worship, to make you accept the situation and say to yourself, 'Let me learn from this man.'"

Arzewski remembered few of the men who conducted the Buffalo Philharmonic while she was there, and almost none of the music she played. The orchestra was then reorganizing after nearly going bankrupt, and the precariousness of that situation combined with her involvement as a new mother put her work life into the background. Five months after moving to Buffalo, moreover, she received a letter from the personnel manager of the Boston Symphony announcing three openings for violinists and inviting her to audition at Tanglewood during the summer. Arzewski sent her daughter off to stay with her grandparents and began to practice six hours a day. She auditioned behind a screen for the orchestra's audition committee (behind-screen auditions had been introduced in the 1960s as American musicians unionized) and was accepted for the last desk in the second violin section by the BSO's music director, William Steinberg.

Four men and another woman were in the finals, according to Joseph

Silverstein, who was on the committee. The members took a secret ballot before discussion and the result was overwhelmingly in favor of the two women. But their first woman violinist had been hired just the year before, and the committee members, Silverstein recalled, were not at all sure about how Steinberg would react to their recommendation. When they met with him, Steinberg asked Silverstein what his views of the two women were, and the concertmaster replied that since both Cecylia Arzewski and Marylou Speaker were his former students, it would be unfair of him to speak. Steinberg then questioned the other members of the committee, who, in Silverstein's recollection, hemmed and hawed. Finally, Steinberg said, "I will tell you what I think. The first man is not a violinist. The others will fill chairs somewhere. As far as the two young women are concerned, those were the finest orchestral auditions I have ever heard, and you should try to keep those two as long as you can."

Bill Moyer, the BSO's personnel manager, announced the decision to the two women and remembered that Marylou Speaker "immediately jumped up and down in glee" while Cecylia "was very concentrated, intense, even a little somber. Her head went down and she had the damnedest look on her face." When Steinberg introduced them to the orchestra at its first rehearsal in the fall of 1970, they received the kind of reception that token women were then receiving in law offices, universities, and corporations across the country. Everyone applauded and then one of the violinists, a man who had just turned sixty, gave a short speech (meant to be jocular) asserting that after remaining the last man in the BSO, he would go out and found an all-male orchestra. It was typical of Cecylia Arzewski that she later developed a fondness for this "institution," who, in 1986 when he was seventy-seven, was still playing in the orchestra. It was typical of the nearly all-male orchestra that the two female violinists—"bubbly" Marylou Speaker and "volatile" Cecylia Arzewski—would be compared to each other for years to come, in the way members of a minority group are often compared by members of the majority.

The Boston Symphony considered itself slightly in advance of other major orchestras insofar as its hiring of women was concerned. Its first female member, a wind player, was hired in 1945. Its first female principal, flutist Doriot Anthony Dwyer, was hired in 1952 (she made headlines as the first female principal in the United States), after trying to obtain an audition with a major eastern orchestra for years. Dwyer later said that she had never been asked to audition because she signed her inquiries "Miss." Her luck changed only when Charles Munch let it be known that he would welcome women into the BSO, and she worked for that audition "like for a doctorate," learning everything she played by heart. Several women had been invited to audition for the position of principal flutist on what the musicians had dubbed "Ladies Day," and, as Dwyer recalled, "Munch was stunned. He had been expecting a lark and instead here were all these excellent players. I played everything I knew and I played well. Then they asked if I would come back and audition a second time. I said no. I thought they'd heard enough, and I didn't want to make another trip cross-country from California. Finally, they hired me, but management kept it a secret for a while. They knew it would upset the applecart."

When Cecylia Arzewski joined eighteen years later, she and Dwyer were the only women with children, and she was grateful for her presence and help. Even in 1986, there were only eighteen women among the 102 players in the Boston Symphony, a figure that everyone concerned with the orchestra kept saying was growing but which has remained as small as the number of women in other top American symphonies. Arzewski's head of tousled black hair was as instantly visible amid the bald pates and receding hairlines in 1986 as it had been in 1970, and, although her playing drew no attention to itself (orchestra members described it as "quiet" or "self-contained"), her facial expressions, the angularity of her body, and the intensity of her regard stood out as well. Silverstein remembered that Arzewski had been perceived as "a free spirit, a vestigial remnant of the sixties," when she first joined the BSO. It was not only that she eschewed brassieres and hung out with a group that smoked dope and asked for water beds on tour. She talked through rehearsals with her stand partner, she was absent a lot, and she made no effort to mask her opinions (especially negative ones) of conductors or fellow musicians. The politics of being a member of an orchestra irritated her and, even had she been interested in them, she lacked the temperament to become a practitioner.

In 1970, the BSO was still known as "the aristocrat of orchestras," the second oldest symphony in the United States (after the New York Philharmonic) in a city that lionized its aristocrats. Its sound was distinctive. It had been molded by Serge Koussevitzky and then preserved by Charles Munch, Erich Leinsdorf, and William Steinberg. Its hall was one of the best in the world and its subscription series consistently filled. "You could have heard a pin drop at those rehearsals," Arzewski said of her first years with the orchestra. "There was no talking, no fooling around. We had no rotation system then, and, every once in a while, the second violins would, if they knew the part, start joining the first violins. That was the extent of fooling around. But people didn't make fun of the conductor. They were very disciplined and the morale was very high."

The first piece she rehearsed with the orchestra was Gustav Holst's *The Planets*. When seventy-one-year-old William Steinberg began conducting the piece (which begins in 5/4 time) and did not clearly convey the beat, Arzewski's first thought was that she was simply not cut out for the job. The famous Boston Symphony sound overwhelmed her, and the first thing she tried to do was just blend in and watch. It took some time for her to develop relationships with the other violinists and to feel comfortable with personalities as varied and as prototypical as in any orchestra. "There was the spastic violinist and the one who had to be the first to get off the stage after a concert or rehearsal even if he had to knock over a few harps to do it. Then you had the guy with bad b.o. and you tried to stay away from him. Then there was the passive-aggressive. He's my favorite: very quiet but every once in a while he lets loose. Then you have the guy whose bow does not like to leave the string—he's always the last to finish the phrase or the piece. And you have the comedian—a wonderful man and great personality. There were also a few people I could pick out immediately who were great musicians, and those were the guys I learned from."

At the time Arzewski joined the symphony, all its members were required to play Pops concerts. The Boston Pops under Arthur Fiedler probably had the largest audience and was the best-known orchestra in the world at the time; it sold records; it was frequently televised; and for many people in Boston, its opening night was the kind of preeminent social event possible only in a still provincial city. Arzewski was, early on, recruited by the orchestra's press office for an interview on WGBH radio, one of the local public radio stations. The interviewer asked her whether she enjoyed playing Pops concerts, and her reply was that she had to stuff her ears with cotton because the brass was so loud. Her answer was typical of her attitude toward the press and the Pops. As far as the former was concerned, the press office learned to steer reporters to less candid members of the orchestra; as for the Pops, she never learned to like it.

"Pops was sheer torture," she said the year she finished paying for her violin and could afford to pass up the work. "Part of it was Arthur Fiedler. Part of it was the music. And part of it was the audience. It was six nights a week in those days, and eight weeks a year. I did not find Fiedler to be either a good conductor or a good musician. He drank. He yelled and screamed at the orchestra. He was the only member of the Boston Symphony ever to be fired. The music—well, the first third was the serious third: A march, then a Beethoven overture, maybe a little bit of Tchaikovsky; the second third was the 'talent show,' when the pianist or the violinist played Saint-Saëns or Grieg or Gershwin or Tchaikovsky; and the third third—the part they all waited for—consisted of Strauss waltzes back then, *My Fair Lady*; *Exodus* was in there sometimes, and did that make me feel strange! Nowadays, of course, it's *Star Wars*.

"My second year in the orchestra, I played a Wieniawski concerto in the second third. You're up there playing and, suddenly, you hear the pop of a champagne bottle. Then someone drops a few glasses. Someone else lets out a loud burp. In those days, you could even *smoke* in the hall. The clientele never goes to real concerts. They probably don't even own a classical record. They come because it's a social event, to sit at a table and drink and eat and listen to music. It's the most disgusting thing that can happen to a serious musician. It's musical prostitution. Because, if I wanted to do this sort of thing seriously, I could go live in L.A. and make about three hundred and fifty thousand dollars a year in the studios playing this stuff, working twenty-five percent less than I do now, taking more vacations, buying more fiddles. And finding myself in that position! There was no choice. I had to do it."

Despite her dislike of the Pops, public relations, and orchestra politics, Arzewski rose quickly within the orchestra, and her playing, several musicians said, was respected without exception. One year after she joined the orchestra, there was an opening in the first violin section. She auditioned for it, again behind a screen, and won it. She was twenty-three then, still the "new player," and, as the last violinist to join the section, she served for a time as "move-up man," filling the seat of any absent violinist up to the second stand. She played beside violinists who had worked in Cleveland under George Szell or in New York when Toscanini was still conducting, and, during breaks, her stand partner would recount to her what each maestro had said about a given phrase or piece. When the orchestra played Ravel's *La Valse* or Berlioz's *Symphonie Fantastique*, they would tell stories about how Charles Munch had brought the house down. To her surprise, she found the scores she played from marked up with notes on important remarks and happenings together with the dates they were recorded, remarks such as "Stagliano (the BSO's famous French horn player) sounds like a moose coming down Mass. Ave." in the score of the Brahms First Symphony. Several of her stand partners insisted on turning pages for her—they saw this as common courtesy, similar to holding a door for a woman—even though as the inside player this was her job, and a few encouraged and applauded her as she began to like the music she was playing and began to play it well.

What made her work particularly rewarding, Arzewski recalled later, was the day-to-day experience of playing with her former teacher, the leader of her section. Joseph Silverstein was, in the view of many of the conductors and orchestra musicians who had worked with him, the best concertmaster in the business and an extraordinary violinist who had lacked only the "flash" necessary for a solo career. He was interested in contemporary music, he was active in civic affairs in Boston, he taught, he played chamber music and recitals, and he was, for Arzewski and many others, a counselor as well as a consummate musician.

"There are these little games one can play in the violin section," she said. "If you know what you're doing, you can take over. All kinds of things go on within a section—covering up, faking, all kinds of intimate, secretive things. But the person I could never do this with—not for one moment—was Silverstein. Of course, there was my respect for him, but the thing was no one could do it. This man was leading a hundred and one percent of the time. He never sat back and relaxed, and he almost always knew the music better than the conductor did. There were times that the conductor got lost, which is, of course, a disaster. Because if the conductor doesn't cue in the oboe, it sets off a chain reaction. The violins may have had to count eighteen bars since their last note and, if they come in only two bars after the oboe, they count two bars after the oboe instead of the eighteen. And it's the same for whoever comes in after the violins. But Joey always knew the score and that chain reaction never happened; he provided a security blanket for the entire orchestra. When a conductor complained about the way we were playing or put us down, he would ask the conductor what, exactly, it was that he was after and he would suggest things to him. He stuck his neck out for us and did it because he wanted to, because he thought that was his job."

After her first year of adjusting to the length of Bruckner and Mahler symphonies—"They're difficult to sit through, especially if you're sitting at the back of the seconds with the brass and percussion blasting into your ears"—and the technical requirements of Bruckner—"You tremolo for half an hour until it feels like your arm's going to fall off and you wonder: *Why did he write this? He must have hated musicians*"—she began to enjoy the repertoire. Although she would never develop a liking for Bruckner, no matter how often his symphonies were programmed, and would remain largely indifferent to modern American composers such as Aaron Copland and Roger Sessions, the repeated performances and rehearsals of Brahms, Beethoven, and Mahler imbued her with a love of their music that she had not thought possible before. She had played Mahler for the first time as a conservatory student and then under William Steinberg, but the music had not greatly moved her. Then, for two years in a row, Claudio Abbado had conducted the Second and Third symphonies and Leonard Bernstein conducted the Ninth. "I had to play a lot of Mahler before I understood him," she said later. "I read a biography of him, *Man on the Margin*, about his background and upbringing, and I began to identify with his life. After playing with Bernstein and Abbado, I began to remember what Steinberg had done. I still have not done Mahler's Fifth very well. Mahler seems simple to me because every nuance and tempo change is marked. Everything you need to know is in the score. In Beethoven, there's almost nothing to work from—people have written doctoral dissertations trying to figure out what his markings mean."

Like most orchestra musicians, Arzewski was tough on the conductors with whom she had played. There were only four who had her unreserved approval—Bernard Haitink, Claudio Abbado, Colin Davis, and Leonard Bernstein. "They know the music, they care about what the composer wanted, they know the structure of the piece and the structure of the orchestra, they don't learn the score on our time, and they know how to put the music together so that when we perform it's all of a piece." Her first experience of first-rate conducting was provided not by William Steinberg—"He was an extraordinary musician and a real presence but just too old by the time I joined the orchestra"—but by Bernard Haitink, when he led the BSO in Strauss's *Ein Heldenleben*. She had never played the music before and had heard of neither Haitink nor the Amsterdam Concertgebouw, but she felt the entire orchestra cohere around a clear conception of the piece, start to finish. "People float into Saturday morning rehearsals to play for him; it's like a vacation." Colin Davis, she remembered, was almost always "magical. Sometimes I thought we were taking off from the stage when we played Haydn and Mozart. What makes an orchestra good is the same thing that makes a soloist good. You have to play pieces that make you work, that allow you to develop musical ideas and style and a certain tone. Mozart allows you that, and Colin Davis was very meticulous, clear, hardworking, and musically serious. When he was our principal guest conductor, we used to get that kind of discipline four weeks or more every year."

Her first encounter with Leonard Bernstein shocked her by its intensity. "I had never seen anyone so extroverted in my life," she recalled. "He knows no boundaries, no limits, and he makes music like that, which is extremely exciting. He is probably one of the most intelligent musicians alive, in a class of his own, knowledgeable on any number of subjects. I think he's a genius."

She sighed when she recalled working with Claudio Abbado. "He's his own man, very much his own person, with the utmost sensitivity and intensity too. He's a bit of a dictator in the sense that he doesn't leave you much room to do anything of your own, but the music is unique, different, fabulous when he conducts—you feel he's holding you by your throat and it's somehow a positive experience. He's not into choreography; he doesn't move his feet off the podium and never turns his profile to the audience as so many of the others do. All of them need feedback from the audience, but Abbado is very sure of himself and seems to need it less."

Arzewski remembered all the programs she had ever played for these four conductors, and, whenever she played a given piece, she would hear it the way each of them had conducted it. She tended to view her work, her colleagues, and life in general in stark black and white; she either loved or hated a thing. As one of the people who had known her since she joined the orchestra pointed out, "Cecylia has people in the orchestra who would die for her, but she's not likely to ever win a popularity contest. She's a personality. She never was bland." This kind of temperament proved exceedingly difficult in a profession where most of the conductors Arzewski played under did not approach, in her view, the artistry of her four favorites and where, especially when the orchestra went on tour, she would have to play a standard work such as Beethoven's Fifth as many as ten times a month. "Most of the time, we don't make music— that's what Silverstein meant about orchestra musicians leading a life of sin. On tour especially, you begin to tune yourself out. You're thinking that the restaurant in your hotel will still be open by the time the concert is over, that there will be room service if it's not and then you can turn on the TV. You think about how many hours of sleep you'll get before

the bus in the morning, and then the concert is over and they're applauding: The audience is happy!" On tour, she tended to hang out with
Ikuko Mizuno, the first woman in the violin section, who had joined the
BSO one year before Arzewski, and with Bill Rhein, a bass player and
manic-depressive who killed himself in 1980. She inspired tremendous
admiration for her playing, which matured and mellowed in the orchestra, yet, at the same time, irritated her colleagues by what they viewed
as "extreme negativity" or "bitterness" or "uncompromising sourness." In
a group of people where everyone was presumed to have high ego needs
and a sizable dose of neuroses, interpersonal skills and diplomacy were
highly valued. Arzewski, of course, let people know whatever was on her
mind without reflecting much on the context or the ramifications of what
she said; to do otherwise was hypocrisy, she felt; and, eventually, she
would suffer the consequences of ignoring orchestra politics.

In 1976, she finally bought herself a great violin. Her father had picked
up her first in Berlin; she did not remember her second; as Ivan Galamian's
student she had played on a Gagliano borrowed from the New York String
Society; and, for one year, Wurlitzer (the violin dealers) had loaned her
a Guadagnini, which was her first taste of a fine violin. Her father had
then bought her another Gagliano, which she played until she decided
it was time to invest in an instrument she really loved. The decision came
with the realization that she, in fact, loved playing the violin. At
twenty-five, she had entered psychotherapy and credited the doctor with
whom she worked six years for untangling her family history and helping
her to discover that she was playing for herself and not for her parents.
She looked at a few violins in the vault of Jacques Français Rare Violins
in New York and found a Guarnerius—a Petrus Guarnerius of Mantua,
made in 1714—which she liked but did not immediately buy. One
month later, she returned on tour with the orchestra and checked the
instrument out for a rehearsal at Carnegie Hall. It was a Pops rehearsal.
Arthur Fiedler was conducting, and the first piece he had chosen to work
on was the *Pizzicato Polka*. "The pizzicatos weren't exactly together, so
for ten or fifteen minutes I sat there going crazy," she remembered. "I
wanted to play and I couldn't play anything but those pizzies. I do that
now when I pick up a new violin. There are things you can hear when
you're pizzing that are very subtle. When I finally started to play, a few
people turned around and asked me what it was I was playing on.

"I brought it back to Boston and every day it was more of an addiction,
every day I felt myself falling more in love with it. Every violin is

different, every violin needs to be stroked in a different way, and it took me about a year to learn to play it. And ten years to pay for it."

By that time, she had determined to aim for a career as concertmaster of an orchestra, a decision which, she later said, coincided with her growing love for the orchestral repertoire. She auditioned, behind a screen, for the position of "inside second stand," or one of the two BSO assistant concertmasters, and won it in 1978. "The unity in those first two stands was incredible," Arzewski recalled. She sat beside Max Hobart, "the best stand partner anyone could dream of," she would later say, "a man of integrity, great respect for the music, and a conductor in his own right." She sat behind Emanuel Borok, a Russian Jewish emigré who had been a member of the Bolshoi Theatre Orchestra and associate concertmaster of the Moscow Philharmonic. And she was able to observe Joseph Silverstein, with whom she had by then been working for ten years, up close.

Musically, Silverstein recalled, Arzewski ripened during those years. "She finally became able to fully express herself on the violin; her playing became more identifiably hers." She gave a solo debut recital in Carnegie Recital Hall in 1978 composed entirely of unaccompanied Bach—"the First Sonata and the First and (gulp!) Second Partitas," wrote the *Village Voice*—and took her program to that year's International Bach Competition, where she was one of the prizewinners. She performed concerti with local orchestras and taught a small number of students, but neither teaching nor performing chamber music attracted her in the way they did many other musicians. "What do I need to belong to another group for? Belonging to an orchestra is enough!" she would say. Too many students also cut into her practice time. She liked to practice three hours a day: Some Bach—which she found as necessary to her well-being as other people find jogging or swimming or yoga—and whatever new music (such as, say, a new work by composer Earl Kim, or the Berg Violin Concerto) she had decided to learn. Her musical style was intense, serious, and solitary. Arzewski was "admirably equipped to play these uncompromising pieces," read the *New York Times* review of her debut recital. "Steady tone, precise intonation, bowing skill and reliable musicianship were combined in performances that maintained admirably high standards throughout." Her colleagues in the orchestra called her playing "elegant," "impeccable," "assured," and Joseph Silverstein asked her, in 1980, to serve as concertmaster of the Worcester Symphony, of which he was music director. The two violinists would drive to Worcester together, listening to Heifetz tapes on the car stereo, and both enjoyed their work.

There had never been a woman concertmaster of a major orchestra any-where in the world, but Silverstein thought that Arzewski had the talent to become the first. "I worked with her in that capacity," he said later. "She understands the role well and she's very good at it. She's an ex-traordinarily gifted person. Perhaps it's been the circumstances under which she auditioned that have not been right. Maybe if she had been born six years later. There are a lot of old curmudgeons around who don't want a woman as concertmaster. When she auditioned for the BSO associate concertmaster, she was terrific. If she had had a different personality profile, she would have gotten the job."

Arzewski's goal of finding a concertmaster's position at a major or-chestra was, in 1986, unachieved. Auditions were not held entirely behind a screen; personality and reputation counted as much as violin playing. She had gotten as far as negotiating a contract at the Montreal Symphony under the conductor Charles Dutoit, but, in the end, the concertmaster's seat had gone to the other finalist in the auditions, a man. She had, on the recommendation of Itzhak Perlman, been invited to audition for Lorin Maazel at the Pittsburgh Symphony, but when she arrived, that orchestra's audition committee asked to hear her first and then recommended that she not be considered by the conductor. That experience, as well as Montreal, had been frustrating for her. There were not more than half a dozen positions in the world that would open up within the next decade, she was sure that sexism played its part in hiring procedures, and she was reluctant to impose her own professional am-bitions and the moves they could entail on her two daughters, the second of whom, Maya, had been born in 1979. The ideal would have been to slowly move up in Boston, but there, too, there were problems.

Joseph Silverstein resigned as concertmaster from the BSO in 1983 and, after the following summer in Tanglewood, left to become music director of the Utah Symphony. Associate concertmaster Emanuel Borok resigned a year later to become concertmaster of the Dallas Symphony. In two years, Arzewski lost half of the unit of players with whom she had become musically enmeshed, a loss which followed that of conductor Colin Davis, who no longer was the orchestra's principal guest conductor. Malcolm Lowe had been appointed concertmaster after Silverstein, and, while she respected his musicianship, there was no way he could replace the former teacher and colleague she had adored. When it came time to audition a replacement for Borok, she determined to try for the position of associate concertmaster.

There were fifty applications for the position, according to BSO personnel manager Bill Moyer, that came from outside the orchestra and seven from within. They auditioned behind a screen, and two men joined the seven BSO musicians, who, according to orchestra policy, automatically were put in the finals. After a secret ballot, three women—Cecylia Arzewski, Nisanne Lowe, and Jennie Shames—reportedly were the finalists, but "Seiji as music director felt he was unable to make a clear decision," said Moyer, "and asked that we readvertise the position and hold auditions later that year." Nisanne Lowe subsequently left the orchestra to join the Chicago Symphony, a second round of auditions was held, the vote was taken, and once again, Arzewski and Shames were voted in, along with a third woman who was concertmaster of the Zagreb Philharmonic. In September 1986, Tamara Smirnova-Sajfar was appointed the new associate concertmaster of the BSO.

"Cecylia had ardent supporters. Not necessarily friends, but people who love the way she plays," said Moyer, "but being a concertmaster requires all kinds of qualities like leadership and reliability. The concertmaster has to inspire an entire orchestra and he has to be able to work with the conductor." The new associate concertmaster, who would serve as concertmaster of the Boston Pops, spoke no English, and it seemed clear to many of the musicians that she had been hired so that "they wouldn't have to hire Cecylia or Jennie Shames." Yet most of them would point out that it was unrealistic to expect music director Ozawa to hire as associate concertmaster a violinist who had let her displeasure with him be obvious over the course of a decade.

Seiji Ozawa was named music director of the BSO three years after Arzewski joined the orchestra, and, like most of the players, she had been delighted with him at first. Ozawa had been a guest conductor with the orchestra for six years and she had played Bartók and Stravinsky with him. "He would rehearse very little and he was fast," she recalled but would then point out that there were few orchestras which were consistently happy with their music directors. The position carried with it inevitable connotations of fatherhood to an orchestra-family, and most orchestras felt that their music director spread himself too thin to give them the attention they needed. "Like all conductors who want to be superstars," Arzewski said, "Ozawa spends very little time with the orchestra— twenty-two weeks—and the quality of that time is poor. He gets off the plane from Paris and starts to rehearse, and when he opens up the score of a symphony, he may not have looked at it since the last time he conducted it a year or maybe four years ago. Very often he repeats sections that don't need to be rehearsed because he wants to check out whether he's got it right. We call it panic time when he's around. His words of comfort to us when he's run out of time and the performance is the next day, you know what he says? 'You be careful; I be careful.'"

Arzewski was not the only person to find fault with Ozawa. Criticism of the music director boiled over into the press in November of 1986 when *Boston*, the city magazine, ran a long profile of Ozawa and interviewed several BSO players. Double bassist Lawrence Wolfe was one of many musicians who pointed out Ozawa's indecisiveness. Principal violist Burton Fine said Ozawa lacked a clear musical vision. Principal second violinist Marylou Speaker Churchill said, "When it comes to the German repertoire, there's a lack of understanding. And yes, we get frustrated. We're desperate to have someone come and conduct us in the German literature and be inspired. It's the backbone of the literature." And violinist Jennie Shames said, "The orchestra is probably a collection of the finest instrumentalists in the world, but they sure don't sound like it. People are not proud to be on the stage right now."

None of these players, however, made their discontent as palpable during rehearsals and concerts as Cecylia Arzewski. "Careful" had never been a word used to describe her, carefulness was not a quality she particularly respected in people, and she found it difficult to understand why it was important for her to be careful in her relations with Ozawa or that it was disagreeable for him to look down from the podium and see contempt written on her face practically under his nose. Years of being the only female first violinist had, some people thought, driven her into a more extreme posture than she might have chosen in a less stressful setting, and, when she bicycled to rehearsals dressed in nothing but glossy black leggings, a loose sweater, and sunglasses, or made one of her scathing critical remarks, people said, "Well, that's Cecylia." Since 1978, she had occupied the Edward and Bertha C. Rose chair at the BSO. Her job was as secure as that of any unionized worker in a financially untroubled company, and she made over $60,000 per year. But, like many musicians who had started out as child prodigies and many nonmusicians nearing middle age and the dead end of their career track, she was often bewildered by, and angry at, where she had ended up. About 175 violinists had auditioned for three openings in the BSO in 1986. One opening was the result of a retirement, one of a move to another city, and the third was occasioned by Joel Smirnoff (who left to join the Juilliard

Quartet). Only one candidate was found suitable by the orchestra, but knowing that did not make her any happier.

Throughout her professional career, she had spent a great deal of time with her daughters and on a personal life that she kept resolutely private. She had not encouraged either Maya or Ilana to pursue the study of a musical instrument, and, even though both had spent summers in Tanglewood and regarded some musicians as extended family, neither wanted to become one. Arzewski also taught a small number of students in the elegant salmon-colored study of her Cambridge apartment, where a large, stark poster titled *Oswiecim* (Auschwitz in Polish) hung near the music stand. She listened to hours of piano music when she was at home: To Glenn Gould or Michelangeli for Bach; to Ivo Pogorelich for Chopin; to Horowitz "for Horowitz, then the piano, then the composer"; to Rubinstein, Lipatti, Josef Hofmann, Pollini, Martha Argerich, Emanuel Ax.

In the last years of her father's life, Stanislaw Arzewski worked as a pianist at The Sign of the Dove, a Manhattan night spot and restaurant. Often his daughter would remember how, after a New York concert with the Boston Symphony, she would walk in and hear him performing the Chopin G minor Ballade at the request of one of the diners. She would remember what he had repeated to her from the time she was small, that "the most important thing in a musician's life is to have pride in himself, to respect himself, and to have the respect of other musicians." Routine had eroded some of the pride she took in her orchestra work, but, she said, ever more pressure, ever shorter rehearsal time, and ever less committed conductors were mostly to blame. "There's never enough money, so they're constantly trying to raise it and make it on the orchestra. Musicians are exploited for business purposes—quality artistry doesn't matter anymore and doesn't, in fact, exist in American orchestras on a regular basis. It's quantity: How many concerts can you squeeze out of us? We play three different programs a week at Tanglewood all summer. Two rehearsals per concert. How do you expect those concerts to be great? I was in Munich recently and I heard Celibidache conduct. He *teaches* the orchestra the piece. They have so much rehearsal that when it comes to the performance, he gets into the passenger's seat. Music like this is simply not performed in this country anymore. At Tanglewood, it's more like a factory, and the worst of it is that it's such a beautiful place. A wonderful place to make music, especially when the weather is nice." And all year long the orchestra members were hungry for conductors with ideas, so hungry that they had begged and petitioned Bernard Haitink to come back and guest conduct during the 1986–1987 season.

For the most part, she worked on her musical development alone at home. She had gone to California to take a class with Heifetz ("in two and a half hours I learned more than I had in seven years with Galamian") and she sought out musical elders in Boston such as Louis Krasner, who had played the premiere of the Alban Berg Concerto in Boston, to work with her. She still tried to practice three hours a day ("I'm quite driven, one might say"), and, occasionally, her work would come into public view. Obtaining concert dates was difficult without a manager and without a press agent, but Arzewski performed concerti with New England orchestras every once in a while and in the spring of 1986 gave a recital that reminded critics of her stature.

"Arzewski has escaped the industrial-strength, all-purpose international style so in vogue at the moment, the kind of technique that approaches the entire repertory as if it were the Tchaikovsky Violin Concerto, and the Tchaikovsky Violin Concerto as if it were only a display piece," wrote the *Boston Globe*. "Arzewski's Bach sounded like Bach, her Beethoven like Beethoven, her Prokofiev like Prokofiev....Arzewski rounded off her program with a gorgeous performance of Nathan Milstein's transcription of a Chopin nocturne, displaying a subtle sureness of rubato no teacher could impart, and Wieniawski's Polonaise Brillante. This was brilliant because she played it as music, and not just a bag of tricks."

The *Boston Herald*, too, gave Arzewski an excellent review, noting that "it was one of those occasions that compelled one into the music, that made one think about what the composer was doing, not just about the fancy finger-and-bow-work of the soloist." That review began with a sentence that could not have been more apt: "Violinist Cecylia Arzewski is one of the superb musicians whose individual gifts are most often hidden within the collective splendor of the Boston Symphony Orchestra."

The BSO and the Boston area are both hard places to leave, and Arzewski might have remained, resigned and on automatic pilot, had Itzhak Perlman not suggested to her in the summer of 1986 to audition for the position which would become available in the fall of 1987 of associate concertmaster of the Cleveland Orchestra. Arzewski thought about the idea for a while. Her experience in Pittsburgh had made her wary of orchestra audition committees, and she called colleagues in Cleveland to ask point blank whether she was likely to encounter sex discrimination there. The answer she received was an unequivocal no. Once again, she began practicing for an audition and in November of

1986 played for members of the Cleveland Orchestra and their music director, Christoph von Dohnanyi. She performed for thirty minutes and was offered the job the same afternoon. In September of 1987, Cecylia Arzewski will become associate concertmaster of the Cleveland Orchestra.

Index

ABOUT THE AUTHOR

Helen Epstein was born in 1947 in Prague, Czechoslovakia, and emigrated to New York City at the age of eight months. She grew up down the street from Lincoln Center and began attending the opera at age three. She made her journalistic debut in August 1968, by writing a first-hand account of the Russian invasion of Czechoslovakia, and subsequently worked as a reporter for the *Jerusalem Post* while she was a musicology student at the Hebrew University in Israel. A graduate of the Columbia Graduate School of Journalism, she taught writing for twelve years at New York University while writing about books and the arts for the *New York Times*, the *Washington Post, Esquire, MS., ARTnews* and other publications. Her first book, *Children of the Holocaust*, has been translated into German, Italian, and Japanese. Her second book, *The Companies She Keeps*, is a theater book. In 1985, she founded the Plunkett Lake Press and, in 1986, translated and published *Under a Cruel Star: A Life in Prague 1941–1968*. She lives in Cambridge, Massachusetts, with her husband and young son.